LANGUAGE LAB

Reading Materials for Easier Learning

Editor: Mahendra Kulasrestha

FIRST ENGLISH DICTIONARY

English-हिन्दी-English

with one sentence

"We envy India's IT stride . . . and the comfort with which English is used by large sections of the population. There is for us a lot of work to do on that front."

– Sun Wiede

Dy. Director, Beijing Olympiad

(*Times of India,* 31 July, 07)

अंग्रेजी सीखना चीनियों के लिए मुश्किल हो सकता है, हम भारतीयों के लिए नहीं। एशिया में भारत सबसे अच्छी अंग्रेजी जानने वाला सबसे बड़ा देश है, जिसका वह विश्व व्यापार में लाभ उठा रहा है। अंग्रेजी भाषा का उच्चारण भी हमारे यहाँ का सबसे अच्छा और स्पष्ट है – जिसे **neutral** उच्चारण कहा जाता है – जिसका लाभ हमें प्राप्त होता है। सामान्य उपयोग की अंग्रेजी जानने के लिए सिर्फ 2–3 हजार शब्द और 2–3 सौ वाक्य सीखने की जरूरत है। इस कोश में उतने ही शब्द चुनकर दिये जा रहे हैं जिनसे आपका काम बखूबी चल सकता है। इसके बाद आप धीरे-धीरे और भी शब्द सीख सकते हैं।

हर शब्द का अर्थ हिन्दी और अंग्रेजी दोनों भाषाओं में दिया गया है और साथ–साथ एक–दो वाक्य भी दिये जा रहे हैं। पहले अंग्रेजी सीखने की आवश्यकता और विश्वास पैदा करें – मन से डर निकाल दें – और समय–समय पर कहानी उपन्यास की तरह किताब के कुछ पृष्ठ पढ़ते रहें, अपने मित्रों के साथ बेहिचक अभ्यास करते रहें, बहुत जल्द आप इस भाषा पर काबू पा लेंगे।

FIRST ENGLISH DICTIONARY

English-हिन्दी-English

with one sentence

VIJAY P. VERMA

Lotus PRESS

4735/22, Prakash Deep Building,
Ansari Road, Daryaganj,
New Delhi - 110002

Lotus Press Publishers & Distributors
Unit No.220, 2nd Floor, 4735/22, Prakash Deep Building,
Ansari Road, Daryaganj, New Delhi- 110002
Ph:- 32903912, 23280047, 098118-38000
Email : lotuspress1984@gmail.com
Visit us : www.lotuspress.co.in

First English Dictionary

ISBN : 81-8382-125-1

***Printed & Published by* : Lotus Press Publishers & Distributors,** New Delhi- 2

भाषा की नई कहानी

अंग्रेज़ी दुनिया की सात प्रमुख भाषाओं में से एक है। आज विश्वीकरण के इस युग में यह मानव–व्यवहार की प्रमुख भाषा बनती जा रही है। हम भारतीयों के लिए इसे सीखना बहुत आसान है, क्योंकि इसे हम लगभग दो सौ वर्षो से जानते रहे हैं। इसी कारण अमेरिका और यूरोप के आई. टी. उद्योग तथा विश्व–व्यापार में आज हमारे युवक–युवतियाँ तेज़ी से आगे बढ़ रहे हैं और सदियों से ग़रीब अपने देश को समृद्ध बना रहे हैं। आप भी इस राष्ट्रीय जुलूस में शामिल हो जाइये और सारी दुनिया को एक बनाने में सहायता तथा नेतृत्व भी कीजिए।

ज़रूरी नहीं है कि आप अंग्रेजी के विद्वान बनने की कोशिश करें। कामकाज के लायक अंग्रेज़ी सीखना बिलकुल मुश्किल नहीं है। अंग्रेजी भाषा की शब्दावली करोड़ शब्दों से अधिक है, और उदार भाषा होने के कारण यह अन्य भाषाओं के शब्दों को हर साल अपने कलेवर में शामिल करती जा रही है – इसमें भारत के भी कई हज़ार शब्द शामिल किये जा चुके हैं – लेकिन दो–तीन हज़ार शब्दों से ही आपका काम अच्छी तरह चल सकता है। 'वॉयस ऑफ अमेरिका' ने सफलतापूर्वक यह प्रयोग किया है। इसी दृष्टि से यह प्रथम अंग्रेजी शब्दकोश तैयार किया गया है – इसमें ऐसे तीन हज़ार शब्दों का चुनाव किया गया है जिनके प्रयोग से हमारा कार्य अच्छी तरह चल सकता है। इन शब्दों के हिन्दी तथा अंग्रेज़ी दोनों के अर्थ तथा वाक्य–प्रयोग दिये गये हैं। कोश के आगामी भागों में स्तर के अनुसार शब्दों की संख्या बढ़ायी जाती रहेगी तथा उनके प्रयोग पर ज़्यादा रोशनी डाली जायेगी।

यह समझना ज़रूरी है कि अंग्रेज़ी मातृभाषा के देशों तथा ऐसे देशों, जिनके

लिए अंग्रेज़ी दूसरी भाषा है, के लोगों के लिए अंग्रेज़ी का ज्ञान और उपयोगिता एक–दूसरे से बिलकुल अलग है। उन सब का उच्चारण भी भिन्न होता है, होना चाहिए। ब्रिटेन की अंग्रेजी से अमेरिकी अंग्रेजी अलग है, आस्ट्रेलिया, अफ़्रीका और एशिया की भी भिन्न है। भारत में बंगाल, पंजाब, महाराष्ट्र, कर्नाटक, तमिलनाडु के उच्चारण तथा प्रयोगों में भी स्पष्ट अंतर हैं। यह स्वाभाविक है और इसे स्वीकार कर ही आगे बढ़ते रहना चाहिए। यह कोश हिन्दीभाषी भारत के उपयोग के लिए तैयार किया गया है और उसके निवासियों की भूमिका तथा आवश्यकताओं का इसमें ध्यान रखा गया है। पंरतु मौलिक आवश्यकताएँ सबकी एक होने के कारण हिन्दी के स्थान पर अन्य भाषाओं को रखकर उनके द्वारा भी इसका उपयोग किया जा सकता है।

हम हिन्दीभाषी उत्तर भारतीय अंग्रेजी सीखने और बोलने के मामले में जरूरत से ज्यादा डरपोक या संकोची हैं। हम इस मामले में घमंडी भी हैं और हमारे अनेक पूर्व साहित्यकारों ने इसे हमेशा हवा दी है– 'धर्मयुग' के एक सम्पादक धर्मवीर भारती इसके अगुवा थे और इन पंक्तियों के लेखक की उनसे, अग्रणी साहित्यिक पत्रिका, 'कल्पना', के पृष्ठों में, साठ के दशक में, लम्बी बहस हुई थी – उन्होंने, उस समय प्रधान मंत्री लालबहादुर शास्त्री जैसे व्यक्ति की, अन्य भारतीय भाषाओं का समर्थन करने को लेकर, कटु आलोचना की थी। यही कारण है कि आज अंग्रेजी से जुड़े व्यापार, आई. टी. आदि सभी क्षेत्रों में दक्षिण भारतीय हिन्दीभाषियों से कहीं आगे हैं। हमें अपना संकोच समाप्त कर द्विभाषी प्रगति के मार्ग पर आगे बढ़ना चाहिए, और पिछला घाटा भी पूरा कर लेना चाहिए।

हर भाषा की कुछ कमियाँ भी होती हैं। इन्हें विस्तार से बताने का यह स्थल नहीं है, इनका इशारा भर किया जा रहा है। पहली महत्वपूर्ण बात यह है कि अंग्रेजी लिपि में सभी शब्दों के दो, कैपिटल और स्मॉल, लेटर्स के प्रयोग की क्या ज़रूरत है ? मेरा यह भी मानना है कि अंग्रेज़ी की लिपि रोमन् के स्थान पर देवनागरी कर दी जाये तो वह उच्चारण में कहीं ज्यादा शुद्ध हो सकेगी। कम–से–कम एशिया की अंग्रेजी में तो यह परिवर्तन किया ही जा सकता है। अंग्रेजी की वर्णमाला में भी संशोधन संभव है। इन परिवर्तनों के बाद अंग्रेजी विश्व–भाषा के रूप में ज्यादा सफ़ल हो सकेगी।

ढीले–ढाले रूप में ही सही, एक विश्वभाषा की दिशा में दुनिया की प्रगति सभ्यता के विकास में एक अत्यन्त महत्वपूर्ण कदम है। भारत की तुलना में चीन इस तथ्य को कहीं अधिक जानता–समझता है और अनेक, कई बार अद्‌भुत

प्रतीत होने वाले उपायों से, इस क्षेत्र में आगे बढ़ने की लगातार चेष्टा कर रहा है। इन्टरनेट और कम्प्यूटर–आधारित कल्पनातीत रूप से आश्चर्यजनक प्रगतियों को इससे जबरदस्त गति और बल प्राप्त हो सकेगा। गैर–पाश्चिमी देशों में अंग्रेज़ी के अपने ज्ञान के कारण भारत इसका आज भी अधिक लाभ उठा रहा है और भविष्य में भी उठाता रह सकता है। वह समग्र गैरपश्चिमी देशों का नेता भी बन सकता है। हमें समय रहते इसका महत्व समझना चाहिए और उसका अधिक से अधिक लाभ उठाने की मानसिकता और योजना बनाना चाहिए।

ये कोश मेरे छोटे भाई के द्वारा तैयार किये जा रहे हैं। वे शिक्षा ज़गत से आजीवन जुड़े रहे हैं। कोश के पाठकों के सुझावों का सदा स्वागत रहेगा। विदेशों में रह रहे हिन्दीभाषी इस कार्य में महत्वपूर्ण योगदान कर सकते हैं।

361/37, फरीदाबाद–121003 — **सम्पादक**

पुनश्च :

ये पंक्तियों लिखने के दिनों में ही 'टाइम्स आफ इंडिया' ने परिवर्तन की पहल कर दी – वे अब 'I' के स्थान पर 'i' का प्रयोग करने लगे हैं। यह अच्छी शुरूआत है। 'दैनिक जागरण' इत्यादि अनेक दैनिक पत्रों ने विद्यार्थियों के पृष्ठों पर विशेष रूप से, तथा अन्य पृष्ठों पर भी, अंग्रेजी का प्रयोग आरंभ कर दिया है। देर आए, दुरुस्त आए।

अंग्रेजी भाषा का, 'कॉर्पस' करोड़ों शब्दों का है परंतु उपयोग में बहुत कम शब्द आते हैं। दूसरी भाषा के रूप में अंग्रेजी का प्रयोग करनेवालों के लिए यह संख्या और भी कम रह जाती है, इसलिए यह शब्दकोश उतने ही शब्दों को चुनकर बनाया गया है जितने से सामान्य व्यक्ति का काम चल जाय। इसमें लगभग तीन हजार शब्द हैं, शब्दों के अर्थ भी वे ही दिये गये हैं जिनका सामान्यतः प्रयोग होता है, बाकी अर्थ छोड़ दिये गये हैं। शब्द का प्रयोग समझाने के लिए एक वाक्य भी दिया गया है।

प्रख्यात कोशकार डॉ. हरदेव बाहरी कहते थे कि भाषा सीखने के लिए कोश को उपन्यास मानकर पढ़ना चाहिए। शब्द बहुत ज़्यादा हों तो ऐसा करना कठिन होता है, परंतु यह कोश उपन्यास की तरह पढ़कर दिमाग में बिठाया जा सकता है। इसमें प्रत्येक अक्षर के आरंभ में चार्ट बनाकर भी कई बातें स्पष्ट की गई हैं। माध्यम की भाषा अंग्रेजी के स्थान पर हिन्दी ही रखी गई है क्योंकि जिन्हें अंग्रेजी सीखनी है, उन्हें अंग्रेजी के ही माध्यम से उसे सीखने में कठिनाई हो सकती है। जैसे, ये आरंभिक नोट्स अंग्रेजी में न होकर हिन्दी में ही दिये जा रहें हैं। ठीक है न!

हर भाषा की अपनी स्वतंत्र विशेषताएं होती हैं। अंग्रेजी वर्णमाला में स्वर और व्यंजन एक साथ मिले–जुले हैं, हिन्दी की तरह अलग–अलग नहीं हैं, और प्रत्येक वर्ण, या अक्षर, के उच्चारण कुछ अक्षरों में केवल एक, और कुछ में एक से ज़्यादा, भी हैं। इसी के साथ एक ही अक्षर के दीर्घ तथा लघु रूप भिन्न हैं और प्रत्येक वाक्य का आरंभ दीर्घ रूप से ही किया जाता है। 'मैं' के अर्थ मे प्रयुक्त 'I' का प्रयोग वाक्य के भीतर भी दीर्घ रूप में ही किया जाता है। इसके अलावा लघु अक्षरों के मुद्रण तथा लेखन रूप भी भिन्न हैं।

इसलिए प्रत्येक अक्षर के आरंभ में एक चार्ट बनाकर इन बातों को स्पष्ट करने का प्रयत्न किया गया है। इसे ध्यान से देखें – इससे भाषा का स्वरूप स्पष्ट होगा और कुछ मनोरंजन भी होगा।

अंग्रेजी अन्य भाषाओं के शब्द लेकर तेज़ी से अपने कलेवर को बढ़ाती जा रही है। हिन्दी से भी उसने हजारों शब्दों को शमिल कर लिया है। कोश के अन्त में ऐसे कुछ शब्दों की सूची दी जा रही है। उसकी प्रगति का एक कारण उसकी यह उदारता भी है – जो हमारे लिए सीखने की बात है।

अंग्रेजी की लिपी बदलने का समय आ गया है

समाचार है कि प्रेसीडेन्ट बुश को संयुक्त राष्ट्र संध में पढ़ने के लिए जो भाषण दिया गया, उसमें अनेक शब्दों के उच्चारण ब्रेकेट में दिये गये जिससे वे पढ़ने में गलती न करें – खास तौर से विदेशी नामों के उच्चारण।

यह रोमन लिपि की कमजोरियों के कारण होता है। इस समस्या का हल है देवनागरी लिपि। यूरोप की माषाओं पर प्राचीन काल से संस्कृत का बहुत प्रमाव है, अब वे देवनागरी की सहायता से अंग्रेजी को और मी सरल बना सकते हैं।

A

a
मुद्रण में प्रयुक्त
लघु रोमन अक्षर

a
लेखन तथा मुद्रण
में प्रयुक्त लघु
इटैलिक अक्षर (जो a से भिन्न है, याद रखें – परंतु ऐसा क्यों?)

मूल उच्चारण **ए**

अ आ प्रयोग में उच्चारण

अंग्रेजी वर्णमाला का प्रथम अक्षर तथा पाँच स्वरों में से पहला स्वर

a (ए) article
एक, one, any, each. *I have ~ pen.*

A-1 or **A-one** (ए–वन) adjective
अति उत्तम, उत्कृष्ट, उच्च कोटि का, बहुत अच्छा, excellent, very good, first class. *His work is certainly ~.*

a (ए) preposition
प्रति, फ़ी, each, every, per, *Four rupees ~ meter.*

A to Z (ए टू ज़ेड)
प्रारंभ से अंत तक, from beginning to end. *I have read this story from ~.*

aback (एबैक) adverb
पीछे, पीछे की ओर, taken surprised, भौंचक्का, आश्चर्यचकित, *I was taken ~ when I saw her.*

abandon (ॲबैन्डन) verb
त्याग देना, to give up entirely, *You should not have ~ed him when he was in trouble.*

abbreviate (एब्रीविएट) verb
संक्षिप्त करना, छोटा करना, shorten, make brief.

abbreviation (एब्रीविएशन) noun
संक्षिप्त रूप, short form. *B.A. is an ~ of Bachelor of Arts.*

ABC (ए बी सी), noun
वर्णमाला, alphabet किसी विषय का प्रांरिभक ज्ञान

abdomen (एबडॅमन) noun
उदर, पेट, belly.

able (एबल) adjective
चतुर, योग्य, clever, skilful. *Raj is an ~ person.*

abnormal (एबनौर्मल) adjective
असाधारण, असामान्य, different from what is normal. *He is very ~ in certain matters.*

abort (अॅबोर्ट) verb
गर्भपात करना, होना, समय से पूर्व नष्ट होना, to remove a fetus.

abortion (अॅबोर्शन) noun
गर्भपात, भ्रूणहत्या, expulsion of human foetus within the first 12 weeks of pregnancy, *Conduct the ~ very carefully.*

about (अॅबाउट) adverb
प्रायः, लगभग, nearly, विपरीत दिशा में, आसपास, संबंधित, बारे में, करीब-करीब, opposite, here and there, regarding, more or less. *Turn ~. ~ 3 o'clock. Don't rush ~.*

above (अॅबव) adjective
उँचे स्थान पर, ऊपर, at higher point. *He is sitting ~.*

abreast (एब्रेस्ट) adjective
बराबर में, साथ-साथ, जानकारी होना. side by side, beside, *Keep ~ of political developments.*

abroad (अब्रौड) adjective
विदेश में, in or to a foreign country. *His son has gone ~.*

abscess (ऐबसेस) noun
फोड़ा, sore, ulcer. *The doctor incised the ~.*

abscond (ऐब्सकांड) verb
भाग जाना, गायब हो जाना, फरार हो जाना, to depart in a sudden and secret manner. *He ~ed from the jail.*

absence (ऐबसैंस) noun
अनुपस्थिति, being away from. *~ from school.*

absent (ऐबसैंट) adjective
अनुपस्थित, not present. *~ from duty.*

absentee (ऐबसैंटी) noun
गैरहाजिर रहने वाला, one who is absent.

absurd (एब्सर्ड) adjective
असंगत, मूर्खतापूर्ण, foolish, unreasonable

abuse (एब्यूज़) noun
गाली, अपशब्द, ill used, कुकर्म, कुप्रथा rape or indecent assault. *Sexual ~ of children.*

A.C. (ए.सी.) noun
एयरकंडीशनर, air conditioner, Aero Club, Ante Christum, ईसा पूर्व alternating current, एक प्रकार की विद्युत धारा. *He travels in A.C. class.*

academy (अकैडॅमी) noun
विद्यालय, विद्वत् परिषद, school for higher learning.

accent (ऐसैन्ट) noun
स्वराघात, किसी व्यक्ति विशेष, जाति विशेष या समूह विशेष के उच्चारण का ढंग, stress given to a syllable, natural different speech styles of various people.

accept (ऐक्सैप्ट) verb
स्वीकार कर लेना, to receive, सही मान लेना।

acceptant (ऐक्सैप्टैन्ट) adjective
स्वीकार करने वाला, willingly accepting.

accessory (ऐक्सैसरी) noun
अतिरिक्त सहायक सामान, articles that are useful. *~ of a car.*

accident (ऐक्सीडैंट) noun
दुर्घटना, unfortunate event, संयोग, chance. *There was a serious bus ~ yesterday.*

accompany (ऐकम्पनी) verb
साथ होना, go with. *Please ~ me.*

account (ऐकाउन्ट) noun
खाता-हिसाब, statement of money, समझना, मानना, to count, to consider.

across (ऐक्रास) adverb
आर-पार, आमने-सामने, सम्मुख, from side to side of, in the presence of. *~ the road.*

act (ऐक्ट) noun
कोई काम करना, process of doing. *She must ~ now.*

active (ऐक्टिव) noun
क्रियाशील, चुस्त, कर्मठ, उद्यमी, constantly engaged in action. *He is a very ~ person.*

activity (ऐक्टिविटी) noun
क्रियाकलाप, गतिविधि, action.

actor (ऐक्टर) noun
अभिनेता, a person who acts in stage plays, motion pictures, television, etc.

actress (ऐक्ट्रेस) noun
a female actor, अभिनेत्री.

actual (ऐक्चुअल) adjective
वास्तविक, असली, सही, real. *Tell me the ~ cost.*

acute (ऐक्यूट) adjective
तीव्र, पैना, तेज, keen, sharp, एकदम तीव्रता को पहुँचने वाली (बीमारी). *She is in ~ pain.*

ad (ऐड) noun
विज्ञापन, advertisement. *Put an ~ in a paper for this.*

A.D.
Anno Domini ईसवी, since Christ was born.

address (ऐड्रैस) noun
पता, व्याख्यान, भाषण देना, speech; name, house no., city, etc., put on letters.

adjective (ऐडजैक्टिव) noun
विशेषण, grammar, qualifying a word.

adjust (ऐडजस्ट) verb
व्यवस्थित करना, तालमेल, अनुकूल बनाना, to set right. *You'll have to ~ yourself in that home.*

admissible (ऐडमिसिबल) adjective
स्वीकार करने योग्य, that can be allowed in judicial proof. *His version is ~ .*

admission (ऐडमिशन) noun
प्रवेश, भर्ती, दाखिला, act of entering in a school or institution.

admit (ऐडमिट) verb
प्रवेश करने देना, मान लेना, permit to enter, to join.

advance (ऐडवांस) noun
समय से पहले किया गया कार्य, उन्नति, प्रगति, अग्रिम रकम. forward movement, progress.

advantage (ऐडवांटेज) noun
लाभ, फायदा, something useful. *Don't take undue ~ of him.*

adverb (ऐडवर्ब) noun
क्रिया विशेषण, part of speech that modifies a verb, an adj., a phrase, etc.

advice (ऐडवाइस) noun
सलाह, परामर्श, निर्देश opinion given about what to do.

advise (ऐडवाइज) verb
सलाह देना, नसीहत देना, सुझाव देना, give counsel to. *~ him carefully about it.*

aerobics (ऐरोबिक्स) noun
तैराकी, जोगिंग, व्यायाम, special exercise.

affair (अफ़ेयर) noun
कार्य, मामला, घटना, business matter. *Mind your own ~s.*

affect (अफ़ेक्ट) verb
प्रभाव डालना, असर करना, have an effect on, to influence. *He was deeply ~ed by the sad news.*

affiliate (अफीलिएट) verb
संबंध करना, to connect with. *Our college is ~d to Agra University.*

afford (अफोर्ड) verb
करने की क्षमता रखना, कर सकना, सामर्थ्य होना, to be able to do. *He cannot ~ so much expense.*

afraid (ॲफ्रेड) adjective
भयभीत, डरा हुआ, full of fear. *I'm not ~ of anybody.*

after (आफ्टर) adjective
के बाद, के पीछे, following, next to. *Don't run ~ him.*

afternoon (आफ़्टरनून) noun
तीसरा पहर, दोपहर बाद का समय, time between noon and evening. *Give me a ring in the ~.*

afterwards (आफ़्टरवर्ड्स) adjective
बाद में, फिर, later, after.

again (अगेन) adverb
फिर, पुनः, दुबारा, once more. *Please do it ~.*

against (अगेन्स्ट) preposition
विरुद्‌ध, खिलाफ, indicating opposition. *You can't move ~ the current.*

age (एज) noun
आयु, length of time a person has lived. युग, period of time. *The Gupta ~.*

agency (एजेन्सी) noun
अभिकर्ता का काम, business or office of an agent. *He has taken the ~ of Tatas.*

agent (एजेन्ट) noun
अभिकर्ता, आम मुख्तार, person who acts for another. *He is working as our ~.*

aggregate (एग्रीगेट) verb
योग होना, amount to total. *His ~ is 55%.*

ago (एगो) adverb
अतीत काल में, पहले, पूर्व, post, gone by. *100 years ~.*

agree (एग्री) verb
एकमत होना, सहमत, consent, say 'yes'. *I do not ~ with his ideas.*

aid (एड) noun
सहायता, मदद करना, help, assist. *Give ~ to the poor.*

aim (एम) noun
निशाना, उद्देश्य, लक्ष्य साधना, point. *My ~ is to throw him out of business.*

alarm (अलार्म) noun
खतरे की घंटी, warning signal. *I'm quite ~ed by his threat.*

alive (अलाइव) adjective
जीवित, अमल में, living, in force. *Keep your claim ~.*

all (औल) adjective
सब, सम्पूर्ण, the whole number. *~ three terrorists were killed.*

almost (ऑलमोस्ट) adjective
लगभग, प्रायः सब, nearly. *Dinner is ~ ready.*

alone (एलोन) adjective
अकेला, without anyone. *I went to him ~.*

along (एलाँग) adjective
साथ-साथ, किनारे-किनारे, by the side of. *Come ~, we both will do it better.*

already (ऑलरेडी) adverb
पहले से ही, previously. *He was ~ there, when I reached the office.*

also (ऑलसो) adverb
भी, too. *You ~ come with me.*

always (ऑलवेज़) adverb
हमेशा, every time. *I am ~ with you.*

am (ऐम) verb
हूँ, strong form of 'be'. *I ~ going.*

amount (एमाउन्ट) noun
योग, सम्पूर्ण परिमाण, total, whole quantity. *Tell me the total ~ you'll need.*

an (ऐन) article
एक, used with a vowel sound. *~ apple.*

anger (एंगर) noun
क्रोध, गुस्सा, नाराजगी, ire. *He is in great ~.*

angle (ऐन्गल) noun
कोण, दृष्टिकोण, space between surfaces that meet. *Right ~.*

anthem (एन्थेम) noun
गान, भजन, musical composition, *National ~.*

any (ऐनी) adjective
कोई भी, किसी भी, कैसी भी, हर एक, सब कुछ, कुछ, one, a, an, same, one or more. *There is hardly ~ food in the kitchen.*

anybody (ऐनीबॉडी) adjective
कोई व्यक्ति, any person. *~ can join us.*

apart (एपार्ट) adjective
दूर, अलग, distant. *He lives ~ from us.*

apology (अपोलोजी) noun
क्षमायाचना, written or spoken one's regret. *Make an ~.*

apple (ऐपल) noun
सेब, a fruit.

apply (ऐप्लाई) verb
आवेदन करना, request for something. *~ for this job.*

appoint (अपौइंट) verb
नियुक्त करना, तय करना, choose, decide, fix. *I'll ~ the best person for the job.*

are (आर) verb
present tense of be, हैं। *They ~ going.*

arise (ऐराइज़) verb
उठना, दृष्टिगोचर होना, get up, come into notice.

arm (आर्म) noun
बाहु, भुजा, limb from shoulder to hand. *Hold your right ~.*

army (आर्मी) noun
सेना, फौज, military force. *An ~ of workmen.*

arrange (एरेंज) verb
क्रम में रखना, to put in order. *~everything in correct order.*

arrive (एराइव) verb
पंहुचना, आना, reach, come. *~ at the station.*

arrow (ऐरो) noun
तीर, बाण, दिशा बताने हेतु प्रयुक्त चिह्न, pointed stick shot from a bow, mark or sign

art (आर्ट) noun
कला, शिल्पकला, चालबाजी, creation of what is beautiful, cunning, trickery. *Magic is an ~.*

article (आर्टिकल) noun
पदार्थ, वस्तु, *~s of clothing.* लेख, writing. *Write an ~ for the magazine.*

as (ऐज़) adverb
उसी प्रकार से, उतना, जैसे, चूँकि, क्योंकि, in the same degree. *~ good ~.*

ash (ऐश) noun
राख, भस्म, powder made after burning.

ask (आस्क) verb
पूछना, याचना करना, enquire, request. *~ him about it.*

asleep (एस्लीप) adverb, preposition
सोया हुआ, sleeping.

ass (ऐस) noun
गधा, donkey, foolish, *The ~ brays.*

assume (एस्यूम) verb
सत्य मान लेना, to take for granted. *I ~ the story is correct.*

assure (एश्यूर) verb
निश्चित रूप से, भरोसे के साथ कहना say positively. *Let me ~ you that what he says is correct.*

at (ऐट) preposition
में, पर, near, towards. *He came ~ 5.00 pm.*

ate (एट) verb
खाया, past tense of eat, *He ~ food.*

attach (अटैच) verb
लगाना, जोड़ना, to join. *~ him to the other office.*

attack (अटैक) noun
हमला, आक्रमण, violent attempt to hurt. *The ~ was serious.*

attempt (अटैम्प्ट) verb
प्रयास करना, कोशिश करना, try.*Your ~ is quite successful.*

attend (अटैंड) verb
ध्यान देना, उपस्थित रहना, look after, to be present. *I'll ~ the meeting.*

attest (अटैस्ट) verb
प्रमाणित करना, तसदीक देना, declare to be true. *He'll ~ the documents.*

attract (अट्रैक्ट) verb
आकर्षित करना, लुभाना, मोहित करना, खींचना pull towards. *A magnet ~s iron.*

audience (औडिएंस) noun
श्रोतागण, listeners. *There was a large ~ at the meeting.*

author (औथर) noun
लेखक, writer. *Who is the ~ of this book?*

auto (औटो) noun
स्वतंत्र अर्थ में प्रयुक्त उपसर्ग, स्कूटर, short form of automobile. *Go by an ~ to the bus stand.*

automatic (औटोमेटिक) adjective
स्वचालित, self moving. *~ watch.*

available (अवेलेबिल) adjective
उपलब्ध, प्राप्त, obtainable. *Blue T-shirt is not ~ in this shop.*

average (ऐवरेज) noun
औसत, मध्यमान, mean.

avoid (एवॉइड) verb
दूर रहना, बचना, escape, to keep away. *Do not ~ meeting him.*

await (एवेट) verb
प्रतीक्षा, इंतजार करना, expect.

awake (एवेक) verb
जगाना, जागृत, सचेत, to rouse from sleep. *Tell me, is he ~?*

award (ॲवार्ड) verb
इनाम देना, दण्ड देना, to give prize or punishment. *He was ~ed the first prize.*

aware (एवेअर) adjective
जानकारी होना having knowledge. *He is ~ of the event.*

away (अवे) noun
दूर, distant. *Go ~, I don't want to see your face.*

axis (ऐक्सिस) noun
धुरी, imaginary line round which a body rotates. *The earth is rotating on its ~.*

❑❑❑❑

B

b मुद्रण में प्रयुक्त लघु अक्षर

मूल उच्चारण **बी**

b लेखन में प्रयुक्त लघु अक्षर

ब प्रयोग में उच्चारण

अंग्रेजी वर्णमाला का दूसरा अक्षर

babe (बेब) noun
नन्हा मुन्ना, शिशु

babu (बाबू)
कार्यालय में काम करने वाले व्यक्ति officeworkers.

baby (बेबी) noun
बहुत छोटा बच्चा, a very young child.

babysitter (बेबीसिटर) noun
बच्चे की देखभाल करने वाला व्यक्ति, a person who looks after a child for some time. *Arrange a ~ for the child.*

back (बैक) noun
पीठ, surface of body from neck to buttock, the part behind of something.

bad (बैड) adjective
बुरा, खराब, evil, not good. *What a ~ weather!*

bag (बैग) noun
थैला, बोरा, sack, pouch, satchel.

bail (बेल) noun
जमानत, sum of money demanded by a law court. *He is now out on ~.*

bake (बेक) verb
पकाना, पकना, सेंकना, cook, be cooked. *~ the bread in an oven.*

balance (बैलेंस) verb
तौलना, संतुलित करना, तराजू, weigh on the machine for weighing. ~ of power.

balcony (बालकनी) noun
छज्जा, platform built on outside wall of building. *We all sat in the ~ to see the picture.*

bald (बाल्ड) adjective
गंजा, नीरस, नंगा, having no or scanty hair on scalp. *A ~ man.*

bale (बेल) noun
बुराई, harmful, *His influence is ~ful.*

bale (बेल) noun
गाँठ, गाँठ बनाना, heap of material pressed and tied.

ball (बॉल) noun
गेंद, गोला, गोली, पिन्ड, solid or hollow sphere.

ball (बॉल) noun
अंग्रेजी नृत्य, gathering for dancing.

balloon (बैलून) noun
गुब्बारा, a bag filled with gas lighter than air.

ballot (बैलट) noun
मतपत्र, a piece of paper used in voting. *Use your ~ properly.*

ball-point pen, (बाल पॉइन्ट पैन) noun
बाल पैन, writing pen that do not use ink.

balm (बाम) noun
मल्हम, ointment for soothing pain.

ban (बैन) verb
प्रतिबंध, रोक लगाना, to prohibit, bar. *The govt. has ~ned this organisation.*

banana (बैनाना) noun
कदली, केला plaintain.

band (बैंड) noun
फीता, तस्मा, पट्टा, वाद्य मंडली, a group of persons who play music, a rubber band. *A ~ of robbers.*

bandage (बैन्डेज) noun
घाव पर बांधने की पट्टी, strip of medicated cloth for binding wounds. *Don't get the wound open, better get it ~d.*

bang (बैन्ग) noun
आघात का शब्द, धम, violent blow. *He ~ed his fist on the table.*

bangle (बैंगिल) noun
चूड़ी, कड़ा, ornamental band worn round the arm or ankle. *~s are very popular in India.*

banian (बनियान) noun
बनियान, jacket. *Wear a ~.*

banyan (बनियान) noun
बरगद का पेड, a very large tree.

bank (बैंक) noun
तट, किनारा, land sloping up along each side of the river

bank (बैंक) noun
बैंक, an institution for keeping money. *Keep your money in a good ~.*

banner (बैनर) noun
पताका, निशान, संकेत वाक्य (कपड़े पर), strip with slogan. *In which ~ is he now working?*

bar (बार) noun
छड़, डंडा किसी वस्तु का, long piece of wood, मदिरालय, शराब घर, room where drinks are served, अदालत, court छोड़कर, omitting. *He is now behind the prison ~s.*

bare (बेअर) adjective
नंगा, खाली, वस्त्रहीन, without clothing. *Do not go there ~ foot.*

bark (बार्क) noun
छाल, outer covering of a tree, भौंकना, चिल्लाना, to speak sharply, कुनैन का पेड़, *The dogs ~ at strangers.*

bargain (बारगेन) noun
सौदा, खरीदने बेचने का समझौता, agreement to buy and sale. *~ before you buy.*

barrel (बैरल) noun
पीपा, round container, cask. *Pack it in a ~.*

barrier (बैरियर) noun
अवरोध, सीमा, आड़, something that prevents. *Show your ticket at the ~.*

base (बेस) noun
आधार, lower part of anything, शिविर, छावनी centres of army, etc. *Vizag is a major naval ~.*

basic (बेसिक) adjective
बुनियादी, मूल, fundamental, *You must learn the ~ principles of mathematics.*

basin (बेसिन) noun
तसला, बड़ा कटोरा, round open dish of metal. *Wash your hands in the ~.*

basis (बेसिस) noun
आधार, बुनियाद, foundation. *Milk is the ~ of cheese and butter.*

bat (बैट) noun
चमगादड़, a mammal with a wing, बल्ला, wooden implement to strike the ball. *Cricket is played with a ~.*

batch (बैच) noun
टोली, जत्था, group. *He is my ~ mate.*

bath (बाथ) noun
स्नान, नहाने का काम, washing the body. *Go and take your ~.*

bathe (बेद) verb
नहाना, पानी से धोना, to take bath, apply water to. *The doctor ~d the wound.*

bathing (बेदिंग) noun
स्नान, act of taking bath. *~ cleans our body.*

battery (बैटरी) noun
फौज की टुकड़ी वाहन हथियारों सहित army unit, बैटरी, portable cell for supplying electricity. *A car ~.*

battle (बैटिल) noun
युद्ध, लड़ाई, संग्राम, struggle, fight between organized forces. *The famous ~ of Trafalgar.*

bay (बे) noun
खाड़ी, part of sea enclosed by a wide curve of coast. *The ~ of Bengal*

bazaar (बाज़ार) noun
बाजार, market, *Go to ~ and bring vegetables.*

be (बी) verb
होना, occur, happen, is, am, are, was, were, linking word, उपसर्ग की भांति प्रयोग जैसे before, behind, below. *They are to ~ married soon.*

beach (बीच) noun
समुद्र तट, किनारा, shore, coast. *Come and sit on the ~.*

beak (बीक) noun
चोंच, hard part of bird's mouth. *The bird is eating with its ~.*

beam (बीम) noun
कड़ी, horizontal piece of iron or timber to bear the weight of the building, तराजू की डंडी, किरण ray. *The sun ~ed down upon the field.*

bean (बीन) noun
सेम, फली, *~s can be eaten for protein.*

bear (बियर) noun
रीछ, अभद्र व्यक्ति, ill mannered person, रखना, have, सहन करना to tolerate. *One has to ~ so many things in life.*

beard (बिअर्ड) noun
दाढ़ी, hair on the lower part of the face. *The thief had a ~ on his face.*

bearer (बिअरर) noun
वाहक, messenger, चैक, *~ of the news.*

beast (बीस्ट) noun
चौपाया, पशु, निर्दय व्यक्ति, animal, cruel person. *A pony is the ~ of burden in the hills.*

beat (बीट) verb
पीटना, मारना, hit. टकराना, strike forcefully, हराना, defeat, चोट, stroke, blow. *Why are you ~ ing him?*

beauty (ब्यूटी) noun
सुन्दरता, खूबसूरती, मनोहरता, loveliness. *~ of painting.*

became (बिकेम) verb
past tense of become, हुआ. *He ~ a doctor when he was twenty five.*

because (बिकॉज़) conjunction
चूंकि, क्योंकि, इस कारण से, for the reason that. *He could not reach the school ~ of heavy rains.*

become (बिकम) verb
होना, हो जाना, बनना, begin to be. *What will ~ of the children if their mother dies?*

bed (बैड) noun
खाट, पलंग, a piece of furniture on which we sleep. *Now you must go to ~.*

bedbug (बैडबग) noun
खटमल, bloodsucking insect. *~s did'nt allow me to sleep.*

bedding (बैडिंग) noun
बिछावन, बिस्तर, bed cloth

bedrock (बैडरॉक) noun
तले की ठोस चट्टान, solid rock at bottom, fundamental principle, मूल सिद्दान्त

bed tea (बैड टी) noun
बिस्तर पर सबेरे पी जाने वाली चाय, tea taken in bed early morning. *Some people are habitual of ~.*

bee (बी) noun
मधुमक्खी, *An insect ~ gives us*

honey and wax.

beef (बीफ) noun
गाय, बैल आदि का गोश्त, flesh of an ox, bull or cow. *Very few people eat ~.*

beep (बीप) noun
भौंपू या विद्युतीय यंत्र की आवाज, warning sound of horn or electronic device.

befit (बिफिट) verb
शोभा देना, अच्छा लगना, be fit for. *My clothes did not ~ the occasion.*

befool (बिफूल) verb
धोखा देना, बेवकूफ बनाना to make a fool of, trick. *In the school boys ~ each other and enjoy.*

before (बिफोर) adverb
पहले, अतीत में, in the past. *The train had arrived ~ I reached the station.*

befriend (बिफ्रेन्ड) verb
मित्र बनना, make friend. *~ing everybody is his hobby.*

beg (बैग) verb
भिक्षा, भीख मांगना, ask for something. *He lived by ~ging.*

began (बिगैन) verb
प्रारंभ किया, past tense of begin. *He ~ working quite late.*

beggar (बैगर) noun
भिखमंगा, one who begs for livelihood *There are too many ~s is India.*

begin (बिगिन) verb
शुरू करना, to start. *Now we can ~ our game.*

behalf (बिहाफ) noun
पक्ष, समर्थन, ओर, तरफ, interest, support, benefit. *You will attend the meeting on ~ of me.*

behave (बिहेव) verb
व्यवहार करना, act, conduct. *Please ~ properly.*

behaviour (बिहेवियर) noun
व्यवहार, बर्ताव, way of behaving. *His ~ is not good.*

beheld (बिहैल्ड) verb
ध्यान से देखा, saw attentively. *I ~ the exhibit and then gave the award.*

behind (बिहाइण्ड) adverb
पीछे, in the rear. *You stand ~ me.*

belief (बिलीफ) noun
विश्वास, भरोसा, श्रद्धा, आस्था, trust, confidence. *To the best of my ~.*

believe (बिलीव) verb
विश्वास करना, किसी का कथन सत्य मानना, to trust, accept something as true. *They ~ his statements.*

bell (बैल) noun
घंटी, घंटा, घड़ियाल, hollow metal vessel to ring. *Ring the ~, the period is over.*

belly (बैली) noun
उदर, पेट, abdomen. *A hungry*

~ *has no ears.*

belong (बिलौंग) verb
किसी के अधिकार में होना, be property of. *That statesman ~s among the great.*

beloved (बिलवेड) adjective
अत्यधिक प्रिय, प्यारा, dearly loved. *He is my ~ friend.*

below (बिलो) preposition
किसी स्थान से नीचे, lower. *People in the rooms ~ are very talkative.*

belt (बैल्ट) noun
पेटी, कमरबंद, something to keep in place clothes or weapons *The warrior's ~ has a sword on it.*

bench (बैंच) noun
बैंच, बैठने का स्थान, long seat of wood to sit, उच्च न्यायालय की न्यायाधीश पीठ. *High court ~. The case is before the ~ for consideration.*

bend (बैंड) verb
मोड़ना, झुकना, to curve. *I can ~ him to my will.*

beneath (बिनीथ) preposition
नीचे, below, अशोभनीय, not worthy of. *It was ~ him to beg.*

benefit (बेनिफिट) noun
लाभ, फायदा, profit, advantage. *Get ~ from the past experience.*

bent (बैन्ट) adjective
टेढ़ा, मुड़ा हुआ, crooked, not straight. *He was ~ on going to theatre.*

berry (बैरी) noun
फली का एक विशेष समूह, a specific group of fruits. *Eat berries and break your fast.*

berth (बर्थ) noun
जहाज या रेल में सोने का स्थान, sleeping place in train or ship. *The M.L.A. could not get a ~ in the train.*

beside (बिसाइड) adverb
समीप, निकट, close to, इसके अलावा भी, moreover, also. *He sat ~ me.*

best (बैस्ट) adjective
सर्वोत्तम, सर्वश्रेष्ठ, most excellent. *He is the ~ teacher to teach English.*

bet (बैट) verb
शर्त लगाना, risk money on a game. *I ~ you will loose.*

betel (बीटल) verb
पान, ताम्बूल, leaf used by Indians for chewing. *Eat this ~ after meals.*

betray (बिट्रे) verb
धोखा देना, दगा देना, be disloyal to. *He ~ed his friends.*

better (बैटर) adjective
उससे अच्छा, comparative degree of good. *He had ~ed my work.*

between (बिटवीन) preposition
बीच में, in the space separating two points. *They*

had Rs.15 ~ them.

beware (बिवेयर) verb
सावधान, सतर्क रहना, be cautious. *~ of dogs.*

beyond (बियान्ड) adjective
परे, सुदूर, farther on. *What is ~ time is difficult to know.*

bias (बायस) noun
पक्षपात, एक तरफ झुकाव, predisposition, prejudice. *He has a ~ against the plan.*

bicycle (बाईसिकिल) noun
साइकिल, two-wheeled machine for riding on.*Get my ~ repaired.*

big (बिग) adjective
आकार में बड़ा, of large size or capacity. *He is working on a ~ post.*

bilingual (बाइलिंगुअल) adjective
दो भाषाओं का, using two languages. *He is ~.*

bill (बिल) noun
पर्चा, हिसाब संबंधी, a statement of money. *Give me the ~ for the amount I have paid.*

billion (बिलियन) noun
सौ करोड़, अरब, a thousand million. *~s of rupees are being spent on defence.*

bin (बिन) noun
अनाज, कोयला या अन्य पदार्थ रखने का पात्र, a large pot to keep things. *Throw dirty papers in the dust ~.*

bind (बाइण्ड) verb
बांधना, कब्जा करना, fasten with a rope. *~ my book properly.*

biodata (बायोडेटा)
जीवन का संक्षिप्त विवरण biographical information. *Prepare your ~ for the job.*

biography (बायोग्राफ़ी) noun
जीवन चरित, person's life-history written by another person. *Tulsidas has written a ~ of Rama.*

biology (बायोलाजी) noun
जीव विज्ञान, जैविकी, science of physical life of animals and plants.

bird (बर्ड) noun
चिड़िया, पक्षी, winged creature. *~s chirp.*

birth (बर्थ) noun
जन्म, पैदायश, process of being born. *My ~place is Nagpur.*

bit (बिट) noun
छोटा टुकडा, small piece of anything. *Give me a ~ of bread.*

bitch (बिच) noun
कुतिया, female dog. *A ~ is more loyal than a dog.*

bite (बाइट) noun
दांतों के काटने की क्रिया, act of biting. *Don't ~ my hand.*

bitter (बिटर) adjective
कड़ुआ, तीता, sour, not sweet.

biweekly (बाइवीकली) noun
पाक्षिक, अर्धसाप्ताहिक, happening

every two weeks, or twice a week.

black (ब्लैक) adjective
काला, अशुभ, opposite to white. *~ money is a curse.*

blade (ब्लेड) noun
चाकू, तलवार आदि का फल, शेव करने का ब्लेड, cutting part of knife, sword, razor. *He cut his cheek by the ~.*

blame (ब्लेम) verb
दोष ढूँढ़ना, find fault with. *The ~d person was punished.*

blank (ब्लैंक) adjective
कोरा, बिना लिखा हुआ, with nothing written on. *I gave him a ~ cheque.*

blanket (ब्लैंकेट) noun
कम्बल, thick woollen covering. *We use ~s in winter.*

blast (ब्लास्ट) noun
तेज झोंका, धमाका, strong, sudden rush of air or weapons. *There were bomb ~s in Bombay.*

bleed (ब्लीड) verb
खून बहना, to lose blood. *His wound was ~ing.*

bless (ब्लैस) verb
आशीर्वाद देना, to ask God's favour for. *God ~ me.*

blind (ब्लाइंड) adjective
अंधा, नेत्रहीन, not having the sense of sight. *A ~ person can move with a stick.*

block (ब्लॉक) verb
बाधा खड़ी करना, make movement difficult. *Police ~ed the road.*

blockage (ब्लॉकेज) noun
गतिरोध, obstruction. *Pak has created ~ in talks.*

blockbuster (ब्लॉकबस्टर)
भवनों को ढहाने वाला काम, something overwhelming, impressive. *This is a ~ film.*

blood (ब्लड) noun
रक्त, खून, रुधिर, fluid circulating in the vascular system of vertebrates. *~ clotting does not occur in haemophilia.*

bloom (ब्लूम) noun,verb
फूल, flower, खिलना, फूलना, flowering. *During spring flowers ~ alround.*

blossom (ब्लॉसम) noun, verb
फूल, flower, पुष्प खिलना. *Marigold ~s in winter.*

blouse (ब्लाउज़) noun
औरतों के पहनने की कमर तक की कुर्ती, outer garment from neck to waist worn by women . *Go and wear the ~.*

blow (ब्लो) verb
बहना, चलना, हवा से उड़ना, move along. *A kite ~s in the air.*

blower (ब्लोअर) noun
धौंकनी, फुंकैया, one that blows. *The ~ melts iron.*

blue (**ब्लू**) adjective
नीला, आसमानी, a colour. *Sky is ~.*

bluff (**ब्लफ**) noun
घुड़की, झाँसा, act of deception. *Dont ~, give me my book.*

blunder (**ब्लंडर**) noun
भारी भूल, stupid mistake. *He did a ~.*

boar (**बोर**) noun
जंगली भैंसा, wild male pig. *Beware of the ~.*

board (बोर्ड) noun
लकड़ी का तख्ता, flat piece of wood, an official group of persons supervising activity, संचालक मंडल. *The ~ sat to decide his case.*

boat (बोट) noun
नाव, नौका, किश्ती, open vessel for travelling on water. *I enjoyed ~ing in the river.*

bob (**बौब**) verb
ऊपर नीचे करना, move up and down, *She ~s her hair to be stylish.*

bodice (**बौडिस**) noun
चोली, अंगिया, woman's close-fitting dress, *The ~ she is wearing is perfect.*

body (**बॉडी**) noun
शरीर, मुख्य भाग, मनुष्यों का समूह, physical entity. *Food is human ~'s requirement.*

bogus (**बोगस**) adjective
नकली, जाली, sham, counterfeit. *It's a ~ firm.*

boil (**बौइल**) verb
उबलना, bubble up, फोड़ा, hard tumour. *Water ~s at 100°C.*

bold (**बोल्ड**) adjective
वीर, निर्भीक, साहसी, brave, enterprising. *Rani was a ~ woman.*

bomb (**बौम्ब**) noun
बम, an explosive device. *Heavy ~ing ruined the city.*

bond (**बौन्ड**) noun
बंधन, समझौता, प्रतिज्ञापत्र, agreement. *Seven year's ~ in service is okay.*

bone (**बोन**) noun
अस्थि, हड्डी, part of skeleton. *There are 206 ~s in our body.*

bonus (**बोनस**) noun
अधिलाभ, extra payment to workers. *One ~ was distributed to workers.*

book (**बुक**) noun, verb
किताब, पुस्तक, printed work of some length. पुस्तक में आदेश दर्ज करना, write down orders. *A good ~ is a boon to learn English.*

boom (**बूम**) verb
गरजना, to make loud sound. *The guns ~ed.*

boon (**बून**) noun
अनुग्रह, वरदान, gift, blessing. *A good friend is a great ~.*

boost (**बूस्ट**) verb
बढ़ावा देना, to raise effect. *Don't ~ the quarrel.*

boot (**बूट**) noun
जूता, covering for foot or ankle made of leather. *Bring my ~s.*

booth (**बूथ**) noun
तम्बू, छप्पर, tent, market stall. *Elections are held in polling ~s.*

border (**बॉर्डर**) noun
किनारा, हद, सीमा, edge, boundary. *Pakistan is on our western ~.*

bore (**बोर**) verb, noun
सूराख, छेद करना, to make a narrow, deep hole, ऊबना, to weary by dullness, अप्रिय, अरुचिकर, uninteresting. *He is a great ~.*

born (**बॉर्न**) verb
जन्म, पैदा हुआ, brought by birth. *Kishan Kumar was ~ in Patna.*

borne (**बोर्न**) verb
सहन कर चुका, लाया हुआ tolerated, carried. *I have ~ your many follies.*

borrow (**बौरो**) verb
उधार लेना, to take a loan. *I will ~ some money.*

bosom (**बूज़म**) noun
सीना, chest, छाती, वक्ष, a person's breast.

boss (**बौस**) noun
मालिक, स्वामी, person who supervises workmen. *My ~ is an honest man.*

botany (**बौटनी**) noun
वनस्पति शास्त्र, science relating to plants.

both (**बोथ**) adjective
दोनों, two together. *Should ~ of you go for tution?*

bother (**बौदर**) verb
परेशान करना, चिन्तित होना, to worry. *Don't ~ about clothes.*

bottle (**बॉटल**) noun
बोतल, container, *Ketchup is in the ~.*

bottom (**बौटम**) noun
तली, आधार, foundation. *There is nothing in the ~.*

bowl (**बोल**) noun
कटोरा, hollow dish. *Bring the ~ for handwash.*

box (**बॉक्स**) noun, verb
सन्दूक, मुक्केबाजी करना, container, to fight with fists. *Keep it in a ~.*

braid (**ब्रेड**) noun
जूड़ा, चोटी, strands of hair.

bray (**ब्रे**) verb
रेंकना, cry of ass. *The ass is ~ing.*

bread (**ब्रैड**) noun
रोटी, चपाती, डबलरोटी, food made of flour. *Give me a ~.*

break (**ब्रैक**) verb
टूटना, तोडना, divide into two or more parts. *Don't ~ the cup.*

breast (**ब्रैस्ट**) noun
स्तन, छाती, वक्षस्थल, milk-secreting organs of women.

breath (**ब्रीद**) noun
सांस, श्वांस, inhale and exhale in respiration. *Take deep ~.*

bribe (ब्राइब) noun, verb
घूस, रिश्वत देना, offer or give something to do a wrong. *~ing is a social evil.*

bride (ब्राइड) noun
दुल्हन, नववधू, newly married woman. *What a pretty ~.*

bridegroom (ब्राइडग्रूम) noun
दूल्हा, newly married man.

brief (ब्रीफ) noun
संक्षेप, जानकारी, summary, जांघिया *Give the news in ~.*

bright (ब्राइट) adjective
चमकीला, shining. *The sun is ~.*

broad (ब्रॉड) adjective
चौडा, wide. *The room is 10' ~.*

bucket (बकेट) noun
बाल्टी, pail. *I want a ~ful of water.*

butter oil (बटर ऑइल) noun
घी, *ghee.*

byte (बाईट) noun
कंप्यूटर विज्ञान में सूचना की इकाई, in computer technology a unit of information.

❑❑❑❑

C

c
मुद्रण में प्रयुक्त
लघु अक्षर

C
लिखने
में प्रयुक्त अक्षर

मूल
उच्चारण **सी**

क और स प्रयोग में उच्चारण ज्यादातर 'क' और कभी-कभी 'स'

प्रश्न : 'सी' का उच्चारण 'क' किस नियम के अनुसार है?

अंग्रेजी वर्णमाला का तीसरा अक्षर

a,o,u,i,r, के पूर्व रखे जाने पर 'क' का उच्चारण तथा e,i,y, के पूर्व रखे जाने पर 'स' का उच्चारण होता है

Roman numeral C = 100
कार्बन का चिह्न

cabin (केबिन) noun
छोटा कमरा, जहाज में, कार्यालय में अधिकारी वर्ग का बैठने का कमरा, रेल फाटक के पास बनी कोठरी, आदि, small roon, cottage. *The boss is in his ~.*

cabinet (कैबिनेट) noun
वस्तुओं को रखने वाला फर्नीचर, almirah, मंत्रिमंडल, group of ministers, *Keep books in the ~.*

cable (केबिल) noun
मजबूत रस्सा, thick rope, संदेश भेजने वाले तार, टीवी, T.V. *The ~ is not in good working condition.*

cadet (कैडेट) noun
सैनिक पाठशाला का विद्यार्थी, student of military or N.C.C. *He is a N.C.C.~.*

cafe (कैफे) noun
छोटा आहार गृह, small restaurant. *Have a cup of tea in the ~.*

cake (केक) noun
चीनी, मक्खन, आटा, अंडे से बनाया केक, टिकिया, soap cake. *The ~ is spongy.*

calculate (केलकुलेट) verb
गणना करना, हिसाब लगाना, find out by working with numbers. *~ his yearly payment.*

calender (कैलेण्डर) noun
तिथिपत्र, पंचांग, जंत्री, table of months, days, weeks and dates. *The ~ is on the wall.*

calf (काफ़) noun
गाय का बच्चा, बछड़ा, young of the cow, पिण्डली, fleshy part at the back of human leg. *It is a lovely ~.*

call (कौल) noun, verb
आवाज, पुकार, बुलाना shout, cry. *~ him to come.*

call of nature (कौल ऑफ नेचर) noun
पेशाब की हाजत, need to urinate. *Relieve me for ~.*

calm (काम) adjective
शांत, शम, प्रशांतता, quiet. *Sit ~.*

calorie (कैलरी) noun
ऊष्मा की इकाई, ऊष्मांक, unit of energy supplied by food. ऊष्मा की वह मात्रा जो एक ग्राम पानी में 1^0C की वृद्धि करती है, *2000 ~s is our daily need.*

camel (कैमल) noun
ऊँट a large-humped quadruped. *People in desert travel on ~s.*

camera (कैमरा) noun
कैमरा, a boxlike instrument to take photographs. *Take its photo by ~.*

camp (कैम्प) noun
शिविर, पड़ाव, a place where people gather for a long time. *We had a yoga ~.*

camphor (कैम्फर) noun
कपूर, a strong smelling white substance. *Bring some ~ for pooja.*

campus (कैम्पस) noun
परिसर, कम्पाउंड, grounds of a school, college or university. *Our school ~ is very big.*

can (कैन) noun, verb
टीन, कनस्तर, container, सकना, be able to. *Fill the ~ with petrol.*

canal (कैनाल) noun,
नहर, channel for carrying water. *I bathed in the ~.*

cancel (कैंसिल) verb
काटना, रद्द करना, निरस्त करना, cross out. *~ the extra answers.*

cancer (कैंसर) noun
कैंसर रोग, malignant tumour, कर्क रेखा Tropic of Cancer.

candidate (कैंडिडेट) noun
प्रार्थी, उम्मीदवार, a proposed person. *He is a ~ for the job.*

candle (कैंडिल) noun
मौमबत्ती, wax stick. *Light the ~.*

candy (कैंडी) noun
मिश्री, चाशनी का टुकडा, sweetened sugar stick. *The child is eating ~.*

cane (केन) noun
टहलने की छड़ी, walking stick. *I go for walking with my ~.*

canned (कैन्ड) adjective
डिब्बाबंद, सीलबंद, preserved and sealed in a can. *This is a ~ vegetable.*

canteen (कैंटीन) noun
जलपान गृह, where food and drinks are sold. *Students take breakfast in the ~.*

canvas (कैनवस) noun
टाट, किरमिच, एक प्रकार का मजबूत कपड़ा, coarse cloth used for tents, bags and for oil paintings. *He has painted a picture on the ~.*

canvass **(कैनवैस)** verb
समर्थन या वोट माँगने के लिए लोगों से मिलना, to solicit votes. *Leaders ~ during elections.*

cap **(कैप)** noun
टोपी, head dress. *He wears a ~.*

capable **(केपेबिल)** adjective
योग्य, समर्थ, competent. *Be ~ for doing your work.*

capacity **(कैपेसिटी)** noun
क्षमता, धारिता, रखने की सीमा, ability to hold. *The ~ of this glass is half a litre.*

capital **(कैपिटल)** noun
राजधानी, seat of the government, अंग्रेजी वर्णमाला के बड़े अक्षर, पूँजी, संपत्ति, व्यापार में लगा धन, wealth that is used for earning more wealth. *Bhopal is a ~ city.*

capricorn **(कैप्रिकॉर्न)** noun
मकर रेखा, Tropic of Capricorn.

captain **(कैप्टिन)** noun
कप्तान, leader or commander. *A ~ controls the entire ship.*

capture **(कैप्चर)** verb
पकड़ना, बंदी बनाना, make prisoner of. *Police ~d the convict.*

car **(कार)** noun
मोटर कार, रेलगाड़ी का डब्बा, गाड़ी, motor car. *This ~ has a music system.*

carat **(कैरेट)** noun
रत्नों के तौलने की माप (=200 mg), pure gold being 24. *I have purchased a 20 ~ topaz.*

carbon **(कार्बन)** noun
कोयला, काजल, black nonmetallic element. *~ is an element.*

carbon copy **(कार्बन कॉपी)** noun
टाइप अथवा हाथ से लिखे मजमून की कार्बन पेपर प्रति, written matter obtained with carbon paper. *Give me a ~ of the letter.*

card **(काड)** noun
मोटा कागज, stiff paper. *I have your visiting ~.*

cardamom **(कार्डमम)** noun
इलायची, an aromatic spice. *~ is an edible spice.*

card board **(कार्ड बोर्ड)**
गत्ता, दफ्ती, thick paper used to make boxes or binding books. *Make a house of ~.*

cardigan **(कार्डिगन)** noun
बिना कालर की बटन वाली ऊनी जैकेट, woollen jacket without collar and with buttons. *Wear your ~.*

care **(केयर)** noun
चौकसी, देखभाल, सावधानी, चिंता, परवाह, देखरेख करना, pay attention. *The ~s of life has aged him.*

careful **(केयरफुल)** adjective
सावधान, होशियार taking care, cautious. *Be ~ about what you say.*

careless **(कैयरलैस)** adjective
लापरवाह, असावधानी से किया गया,

thoughtless. *He is a ~ driver.*

cargo (कार्गो) noun
किसी जहाज या वाहन पर लदा माल, goods carried in a ship. *A ~ should be insured.*

carrom (कैरम) noun
कैरम, an indoor game. *Come and play ~ to enjoy.*

carpet (कारपेट) noun
फर्श, दरी, गलीचा, thick covering of floors. *Set this ~ on the floor.*

carriage (कैरिज) noun
गाड़ी, घोड़ागाड़ी, vehicle with four wheels. *Here is a ~ for goods.*

carrier (कैरियर) noun
किराया लेकर व्यक्ति या माल को एक जगह से दूसरी जगह ले जाने वाली संस्था railway, shipping or aircraft, साइकिल में सामान रखने का फ्रेम, बाजार से सामान लाने के लिए थैला. *Fix a ~ in your car.*

carrot (कैरट) noun
गाजर, edible root. *Prepare ~ juice.*

carry (कैरी) verb
ढोना, ले जाना, move from place to place. *~ the bicycle to home.*

cart (काटे) noun
दो पहियों वाली घोड़ागाड़ी, twowheeled vehicle pulled by a horse. *I enjoyed the ~ journey.*

carton (कार्टन) noun
गत्ते का बक्सा, a cardboard box, *Keep these items in a ~.*

cartoon (कार्टून) noun
हास्य चित्र, व्यंग्य चित्र, a sketch usually humorous satirizing some action. *~ films are good.*

case (केस) noun
प्रकरण, घटना, स्थिति, instance, पेटी, खोल, बक्सा, container. *The culprit was jailed in the ~.*

cash (कैश) noun
धन, मद्रा, रोकड़, money. *Keep your ~ safely.*

cashbook (कैशबुक) noun
रोकड़ बही, account book. *The ~ be updated.*

cashew (कैश्यू) noun
काजू, a nut.

cashier (कैशियर) noun
कोषाध्यक्ष, one who has charge of money. *The ~ absconded with the money.*

casing (केसिंग) noun
रक्षार्थ लगाया गया खोल, covering. *In his house the electric wires are not in a ~.*

cassette (कैसेट) noun
एक प्रकार का टेप, container for magnetic tape. *Keep the ~ in its box.*

cast (कास्ट) verb, noun
फेंकना, त्यागना, throw, drop, नाटक के पात्र, *~ your vote to an honest candidate.*

castle (कैसिल) noun
दुर्ग, महल, किला, a large building. *The ~ of Rana Pratap is very large.*

castor, caster (कैस्टर) noun
नमकदानी, शक्करदानी, container for sugar, salt. *I want salt, give me the ~.*

castor oil (कैस्टर ऑयल) noun
अरंडी का तेल, the oil yielded from castor plant. *The ~ is used as a purgative.*

casual (कैज्युअल) objective
आकस्मिक, सामयिक, happening by chance. *He drinks ~ly.*

casualty (कैज्युअल्टी) noun
दुर्घटना, विशेषतः जिसमें मृत्यु हो जाती है accident involving loss of life. *A ~ occurred in the car accident.*

cat (कैट) noun
बिल्ली, a pet animal, ईष्यालु औरत, spiteful woman *She is a ~.*

catalogue (कैटेलॉग) noun
सूचीपत्र, list of names, places, books, etc. *Print a ~ of books.*

catch (कैच) verb
पकड़ना, लपकना, stop by holding with hands. *The cricket player was ~ out.*

category (कैटेगरी) noun
श्रेणी, वर्ग, grouping, division in a complete system. *He belongs to the scheduled ~.*

cater (केटर) verb
भोजन या खानपान देना, to provide food. *Food was supplied by a ~er.*

cattle (कैटिल) noun
मवेशी, गाय, बैल, bovine animals. *A ~ fair was held in the village.*

cause (कौज़) noun
कारण, हेतु, वजह, that which produces and effects. *What is the ~ of your anger?*

caution (कॉशन) noun
सतर्कता, सावधानी, care taken to avoid danger.*Issue ~ to cadets.*

cautious (कॉशस) adjective
चौकस, सचेत, सावधानी से, to show caution. *Be ~ of pickpockets.*

cave (केव) noun
गुफा, कंदरा, खोह, hollow place under the ground. *Animals live in ~s.*

cavity (केविटी) noun
गुहिका, कोटर, पोल, खोखलापन, small hole. *She has a ~ in her tooth.*

cease (सीज़) verb
अन्त करना, समाप्त होना, bring to an end. *Police ~ed the action.*

ceiling (सीलिंग) noun
भीतरी छत, the inner roof of a room. *Fix a ~ fan.*

celebrate (सेलिब्रेट) verb
समारोह मनाना, उत्सव मनाना, to perform a ceremony. *They are ~ing their golden anniversary.*

celebrity (सेलिब्रिटी) noun
कीर्ति, प्रशंसा, यश, fame, praise, a renowned person, प्रसिद्ध व्यक्ति, *Our president is a ~.*

cell (सैल) noun
कोठरी, जेल या मठ की, कोशिका, minute mass of living matter. *The ~ is a structural and functional unit of life.*

cellulose (सैल्युलोज़) noun
कार्बोहाइड्रेट का प्रकार, inert carbohydrate, पौधों की कोशभित्ति में पाया जाने वाला भाग, the plant cell wall is made of. *Termites eat ~.*

celsius (सेलसियस) noun
सैंटिग्रेड, शतांश तापमान, पानी के जमने पर 0°C तथा उबलने पर 100°C बताता है, pertaining to temperature scale that shows 0°C at freezing and 100°C at boiling point, centigrade, now called celsius.

cement (सीमेंट) noun
ग्लू, सीमेंट, जोड़ने का मसाला, used as building material. *Fix the bricks with ~.*

cemetery (सैमिटरी) noun
कब्रिस्तान, an area used for burials. *Dead body is being taken to the ~.*

censor (सैंसर) noun
प्रकाशन-नियंत्रक, दोषान्वेषक, examining officer who cuts undesirable matter from films, letters, books, etc.*The ~ censures the film's obscene parts.*

censure (सैंसर) verb
दोष लगाना, निन्दा करना, criticise unfavourable things. *Censor ~s the films of undesirable parts.*

census (सैंसस) noun
जनगणना, counting of population. *The ~ was taken in 1991.*

cent (सैंट) noun
अमेरिकन डॉलर का सौवाँ भाग, 100th part of U.S. dollar and many metric currencies. *Give me ten ~s and take the bun.*

centage (सैन्टेज) noun
प्रतिशत दर, rate per hundred. *He got 85% ~ in 12th exam.*

centigrade (सैंटिग्रेड) adjective
सौ अंशों वाला, (0 to 100 degrees), ताप का माप, measure of heat. *Water freezes at 0°~.*

central (सैंट्रल) adjective
प्रमुख, अतिमहत्वपूर्ण, केन्द्रीय, बीच में, near the centre, chief, most important. *He is the ~ person on this occasion.*

centre (सेंटर) noun
केन्द्र, मध्यबिन्दु, धुरी, आकर्षणकेन्द्र, midpoint. *Keep a bouquet on the ~ table.*

century (सैंचुरी) noun
सौ वर्ष, शताब्दी, a period of 100 years. *We are living in the 21st~.*

cereal (सीरियल) noun
अनाज, अन्न, दाल, wheat, barley, gram. *~s are important for our growth.*

ceremony (सैरिमनी) noun
धार्मिक, सामाजिक अनष्ठान, formalities observed on occasions such as wedding, funeral, etc. *Today is his marriage ~.*

certain (सर्टेन) adjective
निश्चित, definite. *I will read this book ~ly.*

certify (सर्टिफाई) verb
प्रमाण पत्र देना, प्रमाणित करना, declare that something is true. *The principal will ~ his character.*

cess (सैस) noun
कर, tax. *A ~ has been imposed on every forest product.*

chain (चेन) noun
जंजीर, चेन, गले की चेन, connected series of links. *A ~ is necessary in the neck of pet dogs, loops, ring, etc.* बेड़ी, हथकड़ी, fetters for prisoners.

chair (चेयर) noun
कुर्सी, seat with arms. *First sit in the ~ and then work.*

chalk (चॉक) noun
खड़िया मिट्टी, white or coloured stick, चॉक. *The teachers use ~ to write on the blackboard.*

challenge (चैलेन्ज) verb,noun
चुनौती देना, चुनौती, play a game, run a race. *Both the teams are playing with a feeling of ~.*

chamber (चैम्बर) noun
बड़ा कमरा, a large room, न्यायाधीश का कमरा, judges room. *Judge is in his ~.*

champion (चैम्पिअन) noun
वीर, योद्धा, person who fights, सर्वोत्तम exceeding all others. *Mr. Anand is our chess ~.*

chance (चांस) noun
संयोग, भाग्य, दैवयोग, by fortune or luck, मौका, अवसर. *This is your last ~ to pass the exams.*

chancellor (चांसलर) noun
विश्वविद्यालय का कुलपति, universitiy's president. *The Governor dismissed the ~.*

change (चेंज) verb
बदलना, परिवर्तन, make or become different. *~ your clothes and go to school.*

channel (चैनल) noun
जलमार्ग, waterway, पहुँचने का रास्ता, means of access, रेडियो या दूरदर्शन पर समाचार भेजने का मार्ग, a band (Radio, T.V.) or frequency. *The English ~ is between England and France.*

chaos (केऔस) noun
अव्यवस्था, गड़बड़ी, गोलमाल, confusion, disorder. *The rioters left the city in a state of ~.*

chapter (चैप्टर) noun
अध्याय, समय की अवधि, division of book, epoch. *The Gupta*

period was the most brilliant ~ in the history of India.

character (कैरेक्टर) noun
चरित्र, प्रकृति, traits and nature of a person. *That lady is of fine ~.*

charcoal (चारकोल) noun
लकड़ी का कोयला, black made by burning of wood. *~ turns into ash after burning.*

charge (चार्ज) verb, noun
अभियोग, दोषारोपण करना, accuse, वस्तु अथवा सेवाओं का मूल्य, काम की सुपुर्दगी, जिम्मेदारी, जोरदार आक्रमण, बिजली संचय यंत्र में बिजली भरना, अंगीकार करना, *After suspension he got the ~ sheet.*

charity (चैरिटी) noun
पुण्य, दान, benevolent feelings. *~ begins at home.*

charm (चार्म) noun, verb
जादू, मोहिनी, मोहित करना, pleasing quality. *She is a ~ing girl.*

chart (चार्ट) noun
नक्शा, तालिका, paper sheet of various information. *Prepare a ~ for English translation.*

charter (चार्टर) noun
राजपत्र, अधिकार पत्र, वायुयान या जलयान किराए पर लेना, hired aircraft or ship, लिखित इकरारनामा, a written deed, लेखा निरीक्षक, chartered accountant. *The Minister travelled in a ~ plane.*

chase (चेज़) verb
पीछा करना, drive away. *Police ~d the man, but couldn't catch him.*

chassis (चेसिस) noun
कार या गाड़ी का ढाँचा, framework. *The ~ of your car is very old.*

chat (चैट) noun, verb
मैत्रीपूर्ण वार्तालाप, friendly talk, gossip. *They ~ for hours together on mobile phone.*

chatter (चैटर) verb
बकवास करना, व्यर्थ की बातें करना, talk foolishly. *Don't ~ here and go.*

cheat (चीट) verb
ठगना, बेइमानी करना, to defraud. *The thief ~ed the man of Rs 500.*

check (चैक) verb
जाँच-पड़ताल करना, to examine. *Go and ~ the examination centre.* चारखाने वाला कपड़ा, crosslined patterned cloth. *This ~ cloth is for your shirt.*

cheer (चियर) verb
प्रसन्न करना, शाबासी देना, to fill with gladness. *Complete the work ~fully.*

cheese (चीज़) noun
पनीर, छैना, solid food made from milk. *Spread the ~ on bread slices.*

chef (शेफ) noun
प्रधान रसोइया, male headcook. *My son-in-law is a ~ in the hotel.*

chemical (**कैमिकल**) noun
रासायनिक, pertaining to chemistry. *In chocolate harmful ~s are mixed.*

cheque (**चैक**) noun
चैक, बैंक को दिया भुगतान पत्र. *The Principal has paid a ~ to him instead of cash.*

cherry (**चैरी**) noun
गोल लाल फल. *The ~ tree is packed with its fruits.*

chess (**चैस**) noun
शतंरज, game of two persons. *He is very fond of ~.*

chest (**चैस्ट**) noun
संदूक, पिटारी, लोहे की तिजोरी, strong box, छाती, सीना, वक्ष, breast. *Keep the cash in the ~.*

chew (**च्यू**) verb
चबाना, to grind with teeth. *~ the food properly in the mouth.*

chick (**चिक**) noun
नन्हीं चिड़िया, small bird. *The ~ is very colourful.*

chicken (**चिकन**) noun
मुर्गी का बच्चा. *People like fried ~ very much.*

chief (**चीफ़**) noun
मुख्य, प्रधान, prominent. *Mr. Gupta is the ~ of staff.*

child (**चाइल्ड**) noun
बालक, शिशु, लड़का या लड़की. infant, boy or girl. *Raju is a mentally sick ~.*

chill (**चिल**) noun, verb
ठंड, काँपना, to feel cold. *The beggar girl died of ~ in the night.*

chin (**चिन**) noun
ठोड़ी, चिबुक, part of body below the mouth. *Mother kissed the ~ of her son.*

chip (**चिप**) noun
किसी वस्तु का छोटा टुकड़ा, electronic chip. *~s are loaded with software in computers.*

choice (**चॉइस**) noun
चुनाव, पसन्द, act of choosing. *These clothes are my ~.*

choke (**चोक**) verb
दम घुटना, unable to breath, पैट्रोल इंजन का ढक्कन, valve in petrol engine. *Four people ~d and died when a mine fell over them.*

choose (**चूज़**) verb
चुनना, to select. *~ the subjects of your liking.*

chop (**चॉप**) verb
टुकड़े करना, to cut, सरकारी सील, official seal. *Give me a plate of ~ped fruits.*

chorus (**कोरस**) noun
समूह गान, गायक दल, group of singers. *Boys were singing in a ~.*

Christ (**क्राइस्ट**) noun
ईसा मसीह, name given to Jesus. *~ was born in Israel.*

chronic (**क्रॉनिक**) adjective
पुरानी बीमारी, disease lasting for a long time. *She expired of ~ diabetes.*

chuckle (**चकिल**) noun
मुंह बन्द करके धीमी हँसी, quiet laugh with closed mouth. *Girls ~ing made everyone laugh.*

church (**चर्च**) noun
गिरजाघर, Christian worship house. *The guilty persons go to the ~ and make confessions there.*

cigar (**सिगार**) noun
धूम्रपान हेतु सिगार, round roll of tobacco leaves for smoking. *Rich people smoke ~s.*

cigarette (**सिगरेट**) noun
सिगरेट, round paper roll with tobacco. *~ smoking is injurious to health.*

cinema (**सिनेमा**) noun
सिनेमाघर, theatre to show films. *Last evening I had gone to the ~.*

cipher (**साइफर**) noun
शुन्य, जीरो, zero. *He got a ~ in maths.*

circle (**सर्किल**) noun
वृत्त, गोला, round figure.

The teacher en~d the wrong words.

circuit (**सर्किट**) noun
परिभ्रमण, परिक्रमा, roundabout, विद्युत परिपथ, closed path for an electric current. *When the ~ is complete, the bulb lights.*

circulate (**सरकुलेट**) verb
भ्रमण करना, चक्कर लगाना, go round. *Heart is the organ through which blood ~s.*

circumstance (**सरकमस्टैन्स**) noun
परिस्थिति, condition. *Her ~s did not allow her to study.*

circus (**सर्कस**) noun
सरकस, आदमियों तथा पशुओं द्वारा खेल दिखाए जाने का स्थान. *To play in a ~ is always risky.*

cite (**साइट**) verb
उदाहरण देना, to quote an example. *~ an example in support of your statement.*

citizen (**सिटिज़न**) noun
नागरिक, person living in a country. *I am a ~ of India.*

citrus (**साइट्रस**) noun
नीबू, खट्टे रस वाले फल, edible fruits such as lemon, orange, lime. *~ fruits fulfil the deficiency of Vit. C.*

city (**सिटी**) noun
शहर, नगर, large town. *Kolkata is a large ~.*

civil (**सिविल**) noun
नागरिक संबंधी, of citizens, civilian. *Wear ~ dress and then go in public, said the police officer.*

claim (क्लेम) verb
अपना अधिकार जताना, दावा करना, to demand one's right. *It is troublesome to get your financial ~ after retirement.*

clamp (क्लैम्प) noun
शिकंजा, दृढ़ता से पकड़ने हेतु यंत्र, band of iron for tightening. *~ the pipe tightly, otherwise the machine will not work.*

clap (क्लैप) verb
ताली बजाना, striking the palms together. *The children ~ped when they saw the magic show.*

clarify (क्लेरिफाई) verb
स्पष्ट करना, make clear. *~ your statement, so you could be saved of the punishment.*

clash (क्लैश) verb
टकराना, collide. *They ~ed with the enemies.*

class (क्लास) noun
श्रेणी, kind of division. *He belongs to the corporate ~.*

classic (क्लासिक) adjective
सर्वोच्च कोटि का, of the class.

classical (क्लासिकल) adjective
शास्त्रीय, of highest excellence. *His work was a ~.*

classify (क्लासिफाई) verb
वर्गीकृत करना, arrange in groups. *Books are ~ied subjectwise in the library.*

clause (क्लॉज़) noun
वाक्यांश, part of sentence. *Change the noun in ~.*

clay (क्ले) noun
मिट्टी, sticky earth. *Bastar ~ pots are made in the olden style.*

claw (क्लौ) noun
पंजा, तीखा, नाखून, palm with nails. *The dog ~ed a hole in the earth.*

clean (क्लीन) adjective
साफ, स्वच्छ, free from dirt, to make clean. *He leads a ~ life.*

clear (क्लिअर) adjective
स्पष्ट, पारदर्शक, easy to see through, remove. *His words are not ~.*

clear-cut (क्लिअरकट) adjective
स्पष्टता से, definite. *Selling secrets of one's country is a ~ example of treachery.*

clergy (क्लर्जी) noun
पादरी, persons ordained as priests. *The ~man was exempted from criminal process before a secular judge.*

clerk (क्लर्क) noun
लिपिक, person employed in any office. *Entire India is ruled by ~s.*

clever (क्लैवर) adjective
चतुर, कुशाग्र बुद्धि, quick in learning. *Are you trying to be ~?*

click (क्लिक) noun
खटखट की आवाज, short sharp sound. *He saluted his officer with a ~ of his heels.*

climate (क्लाइमेट) noun
जलवायु, weather conditions. *Political ~ is not favourable for the ruling party.*

climax (क्लाइमैक्स) noun
उत्कर्ष, चरम सीमा, most intense point. *Their quarrel has reached a ~.*

climb (क्लाइम्ब) verb
चढ़ना, to ascend. *He ~ed to the fourth storey through stairs.*

clinic (क्लिनिक) noun
अस्पताल, चिकित्सालय, hospital. *The doctor is sitting in his ~.*

clock (क्लोक) noun
घड़ी, instrument for measuring time. *I have bought a new ~.*

close (क्लोज़) verb
बंद करना, shut, अन्त, समाप्ति, end. *He wants to ~ his accounts in the bank.*

clot (क्लौट) noun
थक्का, जमा हुआ, coagulated blood. *Snowballs thrown by us ~ted the façade of the house.*

cloth (क्लौथ) noun
कपड़ा, cotton, wool, silk cloth. *Purchase a ~bound register from the shop.*

clothe (क्लोद) verb
कपड़े पहनना, garments for the body. *Gentlemen are always ~d nicely. Hang the ~s here.*

cloud (क्लाउड) noun
मेघ, बादल. *There was a ~ burst in Tamia.*

clove (क्लोव) noun
लौंग, a spice. *Use ~ oil in aching tooth.*

clown (क्लाउन) noun
मसखरा, joker. *Stop this ~ing.*

club (क्लब) noun
सामाजिक सेवा या मनोरंजन हेतु व्यक्तियों का समुदाय, *Rotary ~ donated Rs. 5000/- to flood sufferers.*

clue (क्लू) noun
संकेत, hint. *Police could'nt get a ~ to the murder.*

co (को) prefix
साथ के लिए उपसर्ग, co-education, कंपनी का संक्षिप्त रूप. *There is ~education in this school.*

coach (कोच) noun
यात्री, गाड़ी, बस, passenger car, खेल की शिक्षा देने वाला विशेषज्ञ, trainer. *My ~ trained me in football.*

coal (कोल) noun
पत्थर का कोयला, black mineral. *Smoke causes diseases where most people burn ~.*

coarse (कोर्स) adjective
मोटा तथा भारी, not fine. *Give a ~ cloth to the servant for wet-*

cleaning of the house.

coast (कोस्ट) noun
समुद्र का किनारा, seashore. *Sunset at sea ~ looks good.*

cobbler (कौबलर) noun
मोची, mender of shoes. *The ~ mended the boy's shoes very carefully.*

cock (कॉक) noun
मुर्गा, male fowl, बिगाड़ देना. *They completely ~ed up the arrangements of the party.*

cockpit (कॉकपिट)
हवाई जहाज में पाइलट के बैठने का स्थान। *The pilot sat in the ~ and then there was a blast.*

code (कोड) noun
नियमावली, systematic collection of laws. *A ~ is used in ATM cards.*

coffee (कॉफी) noun
एक पेय पदार्थ, drink with milk and coffee powder. *There is ~ after the meal.*

coffin (कॉफिन)
लाश रखने का ताबूत, box for dead body. *Now keep his dead body in the ~ and take it to the cemetry.*

coil (कॉइल) verb
कुंडली, curl round and round. *My friend's pump motor ~ was burnt.*

coin (कॉइन) noun
सिक्का, मुद्रा, metal money. *The boy asked for a rupee ~ to buy toffee.*

coincidence (कोइन्सीडेन्स) noun
दो घटनाओं में समकालिकता. *That his two-wheeler punctured before a puncture shop, was a ~.*

coir (कौइर) noun
नारियल की जटा, fibres of coconut shells. *Sleeping beds are made of ~ and foam.*

coke (कोक) noun
पत्थर का बुझा हुआ कोयला, kind of soft coal. *~ is made by furning coal in an oven.*

cold (कोल्ड) adjective
ठंडा, शीतल, having low temperature. *My father threw ~ water on my ambitions.*

collaborate (कोलैबरैट) verb
मिलकर कार्य करना, work in partnership. *Both friends are running the medical shop in collaboration.*

collapse (कोलैप्स) verb
ढहना, नष्ट हो जाना, fall down, break. *The roof ~d under the weight of snow.*

collar (कॉलर) noun
गले की पट्टी, part of garment put round the neck. *Don't ask him anything while he is so hot under the ~.*

colleague (कलीग) noun
सहकर्मी, persons working together. *He is respected by his ~s in the office.*

collect (कलैक्ट) verb
संग्रह करना, इकट्ठा करना, gather together. *~ all the waste paper and throw it.*

college (कॉलिज) noun
उच्च शिक्षा या पेशेगत शिक्षा का संस्थान, institution for higher or professional education. *Students of a party killed a professor in ~ elections.*

collide (कलाईड) verb
टकरा जाना, strike, clash. *The cars ~ d in the fog.*

colon (कोलन) noun
बड़ी आँत का निचला भाग, lower part of large intestine. *The ~ is five feet long.*

colonel (कर्नल) noun
कर्नल, army officer above lieutenant. *The lieutenant saluted the ~.*

colony (कॉलोनी) noun
स्वतंत्र नगर, लोगों द्वारा बसाया गया क्षेत्र, plants, animals, humans living together. *There is an Indian ~ in San Francisco.*

colour (कलर) noun
रंग, hue, tint. *Beryl is green in ~.*

column (कॉलम) noun
स्तम्भ, खंभा, upright pillar. *Draw two ~s and then mark the differences.*

comb (कॉम्ब) noun
कंघी, कंघा, instrument for combing hair. *I purchased a ~ of ivory.*

combine (कम्बाइन) verb
जोड़ना, मिलाना, join together. *Some films ~ education with recreation.*

come (कम) verb
आना, पहुँचना, to arrive, to reach. *Where are you ~ing from?*

comedy (कॉमिडी) noun
सुखान्त नाटक, play of amusing kind. *I prefer ~ to tragedy.*

comfort (कम्फर्ट) noun
आराम, सुविधा, relief. *Your father gave me great ~.*

comic (कॉमिक) adjective
हँसी लाने वाला, हास्यास्पद, causing laughter. *There are ~ strips in newspapers.*

comma (कौमा) noun
अल्पविराम, punctuation mark (,)

command (कमान्ड) noun
आदेश, हुक्म, आदेश देना order. *I am at your ~.*

commando (कमान्डो) noun
कमान्डो, फुर्तीले एंव तेज आक्रमण हेतु सैनिक, *~s play a very important part in a country's security.*

commence (कमैन्स) verb
प्रारंभ करना, शुरू करना. to begin, start. *In India the financial year ~ s from April 1st.*

comment (कमैन्ट) noun
टिप्पणी, राय, राय देना, opinion given on an event. *Has anybody to make ~s on my story?*

commerce (कॉमर्स) noun
वाणिज्य, व्यापार, trade between countries. *The cashier should keep all commercial papers under lock and key.*

commission (कमिशन) noun
कोई काम करने का अधिकार, बिक्री से प्राप्त हिस्सा authority for a particular work. *He secured a ~ to design the building.*

commit (कमिट) verb
वादा करना, to promise, to perform. *Mother of four children ~ted suicide.*

committee (कमिटी) noun
समिति, कमेटी, group of persons for some particular work. *We formed a ~ of ten members to look after the expenses.*

commodity (कमोडिटी) noun
सामान, सामग्री, useful things esp. of trade. *He has least ~ requirements.*

common (कौमन) adjective
सामान्य, सार्वजनिक, used for all. *It is of ~ advantage that traffic rules should be followed.*

commune (कम्यून) verb
बातचीत करना, संपर्क करना, मिलन स्थल, to talk in an intimate way. *There is a ~ where we all gather and meditate.*

communication (कम्युनिकेशन) noun
संदेश या समाचार एक से दूसरे के पास भेजना, pass on some news to somebody. *Our ~ with the north has been prevented by heavy snowfall.*

communism (कम्यूनिज्म) noun
साम्यवाद, a system where resources, means of production etc. are under govt. control . *China is ruled by ~.*

community (कम्यूनिटी) noun
एक वर्ग, समाज, समुदाय, a social group. *There is a separate ~ of Indians in America.*

commute (कम्यूट) verb
विनिमय, परिवर्तन (भुगतान की विधि में) to exchange one thing into another. *He ~d his pension for 10 years.*

compact (कम्पैक्ट) noun
समझौता, सौदा, संविदा, agreement सुगठित, closely packed.

companion (कम्पेनियन) noun
साथी, associate. *Now-a-days my ~ is misfortune.*

company (कम्पनी) noun
संगति, साहचर्य, व्यापार की कंपनी, group business, being together with another. *I shall be glad of your ~ on the journey.*

comparable (कोम्परेबल) adjective
तुलना करने योग्य, that which can be compared. *The two characters are not ~.*

compare (कम्पेयर) verb
मिलान करना, तुलना बताना, समानता

बताना, to find out points of similarity or dissimilarity. *Poets have ~ed sleep to death.*

compartment (कम्पार्टमैन्ट) noun
रेल का डिब्बा, partition of railway carriages. *The first class ~s are in the rear.*

compass (कम्पास) noun
कुतुबनुमा, instrument showing magnetic north direction. परकार, *Draw a circle of 2.5 cm. radius with the help of ~.*

compassion (कम्पैशन) noun
करुणा, अनुकंपा, दया, संवेदना, pity, sympathy. *We must have ~ for refugees.*

compatible (कम्पैटिबल) adjective
अनुकूल, संगत, capable of exis - ting together with harmony. *Driving at high speeds is not ~ with safety.*

compel (कम्पैल) verb
दबाव डालना, मजबूर करना, to force. *His boss ~led him not to go on leave.*

compensate (कम्पैन्सेट) verb
क्षतिपूर्ति, भरपाई करना, to recompense for something. *He ~d his homely appearance with fascinating manners.*

competent (कॉम्पिटेंट) adjective
समर्थ, योग्य, निपुण, possessing skill. *Is he a ~ teacher?*

compile (कम्पाइल) verb
संकलित करना, to collect information and arrange in the form of a book or list. *~ a dictionary of spoken English.*

complain (कम्पलेन) verb
शिकायत करना, to express dissatisfaction. *Don't ~ of your youngers.*

complement (कम्प्लीमेंट) noun
पूरक, completing. *They do not have a full ~ of staff.*

complete (कम्प्लीट) adjective
संपूर्ण, पूरा करना, whole. *I need only two words to ~ the puzzle.*

complex (कम्प्लैक्स) adjective
संमिश्रित, जटिल, difficult to understand. *There are endless ~ities in international diplomacy.*

complexion (कप्लैक्शन) noun
रंग, रूप, natural colour and appearance of face. *The ~ of a girl is the base of her marriage.*

compliment (कौम्प्लीमेंट) noun
प्रशंसा, तारीफ़, expression of praise. *The boss paid him ~s while seeing him off at the door.*

comply (कॉम्प्लाई) verb
किसी की आज्ञा, इच्छा, प्रार्थना के अनुसार कार्य करना, act as

requested, on command or somebody's wishes. *You must ~ with the rules.*

compose (कम्पोज़) verb
बनाना, निर्माण करना, form, make up. *He teaches and also ~s poetry.*

composition (कौम्पोज़ीशन) noun
लेख, रचना, a piece of writing or music. *He sang his own ~.*

compound (कम्पाउन्ड) noun
यौगिक वस्तु, बाड़ा, अहाता, enclosed area. *Common salt is a ~ of sodium and chlorine.*

compromise (कम्प्रोमाइज़) noun
समझौता, settlement of dispute. *The contending parties couldn't agree to ~.*

compulsory (कम्पलसरी) noun
अनिवार्य, essential. *English is a ~ subject up to graduation.*

computer (कम्प्यूटर) noun
कम्प्यूटर मशीन, a machine to control, process, or store a system, operation or information by means of electronic device. *We can perform too many programmes with a ~.*

concave (कौनकेव) adjective
अवतल, curved inwards. *Road pits are ~, therefore dirty water is collected in it.*

conceive (कनसीव) verb
किसी विषय पर कल्पना करना, form an idea in mind. गर्भ रह जाना, become pregnant. *The plan you've ~d is good.*

concentrate (कन्सेन्ट्रेट) verb
ध्यान केन्द्रित करना *She was told, she couldn't ~.*

conception (कनसेप्शन) noun
संकल्पना, idea that takes shape in mind, गर्भधारण, become pregnant. *A debator must have a clear ~ of the subject of debate.*

concern (कन्सर्न) verb
चिन्ता, संबध रखना, worry, have relation with. *The problem of dowry should ~ all of us.*

concession (कन्सेशन) noun
छूट, सुविधा, a grant. *Electric fans are selling at ~ prices during the off-season.*

concise (कन्साइज़) adjective
संक्षिप्त, brief, abridged. *Give a quick and ~ narration of the accident.*

conclude (कनक्लूड) verb
अन्त होना, अन्त करना, arrive at a conclusion. bring to an end. *We ~d not to attend the function.*

concrete (कॉन्क्रीट) adjective
जो देखी, छुई जा सके, that can be touched, ठोस, दृढ, कंकरीट, *Building material is made of ~.*

concur (कन्कर) verb
एकमत होना, agree in opinion. *I totally ~ with the speaker.*

condemn (कन्डैम) verb
बुरा बताना, दोषी ठहराना, disapprove. *The city development authority ~ ed his property dealings.*

condense (कन्डैन्स) verb
गाढ़ा, ठोस करना, to make compact, भाषण, पुस्तक का संक्षिप्तीकरण, shorter form. *Give a ~d account of the accident.*

condolence (कंडोलेन्स) noun
शोक प्रकट करना, expressing sorrow. *Please accept my ~s on your father's death.*

conduct (कंडक्ट) noun
व्यवहार, behaviour. *A guide ~ed the visitors around the museum.*

conductor (कंडक्टर) noun
चालक, पथप्रदर्शक, leader, guide. *Copper is a good ~ of electricity.*

cone (कोन) noun
शंकु, of pointed shape. *Give me ice cream in a ~.*

confess (कनफैस) verb
अपराध स्वीकार करना, to admit. *He ~ed his misdeeds to his friends.*

confidence (कौनफिडेन्स) noun
आत्मविश्वास, भरोसा, firm trust. *We should never lose our ~.*

confine (कनफ़ाइन) verb
सीमा के अन्दर रहना, keep within limits.

confirm (कनफर्म) verb
पुष्टि करना, सुदृढ़ करना, make firmer and stronger. *He has been ~ed as a secretary.*

conflict (कनफ्लिक्ट) noun
विरोध, तालमेल न रखना, be in disagreement. *The account of accident ~s with yours.*

confuse (कनफ्यूज) verb
दुविधा पैदा करना, to perplex. *The press reporters ~d the minister.*

congestion (कनजैशन) noun
भीड़भाड़, शरीर के किसी अंग में रक्त का जमाव, crowd, *There was ~ of blood in his lungs.*

congratulate (कनग्रेचुलेट) verb
शुभकामना देना, बधाई देना, to express joy at somebody's fortune. *Staff ~d him for his promotion.*

congress (कॉंग्रेस) noun
सभा, काँग्रेस दल, meeting of representatives for discussion, political party. The ~ party has ruled in India for many decades.

conjugal (कॉन्जुगल) adjective
दाम्पत्य, विवाह संबंधी, relating to marriage. *Their ~ relationship is excellent.*

connect (कनैक्ट) verb
मिलाना, संबंध स्थापित करना, join together. *The two towns have been ~ed by railway.*

conquer (कान्कर) verb
लड़ाई में जीतना, win a war. *The allied forces ~ed Germany.*

conscience (कॉनशेन्स) noun
अंतःकरण, भले बुरे का ज्ञान, विवेक, sense of right or wrong. *Have a clear ~ about your work.*

conscious (कॉन्शस) adjective
जाग्रत, सचेत, सावधान, aware. *He was ~ of his crime.*

consent (कनसैंट) noun
सहमति, स्वीकृति देना, agree, permit. *His parents refused their ~ to the marriage.*

consequent (कॉनसिक्वेन्ट) adjective
परिणास्वरूप, फलतः, following as a result. *The rise in prices is ~ upon the shortage of supply.*

conservation (कनज़रवेशन) noun
संरक्षण, क्षति से बचाव, preservation. *~ of water is necessary for future generations.*

consider (कंसिडर) verb
सोचना, विचार करना, think carefully about. *Please ~ my suggestion.*

consist (कंसिस्ट) verb
का बना होना, be made up of. *A quadrilateral ~s of four sides.*

console (कन्सोल) verb
चिंतित व्यक्ति को सांत्वना देना, show sympathy to worried person. *~ somebody for loss.*

conspiracy (कॉन्सपिरेसी) noun
साजिश, षड्यंत्र, fraud, wrongful act. *He joined the ~ to overthrow the government.*

constant (कॉन्सटैंट) adjective
अडिग, स्थिर, not changing, persistent. *Your complaints are ~ly received.*

constitution (कौनस्टिट्यूशन)
संविधान, रचना, laws and principles to govern a state. *Indian ~.*

construct (कंस्ट्रक्ट) verb
निर्माण करना, build, form. *~ a triangle in given conditions.*

consult (कॉन्सलट) verb
परामर्श लेना, सलाह लेना, to take advice. *I will ~ my lawyer on this point.*

consume (कंज़्यूम) verb
खाना पीना, eat or drink. उपयोग होना. *She ~s a lot of things in entertaining her guest.*

consumer (कंज्यूमर) noun
उपभोक्ता, one who uses a commodity or service. *We all are ~s of several goods.*

contact (कॉन्टैक्ट) noun
सम्पर्क करना, process of coming together. *Where should I ~ Mr. Martin?*

contain (कन्टेन) verb
रखना, धारण करना, hold within

itself. *This book ~s twenty fairly tales.*

contempt (कंटैम्प्ट) noun
नफरत, आदेश की अवहेलना, disrespect, scorn. *A terrorist should be held in ~.*

content (कंटैन्ट) adjective
संतुष्ट, satisfied. *These things ~ me.*

contest (कंटैस्ट) noun
प्रतियोगिता, तर्क, विवाद, argue against, take part in a competition, debate. *The enemy ~ed every inch of the ground.*

continue (कंटिन्यू) verb
जारी रखना, करते रहना, go further, keep doing, *The flood ~d for two weeks.*

contract (कॉन्ट्रैक्ट) noun
सौदा, ठेका, करार, binding agreement, संकुचित होना, become narrower, tighter. *Metals ~ as they become cool.*

contrary (कान्ट्रेरी) noun
विपरीत, विलोम, opposite in nature. *The ship was delayed owing to ~ winds.*

contrast (कॉन्ट्रास्ट) noun
प्रतिकूलता, विषमता, *~ these imported goods with the home-made ones.*

contribute (कन्ट्रिब्यूट) verb
जनहित में सहायता देना, give for common use. *~ food & clothing for the victims of flood.*

control (कन्ट्रोल) verb
नियंत्रण करना, check, अधिकार, authority. *The Government ~s trade and industry.*

controversy (कंट्रोवर्सी) noun
लंबा विवाद, long argument. *His appointment as minister has aroused a lot of ~.*

convenience (कनवीनिएन्स) noun
सुविधा, आराम, facility. *It is a great ~ to have the bus stand near our house.*

converse (कन्वर्स) verb
किसी व्यक्ति से बातचीत करना, to talk together. *What were you ~ing with the gentleman about.*

convert (कन्वर्ट) verb
बदलना, परिवर्तन करना, to change. *Many Christians were ~ed to Hinduism.*

convex (कॉन्वैक्स) adjective
उत्तल, बाहर की ओर उभरा. curved like a ball. *There is a hill ~ in shape.*

convey (कनवे) verb
पहुँचाना, ले जाना, take, carry. *Please ~ my good wishes to him.*

conveyance (कन्वेएंस) noun
वाहन, परिवहन, anything that carries people, *Whose ~ will you use to reach us?*

convict (कनविक्ट) verb
अपराधी सिद्ध करना, अपराधी, to

declare guilty, the guilty. *He was ~ed for felony.*

convince (कनविन्स) verb
समझाना, कायल करना, to make somebody realize. *I ~d him of his folly.*

cook (कुक) verb
खाना पकाना, खाना बनानेवाला, फर्जी हिसाब बनाना, to prepare food, one who makes food. *What is ~ing at the club?*

cool (कूल) adjective
ठंडा, शीतल. cold, calm, unexcited. *She has a ~ head.*

cooler (कूलर) noun
ठंडा रखने का यंत्र, शीतक, anything that cools. *We will take the beer to the picnic in a ~.*

coolie (कुली) noun
कुली, मजदूर, unskilled labour. *The ~ took our luggage out of the station.*

copy (कोपी) noun
नकल करना, imitate. *The students copied what was written on the black board by the teacher.*

cord (कौर्ड) noun
रस्सी, string made of several strands. *The ~ was quite strong, so the thieves could climb up.*

core (कोर) noun
केन्द्रीय, central. *This I speak from the ~ of my heart.*

cork (कौर्क) noun
बोतल की डाट, काग. *Pull out the ~ and open the bottle.*

corn (कॉर्न) noun
अन्न, अनाज, grain chiefly wheat, rice, oat, maize, मकई *Your child can eat ~flakes in the breakfast.*

corner (कॉर्नर) noun
कोना, कोण, nook. *That question ~ed me.*

coronary (कौरोनरी) adjective
मुकुट संबंधी, of the crown. हृदय को रक्त पहुँचाने वाली धमनी, *He had a severe heart attack due to the blockage of ~ artery.*

corporal (कौरपोरल) adjective
शारीरिक, physical, also corporeal. *~ punishment to children has been banned by court.*

correct (करैक्ट) adjective
सत्य, सही, true, right. *He ~ed my essay.*

correlate (कौरिलेट) verb
परस्पर संबंध बिठाना, to bring mutual relationship. *His conclusion in the case does not ~ with mine.*

corridor (कौरिडोर) noun
गलियारा, passage which opens into many rooms. *He always walks in the ~s of power.*

corrupt (करप्ट) noun
भ्रष्ट, भ्रष्ट करना, बिगाड़ना, घूस देना, impure, dishonest, taking of bribes. *He tried to ~ the official.*

cosmetic (कॉस्मेटिक) adjective
श्रृंगार का सामान, designs to make beautiful. *The reforms the government claims to have made are merely ~.*

cosmic (कॉस्मिक) adjective
ब्रह्मांड संबंधी, of the material universe. *~ radiations fill our space more compactly than solid matter.*

cost (कॉस्ट) noun
कीमत, लागत, price, मूल्य, व्यय *The ~ of living in big cities is high.*

costume (कौस्ट्यूम) noun
पोशाक, dress. *Actors wear fashionable ~.*

cosy (कोज़ी) adjective
आरामदायक, warm and comfortable. *The body felt all ~ tucked up in the bed.*

cotton (कौटन) noun
कपास, soft fibrous substance. *Insects don't attack B.T. ~.*

couch (कोच) noun
सोफा, a long bedlike seat for sitting or lying. *Sit in this ~ with full rest.*

cough (कॉफ़) noun
खांसी *Due to cold she was ~ing.*

could (कुड) verb
past tense of can. सका, कर सकता, *He ~ do it.*

council (काउन्सिल) noun
समिति, परिषद्, a body of persons to make rules.

counsel (काउन्सल) noun
परामर्श, कानूनी सलाहकार, advisor, *He ~ed the group during the crisis.*

count (काउन्ट) verb
गिनती गिनना, to say the numerals. *~ your change before leaving the counter.*

counter (काउन्टर)
मेज या खिड़की जहाँ बैठकर ग्राहकों की सेवा की जाती है, table or window in a bank or shop to serve customers. उल्टा, प्रतिकूल, विरोध करना *Acting ~ to my orders.*

country (कन्ट्री) noun
देश, land occupied by a nation. *India is my ~.*

coupe (कूपे) noun
डिब्बा जिसमें दो आदमियों के बैठने के लिए एक सीट हो, compartment with one seat for two persons. *He got full rest in the A.C. ~ in the train.*

couple (कपल) noun
जोड़ा, दो, मियाँ-बीवी की जोड़ी, married persons of opposite sex. *There were several ~s on the dancing floor.*

courage (करेज) noun
साहस, हिम्मत, दिलेरी, spirit to face difficulty. *He didn't have the ~ to disobey me.*

course (कोर्स) noun
गति, चाल, forward movement. *The road is in ~ of construction.*

court (कोर्ट) noun
आंगन, प्रांगण, अदालत, open space in homes, place where legal cases are heard. *The ~ is trying an important case.*

courtesy (कर्टसी) noun
नम्रता, अदब, विनय, politeness. *By ~ rather than by right.*

courtship (कोर्टशिप) noun
प्रणय निवेदन, the wooing of a woman by a man. *After a year of ~ they got married.*

cover (कवर) verb
ढकना, to place one thing over another, ढक्कन, wrapper. *The old book needs a ~.*

coverage (कवरेज) noun
समाचारों का प्रसारण, covering of events. *The newspapers did a nice ~ of news of strike.*

cow (काउ) noun
गाय, female of an ox. *For the Hindus ~ is a sacred animal.*

coward (कॉवर्ड) noun
कायर, डरपोक, weak-hearted person, भीरु, शौर्यहीन, *I am a ~ when it comes to attending funerals.*

coy (कॉय) adjective
शर्मीला, विनीत, shy, modest *She always acts like a ~ girl.*

crack (क्रैक) noun
दरार, चटकने का निशान, broken. *You have ~ed the window pane.*

cracker (क्रैकर) noun
पतला कुरकुरा बिस्कुट, crisp biscuit, पटाखा. *We burn ~s on Diwali night.*

cram (क्रैम) verb
रटना, learn by heart, भरना, make too full. *She ~med Mendel's Laws for the examination.*

cramp (क्रैम्प) noun
मांस-पेशियों की ऐंठन, sudden painful contraction of muscles. *The racer seized with ~s.*

crane (क्रेन) noun
सारस, भारोत्तोलन यंत्र, large water bird, machine to lift heavy loads. *The ~ took out the fallen truck from the river.*

crawl (क्रौल) verb
रेंगकर चलना, move slowly on the belly, hands, knees. *The wounded soldier ~ed into the bunker.*

craze (क्रेज़) noun
गहरी रुचि, सनक, strong desire. *He was ~ed by the desire of drugs.*

cream (क्रीम) noun
मलाई, सार, सर्वोत्तम अंश, a cosmetic. *Doon school admits only students who are the ~ of society.*

create (क्रिएट) verb
उत्पन्न करना, जन्म देना, to give birth, सृजन करना *God has ~d this world.*

creative (क्रिएटिव) adjective
सृजन शक्ति, having power to create. *The teacher must develop creativity in their students.*

creature (क्रीचर) noun
जीव, प्राणी, living animal. *This man is an honest ~.*

credit (क्रैडिट) noun
उधार, borrow, खाते में जमा करना, to deposit, *No ~ is given on this shop.*

creep (क्रीप) verb
रेंगना, सरकना, crawl. *The snake ~s quietly to the frog.*

cricket (क्रिकेट) noun
झींगुर, क्रिकेट का खेल, *~ is very popular in India.*

crime (क्राइम) noun
अपराध, offense. *It would be a ~ to ask a boy to go out in severe cold.*

criticize (क्रिटिसाइज़) verb
आलोचना करना, दोष निकालना, find fault with. *To ~ somebody's work.*

crop (क्रॉप) noun
फसल, उपज, seasonal produce of grain, fruits, etc. *The land is out of ~.*

cross (क्रौस) noun
गुणा का निशान, पार करना to pass to the other side. *The place is marked on the chart with a ~.*

cross-bar (क्रॉस बार) noun
आड़ी कड़ी, टेक, अर्गला, horizontal bar.

crow (क्रो) noun
कौआ, a large black bird, शोर मचाना, to shout. *His success is something to ~ about.*

crowd (क्राउड) noun
भीड़, मजमा, gathering. *Our buses are very ~ed.*

crown (क्राउन) noun
मुकुट, सम्मान प्रदान करना, to put a crown on the king or queen. *They ~ed him king.*

cruel (क्रुएल) adjective
निर्दय, क्रूर, pitiless. *A ~ remark.*

crush (क्रश) verb
कुचलना, रौंदना, to press with force. रस निकालना, *The dog was ~ed under the wheels of the car.*

cry (क्राई) verb
चीखना, चिल्लाना, make loud sounds. *The baby cries as soon as it is born.*

crystal (क्रिस्टल) noun
रत्न, पारदर्शी पत्थर, clear transparent mineral. *A necklace of ~s.*

cube (क्यूब) noun
घनाकृति, किसी संख्या का घन, solid body having six equal square sides. *The cube of 5 (5^3) is 5×5×5 or 125.*

cuckoo (कुकू) noun
कोयल, a bird whose call is very sweet. *She can mimic the call of a ~.*

cucumber (कुकम्बर) noun
ककड़ी, खीरा, a flesh fruit. *~ is eaten as salad.*

culprit (कलप्रिट) noun
अपराधी, मुलजिम, offender. *The ~ was caught by neighbours.*

culture (कलचर) noun
संस्कृति, social advancement. Indian ~.

cum (कम) preposition
साथ, सहित, together with, or plus. *This is my study ~ drawing room.*

cup (कप) noun
प्याला, कटोरा, a small vessel. *He ~ped his hands to catch the ball.*

curd (कर्ड) noun
दही, छैना, substance made from milk. *~ is used to prepare cheese.*

curl (कर्ल) noun
घुंघराले, twist into ringlets. Lord Krishna had ~y hair.

currency (करेंसी) noun
चलन, रिवाज, मुद्रा, money in circulation. *Rupees and paise are India's ~.*

curry (करी) noun
तरकारी, शोरबा, dish cooked with spices. *Chicken ~.*

curse (कर्स) noun
अभिशाप, शाप देना, doom, misfortune. *Gambling is a ~.*

curtain (कर्टेन) noun
पर्दा, piece of cloth to cover doors. *Please draw the ~ because there are ladies behind.*

curve (कर्व) noun
टेढ़ी रेखा, मोड़, घुमाव, turning. *The river ~ s round the village.*

custom (कस्टम) noun
चलन, रिवाज, tradition. *He is a slave to old ~s.*

customer (कस्टमर) noun
ग्राहक, क्रेता, purchaser. *He is an old ~ of this shop.*

cut (कट) verb
काटना, divide or separate, to make an opening. *He ~ his face while shaving.*

cycle (साइकिल) noun
घटना चक्र, series of events, बाइसिकिल

□□□□

D

d
मुद्रण में प्रयुक्त
लघु अक्षर

d
लिखने में प्रयुक्त
लघु अक्षर

मूल उच्चारण **डी**

ड प्रयोग में उच्चारण

अंग्रेजी वर्णमाला का चौथा अक्षर

dacoit (**डॅकोइट**) noun
डाकू, armed robber. *~s looted the bank.*

dad (**डैड**) noun
father, daddy, पिता, बाप, अब्बा *His ~ works in the education department.*

dagger (**डैगर**) noun
कटार, छुरा, twoedged knife. *The policeman looked at the ~ of the thief.*

daily (**डेली**) adjective
रोजाना, प्रतिदिन, everyday. *He has done his ~ work.*

dairy (**डेरी**) noun
दुग्धशाला, where milk and milk products are made. *He runs a ~ farm.*

dais (**डायस**) noun
मंच, चबूतरा, a raised floor. *The leader delivered the speech from the ~.*

damage (**डैमेज**) noun
हानि, क्षति, harm, injury. *The storm did a great ~ to the crop.*

damfool (**डैमफूल**) noun
मूर्ख, बेवकूफ, fool. *You are a ~.*

damp (**डैम्प**) adjective
गीला, नम, wet, moist. *Don't sleep outside in the ~.*

dance (**डान्स**) noun
नृत्य, नाच, move with steps in music. *The leaves were ~ing in the wind.*

dandruff (**डैन्ड्रफ़**) noun
रूसी, dead pieces of skin in hair. *~ is caused by infection.*

danger (**डेन्जर**) noun
खतरा, भय, risk. *Is there any ~ for life?*

dare (**डेयर**) verb
हिम्मत करना, to be brave and act.

He didn't ~ to go there.

dark (**डार्क**) noun
अँधेरा, absence of light. *Small children are afraid of the ~.*

darling (**डार्लिंग**) noun
बहुत प्रिय, person very much loved. *She is a little ~.*

dash (**डैश**) noun
अचानक आक्रमण, sudden violent movement.
He made a ~ at the foe.

data (**डेटा**) noun
आंकड़े, facts. *Sufficient ~ is available.*

date (**डेट**) noun
तिथि, तारीख, दिनांक, खजूर, छुआरा, statement of the day, a small brown fruit. *Never forget to ~ your letters.*

daughter (**डॉटर**) noun
पुत्री, बेटी, female child, *His ~ is studying in 12th class.*

dawn (**डॉन**) noun
सवेरा, प्रातःकाल, दिन का प्रारंभ, daybreak. *He works from ~ to dusk.*

day (**डे**) noun
दिन, time between sunrise and sunset. *I have been reading all ~.*

dead (**डेड**) adjective
मृत, प्राणहीन, no longer living. *The bomb left ~ many people.*

deaf (**डेफ़**) adjective
बहरा, hard of hearing. *He is both ~ and dumb.*

deal (**डील**) verb
कार्यवाही करना, ताश के पत्तों का बाँटा जाना, to take action on, playing cards, *It's your ~ this time.*

dealer (**डीलर**) noun
व्यापारी, trader. *He got the ~ a shop in the area after his credit status had been verified.*

dean (**डीन**) noun
शिक्षण संस्था में किसी विभाग का अध्यक्ष, head of department. *He is the ~ of the faculty of science.*

dear (**डियर**) adjective
प्रिय, प्यारा, loved, lovable. *My ~ John.*

death (**डैथ**) noun
मृत्यु, देहान्त, end of life.
The murderer was sentenced to ~.

debar (**डिबार**) verb
निकाल देना, prevent. *He was ~red from the examinations due to short attendance.*

debate (**डिबेट**) noun
वाद-विवाद, formal discussion. *They held a ~ in the school about the parliamentary system of India.*

debility (**डेबिलिटी**) noun
दुर्बलता, weakness of health. *T.B. is a ~ causing disease.*

debit (डेबिट) noun
खाते में से पैसा निकालना, opposite of credit. *Shyam's account was ~ed by Rs.100.*

debt (डेट) noun
ऋण, कर्ज, money owed. *I cannot easily discharge my ~ to him for helping me.*

debut (डेब्यू) noun
रंगमंच पर पहली बार आना, first appearance on stage. *He is making his ~ in a T.V. serial.*

decade (डिकेड) noun
दशक, period of 10 years. *The Congress party is in power for several ~s.*

decay (डिके) verb
क्षय होना, decline. *Our energy ~s in old age.*

deceive (डिसीव) verb
धोखा देना, ठगना, mislead. *His engaging manners easily ~d us.*

decency (डीसैंसी) noun
शालीनता, भद्रता, modesty. *You must have the ~ to attend the funeral.*

decide (डिसाइड) verb
निर्णय करना, तय करना, settle, finalise. *The judge has ~d the case.*

decimal (डैसिमल) noun
दशमलव प्रणाली का दशमिक, of tens or one tenths. *The ~ system.*

decision (डिसिज़न) noun
फैसला, निर्णय, judgment. *He made a poor ~.*

declare (डिक्लेयर) verb
घोषणा करना, announce. *I ~ the meeting closed.*

decline (डिक्लाइन) verb
मना करना, refuse. *He ~d the invitation with thanks.*

decode (डिकोड) verb
किसी गुप्त भाषा का अर्थ निकालना, to decipher. *It is not easy to ~ the old script.*

decor (डेकौर) noun
सजावट, finishing. *The ~ is good.*

decrease (डिक्रीज़) verb
कम करना, घटाना, to become less, shorten. *Your thirst ~s as you drink the water.*

deed (डीड) noun
काम, कार्य, act. *His ~s are praise-worthy.*

defeat (डिफीट) verb
हराना, पराजित करना, obtain victory over. *The Australian team suffered ~.*

defect (डिफैक्ट) noun
अवगुण, दोष, fault, short-coming. *Some soldiers ~ed from Germany to France.*

defence (डिफैन्स) noun
बचाव, रक्षा, protection. *The prisoner said nothing in his ~.*

define (डिफाइन) verb
परिभाषा करना, state clearly. *~ a verb and tell its kinds.*

definite (**डैफिनिट**) adjective
निश्चित, clear. *Be ~ before you speak.*

defraud (**डिफ्रॉड**) verb
ठगना, धोखा देना, cheat. *I was ~ed by a trickster.*

degrade (**डिग्रेड**) verb
मान या पद घटाना, debase. *He was ~ed from his post of Principal Secretary.*

degree (**डिग्री**) noun
अंश, कोण नापने की इकाई, the measure of an angle. *Water freezes at 0~C.*

delay (**डिले**) verb
देर करना, be slow, late. *We must ~ our journey until weather is favourable.*

delete (**डिलीट**) verb
काटना, निकाल देना, strike out. *~ these four words from the letter.*

delicate (**डैलिकेट**) adjective
कोमल, नाजुक, soft, tender. *The ~ skin of a baby.*

delight (**डिलाइट**) noun
प्रसन्नता, खुशी, joy, pleasure. *To his great ~ his article was accepted for publication.*

delivery (**डिलीवरी**) **noun**
वितरण, distribution of goods, letters. *Prompt ~ of goods.*

demand (**डिमान्ड**) noun
माँग, earnest claim. *He ~ed payment of the debt.*

demerit (**डीमैरिट**) noun
दोष, अवगुण, fault, defect, culpability. *This is his great ~.*

democracy (**डिमोक्रेसी**) noun
जनतंत्र, लोकतंत्र, a goverment by the people. *India is a ~.*

demonstrate (**डिमांस्ट्रेट**) verb
उदाहरण द्वारा प्रस्तुत करना, प्रदर्शन करना, show clearly by giving proof. *How would you ~ that the earth is round?*

demurrage (**डिमरिज**) noun
विलम्ब शुल्क, a charge for delay. *First pay the ~, then collect the goods.*

denial (**डिनाइल**) noun
अस्वीकार, इन्कार, refusal. *He repeated his ~ of the charge framed against him.*

denote (**डिनोट**) noun
अंकित करना, जताना, be the sign or symbol of. *Frequent late coming ~s your negligence.*

density (**डैनसिटी**) noun
घनापन, quality of being dense. *The ~ of water is 1 gm/cc.*

dent (**डैन्ट**) noun
दाँत, कटाव, a notch. *His reputation suffers a ~.*

deny (**डिनाई**) verb
न मानना, refuse. *He ~ied knowing anything about the matter.*

depart (**डिपार्ट**) verb
प्रस्थान करना, चले जाना, go away, leave. *The bus will ~ at noon.*

depend (डिपैन्ड) verb
निर्भर करना, आश्रित होना, भरोसा करना, trust. *Children ~ on their parents.*

deposit (डिपौजिट) noun
जमा, धनराशि, money that is put in a bank. *~ all the spare money.*

depot (डिपो) noun
गोदाम, भंडार, storehouse, warehouse. *Sahni Book ~ is on the road.*

depression (डिप्रैशन) noun
उदासी, मायूसी, being in low spirits. *He committed suicide during a fit of ~.*

deprive (डिप्राइव) verb
वंचित कर देना, prevent from using. *I was ~d of parental love.*

depute (डिप्यूट) verb
प्रतिनिधि नियुक्त करना, give another person the authority. *Four students were ~ed to meet the Principal.*

derive (डिराइव) verb
लिया जाना, लेना, प्राप्त करना, get, obtain. *Thousands of English words are ~d from Latin.*

describe (डिसक्राइब) verb
वर्णन करना, बयान करना, to narrate. *~ the story of Ashoka.*

desert (डिजर्ट) verb
त्यागना, चले जाना, leave, मरुस्थल, रेगिस्तान, barren land, दंड या पुरस्कार, reward. *My friends have ~ed me.*

deserve (डिजर्व) verb
योग्य होना, काबिल होना, be entitled to. *He ~s the punishment for life term.*

desire (डिजाइर) noun
चाह, अभिलाषा, इच्छा, long for, wish. *First deserve and then ~.*

desk (डेस्क) noun
डेस्क, छोटी मेज़, विभाग, small table, department. *He looks after the Pakistan ~ in the foreign ministry.*

despair (डिस्पेयर) verb
उम्मीद न होना, हताशा, निराशा, to lose hope. *Don't ~.*

dessert (डिजर्ट) noun
भोजन के बाद खाए जाने वाले फल, मिठाई आदि, fruits, icecream taken after the meal.

destroy (डिस्ट्राय) verb
नष्ट, बर्बाद करना, break to pieces. *The forces ~ed a lot of terrorists in Sri Lanka.*

detach (डिटैच) verb
अलग-अलग करना, separate, unfasten. *Men were ~ed to defend the bridge.*

detail (डिटेल) noun
विवरण, जानकारी, particular fact. *Let me know all the ~s of the incident.*

detain (डिटेन) verb
रोकना, इन्तजार में रखना, to keep waiting. *The question need not ~ us long.*

detect (डिटैक्ट) verb
पता लगाना, to discover. *Police has ~ed the crime.*

develop (डेवेलप) verb
विकसित होना, grow larger, fuller. *Plants ~ from seeds.*

device (डिवाइस) noun
औजार, रचना, युक्ति, साधन, plan, scheme. *T.V. is a good ~ for entertainment.*

devil (डेविल) noun
शैतान, evil spirit. *What the ~ are you saying?*

devoid (डिवॉइड) adjective
बिना, रहित, रिक्त, without, lacking. *He is ~ of common sense.*

devote (डिवोट) verb
लगन, वफादारी दिखाना, show loyalty. *He is ~d to his studies.*

diagnose (डायग्नोस) verb
निदान, रोग की पहचान करना, determine the nature of disease. *The doctor ~d the illness as typhoid.*

diary (डायरी) noun
दैनन्दिनी, डायरी, daily record. *The teacher writes his ~ everyday.*

dictate (डिक्टेट) verb
बोलकर लिखाना, to speak to another person to write down. *The teacher ~ed an essay to students.*

die (डाई) noun
ठप्पा, stamp, मर जाना, खत्म होना, cease to live. *The laughter ~d at their lips.*

diet (डाइट) noun
आहार, खुराक, भोजन, regular food. *Milk is an important article of ~.*

differ (डिफर) verb
भिन्न-भिन्न मत रखना, to disagree. *I beg to ~ from you on this point.*

difficult (डिफीकल्ट) adjective
कठिन, hard to solve. *The place is ~ to reach.*

digit (डिजिट) noun
एक अंक, one number. *The number 376 contains three ~s.*

dim (डिम) adjective
धुँधला, not bright. *Eyes ~ with tears.*

dine (डाइन) verb
भोजन करना, to have dinner. *They will ~ with me tonight.*

dip (डिप) verb
डूबना, डुबाना, गोता स्नान, quick bath. *~ the pen into the ink.*

diploma (डिप्लोमा) noun
शिक्षा का प्रमाण पत्र, educational certificate. *A ~ in teaching.*

dire (डायर) adjective
भयानक, खौफनाक, dreadful, बहुत जरूरी, extreme. *Water is the ~*

necessity of life.

direct (डाइरेक्ट) adjective
सरल, सीधा, बिना मुड़े, straight, मार्गदर्शन करना, to show the way. *Can you ~ me to the railway station.*

dirt (डर्ट) noun
धूल, गर्दा, dust, soil, mud. *His head was covered with ~.*

disability (डिसेबिलिटी) noun
अयोग्यता, incapacity. *Mr. John has a ~ and is getting pension from the government.*

disappear (डिसेपियर) verb
अदृश्य होना, go out of sight. *Our difficulties will ~ soon.*

disappoint (डिसेपॉइन्ट) verb
निराश होना, मायूस करना, to frustrate. *I was ~ed not to find you at home.*

disc (डिस्क) noun
चकती, thin flat round plate. *The sun's ~.*

discharge (डिस्चार्ज) verb
मुक्त होना, unload. बैटरी का डिस्चार्ज होना, *The Nile ~s in the Mediterranean sea.*

disciple (डिसाइपल) noun
शिष्य, चेला, follower. *Plato was the ~ of Socrates.*

disclose (डिसक्लोज) verb
प्रकट करना, make known. *He refused to ~ his name and address.*

discount (डिसकाउन्ट) noun
मितीकाटा, छूट, deduction. *A bill for Rs. 500 was ~ed for Rs.480.*

discourage (डिसकरेज) verb
हतोत्साहित करना, हिम्मत तोड़ना, dishearten. *Let not one ~ the failure.*

discus (डिसकस) noun
लकड़ी की भारी तश्तरी, *He came first in ~ throw.*

discuss (डिसकस) verb
तर्क करना, examine and argue. *They ~ed the dainty dishes.*

disease (डिसीज़) noun
व्याधि, बीमारी, ailment, illness. *Influenza is a common ~.*

disgrace (डिसग्रेस) noun
अपमान, बदनामी, shame, ignominy. *These slums are a ~ to the city of Taj.*

dish (डिश) noun
प्लेट, तश्तरी, shallow vessel, खाद्य, भोजन, food, *His favourite ~ is soup.*

dishonest (डिसऑनेस्ट) adjective
बेईमान, धोखेबाज़, not honest. *He is a ~ person.*

disinfect (डिसइन्फैक्ट) verb
छूत के रोगाणुओं को दूर करना, to make free from infection. *Wash the floor with phenyl water to ~.*

dislike (डिसलाइक) verb
पसन्द न करना, घृणा करना, feeling for aversion. *He has a strong ~ for classical music.*

dismiss **(डिसमिस)** verb
सेवा समाप्त करना, give permission to depart. *He was ~ed for his dishonesty.*

disorder **(डिसऑर्डर)** noun
गड़बड़, अनियमितता, confusion. *He has a kind of mental ~.*

dispatch **(डिसपैच)** verb
संदेश भेजना, रवाना करना, send something or message. *Please hurry up the ~ of these telegrams.*

dispensable **(डिसपेंसिबिल)** adjective
गैरज़रूरी, not very necessary. *The cook is ~ at present.*

display **(डिसप्ले)** verb
प्रदर्शित करना, show, exhibit. *The matter has been beautifully ~ed on a full page.*

disposal **(डिसपोज़ल)** noun
अधिकार देना, to be used by some other person. *My car shall be at your ~ during your daughter's marriage.*

dispute **(डिसप्यूट)** noun
विवाद, झगड़ा, तर्क, quarrel, बहस करना, argue, debate. *His professional capacity is beyond ~.*

disqualify **(डिसक्वालिफ़ाई)** verb
अयोग्य ठहराना, declare unsuitable. *His weak eyesight will ~ him for military service.*

dissimilar **(डिससिमिलर)** adjective
भिन्न, असमान, different. *People with ~ tastes.*

dissolve **(डिसॉल्व)** verb
घुलना, घोलना, soak into. *Salt ~s in water.*

distance **(डिसटैन्स)** noun
दूरी, फ़ासला, amount of space between two points. *The ~ between Agra and Delhi is 190 km.*

distinct **(डिसटिंक्ट)** adjective
सुस्पष्ट, सुव्यक्त, plain, clearly marked. *There is ~ improvement in his health.*

distant **(डिस्टैन्ट)** adjective
सुदूर, far away. *The post office is four kilometres ~ from the hospital.*

distinguish **(डिस्टिंग्विश)** verb
भिन्नता समझ पाना, to mark difference. *It is not easy to ~ cultured pearls from genuine pearls.*

distress **(डिस्ट्रैस)** noun
दुःख, कष्ट, sorrow, pain. *My friend's untimely death ~ed me much.*

distribute **(डिस्ट्रीब्यूट)** verb
बाँटना, divide and give out in shares. *~ these blankets among the poor.*

district **(डिस्ट्रिक्ट)** noun
जिला, part of a country. *Bhopal is an industrial ~.*

disturb (डिस्टर्ब) noun
परेशान करना, बाधा डालना, to upset. *I am ~ed on hearing the news.*

dive (डाइव) noun
डुबकी, गोता, act of plunging. *He ~ed for the ball.*

divide (डिवाइड) verb
अलग करना, टुकड़े करना, बांटना, to separate. *We ~ed the money between ourselves.*

divine (डिवाइन) noun
ईश्वरीय, दैवी, godly. *She looks ~ in her new dress.*

do (डू) verb
करना, to perform. *What were you ~ing there?*

dog (डॉग) noun
कुत्ता, domestic animal. *~ is a very faithful animal.*

doll (डॉल) noun
गुड़िया, toy, baby. बहुत सुन्दर लड़की, *She was all ~ed up for the party.*

domestic (डोमेस्टिक) adjective
घरेलू, पारिवारिक, of the household. *Cow is a ~ animal.*

door (डोर) noun
द्वार, दरवाज़ा, solid barrier for closing and opening a building. *Open the ~ and let the servant come in.*

dot (डॉट) noun
बिन्दु, small round mark.

double (डबल) noun
दुगना, दुगना करना, become twice. *He has ~d his income.*

doubt (डाउट) noun
शक, संदेह, uncertainty of mind. *I have no ~ about your success.*

dove (डव) noun
पेडुकी, फ़ाख्ता, kind of pigeon. अबोध, भद्र, कोमल व्यक्ति, *He is a ~ in manners.*

down (डाउन) noun
उदास, दुःखी, dejected, नीचे की तरफ, downward. *Her face wore a ~ expression.*

dozen (डज़न) noun
दर्जन, बारह, twelve. *Also take a ~ bananas.*

draft (ड्राफ़्ट) noun
हुन्डी, डिज़ाइन, written order for payment of money, design, मसौदा लिखना, *~ a letter to the secretary.*

drama (ड्रामा) noun
नाटक, play. *I am very much interested in ~.*

draw (ड्रॉ) noun
नम्बर निकालना, खींचना, बाहर निकालना, to extract. न जीतना, न हारना, without a win or defeat. *The cricket match was a ~.*

drawback (ड्रॉबैक) noun
कमी, नुकसान, असुविधा, disadvantage. *His house has no ventilation, it is a big ~.*

dream (ड्रीम) noun
स्वप्न, imagination in sleep or vision. *I saw a horrible ~ and woke up.*

dress **(ड्रैस)** noun
पोशाक, कपड़े पहनना, clothing to wear, put on clothes. *O boy, come in proper school ~.*

drink **(ड्रिंक)** noun
पेय, पीना, take into the mouth, liquid for drinking. *We can't live without food and ~.*

drop **(ड्रॉप)** verb
बूँद-बूँद गिराना, बूँद, small particle of liquid. *Give him five ~s of medicine with half a cup of water.*

dry **(ड्राई)** adjective.
सूखा, not wet. *Is this coal ~ enough to burn?*

due **(ड्यू)** adjective
अभी देय, immediately owed. *Your ~s are still unpaid.*

dust **(डस्ट)** noun
धूल, dirt. *The car left heavy ~ behind it.*

dye **(डाई)** verb
रँगना, to colour by dipping in liquid. *Go to the market and get this cloth ~d.*

□□□□

E

e मुद्रण में प्रयुक्त लघु अक्षर

e लिखने में प्रयुक्त लघु अक्षर

मूल उच्चारण **ई**

अ,आ, इ,ई, ए,ऐ — प्रयोग में ये अनेक उच्चारण सुविधानुसार, जो चाहे कीजिये, कोई फर्क नहीं पड़ता

अंग्रेजी वर्णमाला का पाँचवाँ अक्षर और पाँच स्वरों में दूसरा स्वर

each (ईच) adjective
प्रत्येक, everyone of two or more, *We ~ took a dip in Ganges.*

eager (ईगर) adjective
उत्सुक, इच्छुक, keen, ardent in desire. *I am ~ to meet my old friend.*

ear (ईअर) noun
कान, organ of hearing. *My pleas to raise salary fell on deaf ~s.*

early (अर्ली) adjective, adverb
आंरभिक, शुरू का, जल्दी, पूर्व, sooner, *He is an ~riser.*

earn (अर्न) verb
कमाना, अर्जित करना, get in return of one's labour. *He spends all his ~ ings on drinking.*

earth (अर्थ) noun
पृथ्वी, ground भूमि, जमीन, *The ~ goes round the sun.*

ease (ईज़) verb
आराम देना, सुविधा पहुँचाना, to give relief to the body or mind. *Can I ~ you of your burden?*

east (ईस्ट) noun
प्राची, पूर्व, पूरब दिशा, direction in which the sun rises. *Sun rises in the ~.*

easy (ईज़ी) adjective
आसान, not difficult. *This question is very ~.*

eat (ईट) verb
खाना खाना, भोजन करना, to have meals. *We ~ to live.*

echo (इको) noun
गूँज, प्रतिध्वनि, sound reflected. *The Prime Minister's speech ~ed all over.*

eclipse (इक्लिप्स) noun
ग्रहण (चन्द्र या सूर्य), आंशिक अंधकार, total or partial obscuration of light of sun or moon. *Lunar ~ falls on full moon day.*

economy (**इकोनॅमी**) noun
बचत, किफ़ायत, आर्थिक स्थिति, avoidance of waste of money, economics. *He gave up a large house for economic reasons.*

edge (**एज**) noun
सिरा, किनारा, धार, brink or verge of blade, sword or razor.
On the ~ of the chair.

edible (**ऐडिबल**) adjective
खाने योग्य, fit to be eaten. *~ oil.*

edit (**ऐडिट**) verb
सम्पादन करना, prepare for publication. *~ a magazine.*

effect (**इफैक्ट**) noun
परिणाम, प्रभाव, result, outcome. *Our arguments had no ~ on him.*

efficiency (**ऐफीशेंसी**) noun
कुशलता, दक्षता, competency in performance. *The workers are graded on their ~.*

effort (**ऐफर्ट**) noun
प्रयत्न, कोशिश, attempt. *Requiring no ~.*

egg (**एग**) noun
अन्डा, ovum. *Birds and reptiles lay ~s.*

e.g. (**ई.जी.**)
उदाहरण के लिए, for example.

ego (**ईगो**) noun
अहम्, self image. *He is on one of his ~ trips.*

eight (**एट**) noun
आठ, seven plus one.

either (**आइदर**) adjective, pronoun
दो में से कोई एक, one or the other. यह या वह, *In ~ of these events you will benefit.*

elastic (**इलैस्टिक**) adjective
लचीला, flexible. *Rubber is ~.*

elder (**ऐल्डर**) adjective
परिवार का बड़ा सदस्य, senior in a family. *Always obey your ~s.*

eldest (**एल्डेस्ट**) adjective
परिवार में सबसे बड़ा, of greatest age. *~ brother.*

elect (**इलैक्ट**) verb
चुनना, पसन्द करना, choose by vote. *He has ~ed to become a surgeon.*

electron (**इलैक्ट्रन**) noun
विद्युत अणु, atomic sub particle of matter. *~s are charged particles.*

electronic (**इलैक्ट्रॉनिक**) adj.
इलैक्ट्रौन की क्रिया पर निर्भर साधन, *Computer is an ~ device.*

element (**ऐलिमन्ट**) noun
तत्व, substance that can't be split in simple form. *Water is a compound consisting of hydrogen and oxygen ~s.*

elementary (**एलीमैंटरी**) adjective
सरल, प्रांरभिक, in the beginning stage. *He is in the ~ stage of T.B.*

elephant **(ऐलीफैन्ट)** noun
हाथी, largest four-footed animal.

eligible **(ऐलिजिबल)** adjective
योग्य, वांछनीय, qualified to be selected. *~ for promotion.*

embarrass **(ऐमबैरेस)** verb
घबरा देना, शर्मिंदा करना, कठिनाई में डालना, cause confusion and shame to. *Inexperience will ~ his progress.*

emerge **(इमर्ज)** verb
प्रकट होना, निकलना, to come to notice. *Several ideas ~ from discussion.*

empire **(ऐम्पायर)** noun
साम्राज्य, single supreme authority over many countries. *British ~.*

employ **(ऐम्प्लॉय)** verb
नियुक्त करना, काम में लगाना, give work to. *How do you ~ your workers?*

empty **(एम्पटी)** noun
रिक्त, खाली, containing nothing. *Words ~ of meaning.*

enable **(इनेबल)** verb
योग्य बनाना, समर्थ करना, make able. *A stick ~d him to walk quickly.*

enclose **(एन्क्लोज)** verb
नत्थी करना, attach. *The R/R is ~d herewith.*

encroach **(एन्क्रोच)** verb
अतिकमण, सीमाओं को लांघना, to advance beyond limits. *He always tries to ~ on other's rights.*

end **(एण्ड)** noun
सिरा, छोर, last part, अंत, मौत, death. *At 9 P.M. the meeting came to an ~.*

endure **(एन्ड्योर)** verb
झेलना, to tolerate. *I can't ~ this.*

enemy **(एनिमी)** noun
शत्रु, दुश्मन, opponent. *The ~ was forced to surrender.*

energy **(एनर्जी)** noun
बल, शक्ति, power. *He has ~ enough to work for ten hours.*

engage **(एनगेज)** verb
व्यस्त करना, सेवा में लेना, take into service. प्रणय सूत्र में बंधना, *Rajesh is ~d to Uma.*

engine **(एन्जिन)** noun
इंजन, machine that changes energy into power to motion. *An oil ~.*

enjoy **(एन्जॉय)** verb
खुशी मनाना, आनन्द लेना, take delight in. *Students ~ talking in their free periods.*

enough **(इनफ़)** adjective
काफी, पर्याप्त, sufficient, needful. *There is ~ milk in the jug.*

enter **(एन्टर)** verb
प्रवेश करना, शुरुआत करना, go into. *Where has the bullet ~ed in the body?*

entertain **(एन्टरटेन)** verb
मनोरंजन करना, स्वागत करना, to treat as guest, amuse, interest. *We were all ~ed by his funny tricks.*

entire **(ऐन्टायर)** adjective
पूरा, सम्पूर्ण, whole, complete. *The ~ village was destroyed in fire.*

entity **(एन्टिटी)** noun
अस्तितत्व, हस्ती, distinct existence. *I have a separate ~.*

entry **(ऐन्ट्री)** noun
प्रवेश, coming or going in. *The thieves had a forced ~ in the house.*

envelope **(एलवैलप)** **noun**
आवरण, लिफाफा, covering for a letter. *Fold the letter properly and put it in an ~.*

environment **(एनविरनमैन्ट)** noun
वातावरण, surroundings. *There is always a healthy mind in a healthy ~.*

envy **(ऐनवी)** noun
ईर्ष्या, jealousy. *Her looks made her the ~ of her classmates.*

equal **(ईक्वल)** adjective
एक सा, समान, बराबर, same in size, shape, etc. *There must be ~ pay for ~ work.*

erase **(इरेज़)** verb
मिटाना, खुरचना, rub, scrap out. *~ all the messages from my mobile phone.*

error **(ऐरर)** noun
त्रुटि, भूल, गलती, mistake. *There is an ~ in your judgement.*

escape **(एस्केप)** verb
पलायन, बचना, get free, run away. *He had a narrow ~ from the accident.*

essay **(ऐसे)** noun
निबंध, खोजपूर्ण लेख, composition. *His ~ on friendship was liked by all.*

essential **(एसेन्शल)** adjective
अतिआवश्यक, सारभूत, most important. *Ahimsa is an ~ part of Indian character.*

estimate **(ऐस्टीमेट)** noun
आकलन, अनुमान, approximate calculation. *A rough ~ of the construction.*

etcetera **(एटसैटरा)**
आदि, इत्यादि, and other things.

even **(ईवन)** adverb
फिर भी, एक सा, चिकना, समतल, still, smooth. संन्ध्या evening. *It is a perfectly ~ table.*

event **(इवैन्ट)** noun
महत्वपूर्ण घटना, an occurrence, *Marriage is an important ~ in life.*

ever (ऐवर) adverb
कभी भी, किसी भी समय, at any time. *Nothing ~ happens in this village.*

every **(ऐवरी)** adjective
प्रत्येक, each one of a whole. *I have read ~ book on that*

shelf.

evidence (ऐविडेन्स) noun
प्रमाण, साक्ष्य, proof. *You must produce ~ in your support.*

evil (ईविल) adjective
दुष्ट, हानिकारक, wicked, harmful, bad. *He lives an ~ life.*

exact (एग्ज़ैक्ट) adjective
ठीक, यथार्थ, correct, free from error. *What is the ~ size of this table?*

examination (एग्ज़ामिनेशन) noun
परीक्षा, जॉच, act of test. *When your annual ~s will start?*

example (एक्जाम्पिल) noun
उदाहरण, दृष्टान्त, instance, pattern. *Let this be an ~ to others.*

exceed (एक्सीड) verb
से क्षेष्ठ होना, be greater than. *New York ~s Delhi in size and population.*

excel (एक्सेल) verb
दूसरों से अच्छा होना, do better than. *He ~s in courage.*

except (एक्सैप्ट) preposition
सिवाय, से अलग, apart from, excluded from. *All were present ~ John.*

excess (एक्सैस) noun
अधिकता, more than expected. *The ~es committed by police can't be ignored.*

exchange (एक्सचेंज) noun
बदला, आदान-प्रदान, लेन-देन, barter, give and take, विनिमय. *Five big oranges for two rupees is a fair ~.*

exclude (एक्सक्लूड) verb
वर्जित करना, वंचित, महरूम रखना, prevent someone or keep something out. *Please ~ all possibilities of doubt.*

exclusive (एक्सक्लूसिव) adjective
केवल, विशेष, एकान्तिक, in which no other have share. *He moves in ~ social circles.*

excuse (एक्सक्यूज़) verb
क्षमा करना, to overlook a fault, बहाना, pretence, *Please give them my ~s.*

exercise (एक्सरसाइज) noun
व्यायाम, कसरत, practice of physical and mental powers अभ्यास, practice. *Walking is a good ~.*

exit (ऐक्ज़िट) noun
बाहर जाने का द्वार, प्रस्थान, way out, go out. *Make an ~.*

expand (एक्सपैंड) verb
फैलना, फैलाना, विस्तार करना, spread out. *The petals of many flowers ~ in sunshine.*

expect (एक्सपैक्ट) verb
आशा करना, to look forward to. *I ~ed you yesterday.*

expend (एक्सपैंड) verb
व्यय करना, spend. *~ your income wisely.*

expense (एम्सपैंस) noun
लागत, खर्चा, cost. *Children in*

Russia are educated at public ~.

expert (ऐक्सपर्ट) noun
विशेषज्ञ, माहिर, skillful. *He is an ~ in skin diseases.*

expire (ऐक्सपायर) verb
मरना, अन्त होना, die, come to an end. *His term of office as Chief Minister ~s next month.*

explain (ऐक्सप्लेन) verb
समझाना, make clear. *Please ~ this poem to me.*

export (ऐक्सपोर्ट) verb
निर्यात करना, sending goods abroad. *There is a ban on the ~ of opium.*

expose (ऐक्सपोज़) verb
भंडाफोड़ करना, revelation of something. *Please don't ~ my secrets.*

express (ऐक्सप्रैस) adjective
विचार प्रगट करना, to put into words, तेज़ चाल वाला, high speed. *She can ~ herself eloquently.*

extend (ऐक्स्टैंड) verb
विस्तार करना, फैलाना, spread out *My orchard ~s as far as the canal.*

extra (एक्स्ट्रा) adjective
अतिरिक्त, additional. *I have been paid ~ for my work.*

eye (आई) noun
नेत्र, organ of sight,

eye witness (आईविटनैस) noun
चश्मदीद गवाह, प्रत्यक्ष साक्षी, person who has acually seen some act. *The ~ of the murder was shot dead.*

❑❑❑❑

F

f
मुद्रण में प्रयुक्त
लघु रोमन अक्षर

f
लिखने में प्रयुक्त
लघु अक्षर

मूल
उच्चारण **एफ़**

फ़ प्रयोग में
उच्चारण
एक ही,
ग़नीमत है!

अंग्रेजी वर्णमाला का छठा अक्षर

face (फ़ेस) noun
चेहरा, मुख, from the forehead to the chin, सामने देखना, be opposite to. *Turn round and ~ me.*

facility (फैसिलिटी) noun
आसानी, सुविधा, ease, freedom from difficulty. *He has the ~ of free travel.*

fact (फ़ैक्ट) noun
सच्चाई, तथ्य, something known to be true. *No one can deny the ~s.*

factor (फ़ैक्टर) noun
खंड, divisor. *6 and 3 are ~s of 18.*

faculty (फ़ैकल्टी) noun
विभाग, department, क्षमता, योग्यता, विद्या विभाग के सदस्य, *The ~ of science.*

fail (फ़ेल) verb
असफल होना, अनुत्तीर्ण होना, failure as to performance. *I will reach the station without ~.*

faint (फ़ेन्ट) verb
बेहोश हो जाना, loose conscio-usness, कम, क्षीण, less. *There is a ~ hope of her success.*

fair (फेयर) adjective
ठीक, सही, just, साफ, clean, सुन्दर, beautiful. *To do such a thing is not ~.*

fairy (फेयरी) noun
परी, अप्सरा, small imaginary being with supernatural powers. *The report of the flying saucers coming to the earth from outer space are ~ tales.*

faith (फ़ेथ) noun
भरोसा, trust. *Have ~ in God.*

fake (फ़ेक) noun
नकली, मनगढ़ंत, a copy of something. *She tried to borrow Rs. 100 for a ~ purpose.*

fall (**फ़ॉल**) verb
गिरना, पतन, गिरावट, a lowering, decline. *The ~ of an apple from the tree.*

false (**फ़ॉल्स**) adjective
मिथ्या, झूठा, not right, deceiving, lying. *His witnesses were ~.*

fame (**फ़ेम**) noun
कीर्ति, शोहरत, good name, reputation. *He bears ~ as a good orator.*

family (**फ़ैमिली**) noun
परिवार, कुटुम्ब, कुल, parents and their children. *The cat is a member of tiger ~.*

famous (**फ़ेमस**) noun
प्रसिद्ध, मशहूर, known widely, first rate. *Amritsar is ~ for its Golden Temple.*

fan (**फ़ैन**) noun
पंखा, rotating device, भक्त, प्रशंसक, admirer, supporter. *A ceiling ~.*

fancy (**फ़ैंसी**) adjective
मनोहारी, अलंकृत, of fine quality. *~ goods.*

fantastic (**फ़ैन्टैस्टिक**) adjective
अनोखा, strange, अति उतम, excellent, काल्पनिक, fancy, imaginative. *She is a ~ girl.*

far (**फ़ार**) adjective
दूर, distant, remote, *How ~ did you go?*

fare (**फ़ेयर**) noun
यात्रा भाड़ा, यात्रा करना, money charged for travelling, सफल होना progress. *How did you ~ in your journey?*

farm (**फ़ार्म**) noun
पशुपालन तथा कृषि क्षेत्र, land for growing crops, rearing animals. *He has a lot of ~ land.*

farther (**फ़ार्दर**) adverb
और अधिक दूरी पर, at a greater distance. *He went ~ into the jungle.*

fascinate (**फ़ैसीनेट**) noun
वश में करना, सम्मोहित करना, charm, attract. *A magician has great fascination for children.*

fashion (**फ़ैशन**) noun
कार्य प्रणाली, ढंग, manner of doing, वेशभूषा की शैली, style of dress, *Dressed in the latest ~.*
He talks in a peculiar ~.

fast (**फ़ास्ट**) adjective.
तेज, शीघ्रगामी, moving quickly. *The train is super~.*

fast (**फ़ास्ट**) noun
उपवास, रोज़ा, व्रत, abstain from food. *Act of ~ing.*

fat (**फ़ैट**) adjective.
स्थूल, मोटा, plump, thick, चर्बीदार, greasy. *He is a ~ man.*

fate (**फ़ेट**) noun
किस्मत, तकदीर, destiny, fortune, lot. *Death is man's ~.*

father (**फ़ादर**) noun
पिता, बाप, male parent. महत्वपूर्ण व्यक्ति, important person. *Prof*

Rai is known as the ~ of economics.

fatigue (फ़ैटीग) noun
थकावट, being tired. *Many athletes dropped with ~ in the long march.*

fault (फ़ॉल्ट) noun
त्रुटि, कमी, दोष, blemish, flaw. *I could not find any ~.*

favour (फ़ेवर) noun
पक्षपात, सद्भाव, कृपादृष्टि, a kind act. *He is trying to win the ~ of the boss.*

fear (फ़िअर) noun
भय, डर, alarm, awe. *The boy stood in ~ before his father.*

feast (फ़ीस्ट) noun
दावत, rich meal, धार्मिक पर्व, त्यौहार, religious festival. *The ~ of Christmas.*

feather (फ़ेदर) noun
पंखा, plumage, *Peacock's colourful ~s.*

feature (फीचर) noun
लक्षण, characteristics. *Her eyes are her best ~.*

fee (फ़ी) noun
शुल्क, मेहनताना, payment for professional services. *Entrance ~ in circus.*

feed (फ़ीड) verb
खाना खिलाना, give food to, चारा, fodder. *There is not enough ~ left for the cows.*

feel (फ़ील) verb
अनुभव करना, be aware of. स्पर्श, sense of touch. *You can't say anything by the ~ of it.*

feet (फ़ीट) noun
पैर, plural of foot, *Sit at someone's ~.*

fellow (फ़ैलो) noun
व्यक्ति, आदमी person, man or boy, साथी, शोध छात्र person of the same group. *He is my class ~.*

felt (फ़ैल्ट) verb
अनुभव किया, past tense of feel. *I ~ happy on her selection as sub inspector.*

felt (फ़ैल्ट) noun
नमदा pressed wool to cover with. *He wears a ~ hat.*

female (फ़ीमेल) adjective
स्त्री, मादा, feminine, *A ~ child.*

ferry (फ़ैरी) noun
नौका, नाव, किश्ती boat. *The ~ crosses the river.*

festival (फ़ैस्टिवल) noun
त्यौहार, खुशी का अवसर, समारोह religious or any other kind of performance. *A ~ of drama.*

fetch (फ़ैच) verb
जाकर लाना, to go and bring back, *Please ~ the children from school.*

fever (फ़ीवर) noun
ज्वर, ताप, बुखार abnormal body temperature condition. *To suffer from ~.*

few (फ़्यू) adjective
कुछ, थोड़े से, कम, बहुत कम, not much. *He is a man of ~*

words.

fiance (फ़ीऐंसे) noun
मंगेतर, boy to whom a girl is engaged.

fiancee (फ़ीऐंसी) noun
वाग्दत्ता, girl to whom a boy is engaged.

fibre (फ़ाइबर) noun
रेशा, महीन धागा, yarn.

fiction (फ़िक्शन) noun
कहानी-उपन्यास, कल्पित, काल्पनिक, stories and novels, imagined, invented. *Fact is often stranger than ~.*

field (फ़ील्ड) noun
खेत, चरागाह, crop or pasture area, खुला मैदान, open space, खेल में गेंद खेलना, रोकना. *What a fine ~ of wheat!*

fierce (फ़िअर्स) adjective
भंयकर, बर्बर, भीषण, प्रचंड, उग्र, violent and angry. *He wears a ~ look on his face.*

fifth (फ़िफ्थ) adjective
पाँचवाँ, ordinal of five, पंचभागी, देश द्रोहियों का दल, fifth column, traitors. *In the ~ place.*

fig (फ़िग) noun
अंजीर, गूलर, a pear-shaped fruit. *~ is rich in iron.*

fight (फ़ाइट) verb
लड़ना, to use physical force. *The boys were ~ing over a ball.*

figure (फ़िगर) noun
बनावट, आकृति, संख्या, shape, form, number. *His income is in four ~s.*

file (फ़ाइल) noun
रेती, tool for smoothing surface, मिसिल, cover to keep documents. *Use a ~ on it. ~ these applications.*

fill (फ़िल) noun
भरना, to make full. *~ up the tank.*

film (फ़िल्म) noun
परत, झिल्ली membrane, फोटो फिल्म, चलचित्र, motion picture. *A ~ of dust on the table.*

filter (फ़िल्टर) noun
छन्ना, छानना, apparatus for sifting. *Use a ~ for purifying water.*

final (फ़ाइनल) adjective
अंतिम, आखिरी, coming at the end. *The matter was ~ly decided.*

finance (फ़ाइनैन्स) noun
अर्थ, अर्थ व्यवस्था, money, management of money, राजस्व *Our country's ~s are sound.*

find (फ़ाइन्ड) verb
तलाश करके पाना, to obtain by search, मार्ग ढूँढ़ लेना, *Rivers ~ their way to sea.*

fine (फ़ाइन) noun
जुर्माना, अर्थदण्ड, penalty, उत्तम, स्वच्छ, साफ़, pleasing, splendid. *He was ~d for rash driving.*

finger (फ़िंगर) noun
उँगली, long parts at the end

of a hand. *Four ~s in a hand.*

finish (फ़िनिश) verb
समाप्त करना, समाप्त होना, complete, bring to an end. *He ~ed his work in time.*

fire (फ़ायर) noun
अग्नि, जलने की स्थिति condition of burning. *Set on ~. ~ bricks in a kiln.*

firm (फ़र्म) adjective
ठोस, सख्त, solid, hard, अडिग, not easily changed, व्यवसाय, संघ, कम्पनी, फर्म. *As ~ as a rock. A big business ~.*

first (फ़र्स्ट) noun
प्रथम, पहला, coming before all others. *He stood ~ in relay race.*

fish (फ़िश) noun
मछली, मत्स्य, coldblooded water animal. *The flesh of ~es is used as food.*

fission (फिशन) noun
विभाजन splitting or division. *Atom bomb is made of the ~ technique.*

fit (फ़िट) adjective
ठीक, सही, उचित, good enough, suitable, दौरा, मूर्च्छा, sudden attack of illness. *The food was ~ to eat. A fainting ~.*

five (फ़ाइव) noun
पाँच, four plus one, a cardinal number. *He paid Rs. ~ for lower class in the cinema hall.*

five-star (फाइव-स्टार) noun
पाँच सितारों वाला, five stars to indicate rank. *His marriage ceremony was performed in a ~ hotel.*

fix (फ़िक्स) verb
जमाना, बैठाना, बाँधना, make firm or fast. कठिनाई, दुविधा dilemma. *~ a nail to the wall. You have put me in a ~.*

flag (फ़्लैग) noun
झण्डा, ध्वज, national banner. *~ day.*

flame (फ़्लेम) noun
लपट, लौ, burning gas. *The shop was in ~s.*

flash (फ़्लैश) noun
क्षणिक तेज़ प्रकाश, sudden burst of flame. *The lightning ~ed along the sky.*

flat (फ़्लैट) adjective
फीका, बेमज़ा, without vitality, lifeless, बड़ी इमारत में रहने का एक भाग a block in big building. *~ writing. A block of ten ~s.*

flatter (फ़्लैटर) verb
चापलूसी करना, praise too much in order to please. *He ~ed his boss to get promotion.*

flavour (फ़्लेवर) noun
सुगंध, स्वाद का एहसास, sensation of taste or smell. *~ of garlic.*

flaw (फ़्लॉ) noun
दरार, कमी, crack, defect. *There were several ~s in their arguments.*

flesh (**फ़्लॅश**) noun
माँस, गोश्त, meat. *Lions are ~eating animals.*

flirt (**फ़्लर्ट**) verb
प्रेम करना act amorously. *Butterflies are ~ing from flower to flower.*

float (**फ़्लोट**) verb
तैरना, बहना, बहाना, to move in air or water. *The boat ~ed down the river.*

flood (**फ़्लड**) noun
बाढ़, जलप्लावन, overflowing of water over a dry place. *Applications ~ed in.*

floor (**फ़्लोर**) noun
तल, तह, फ़र्श, a flat bottom's surface on any structure. *She danced on the ~ of the stage.*

flour (**फ़्लोर**) noun
आटा, ground wheat. *Make chapaties if there is some ~ in the kitchen.*

flow (**फ़्लो**) verb
बहना, प्रवाहित होना, move along. *Rivers ~ into the sea.*

flower (**फ़्लावर**) noun
फूल, पुष्प, plant of part producing seeds. यौवन, peak, the prime. *She had a rose ~ in her hair. She was blooming like a ~ in her youth.*

flu (**फ़्लू**) noun
इन्फलूएंजा, influenza.

fluent (**फ़्लुएंट**) adjective
धारावाही, धाराप्रवाह, command of something. *A ~ speaker.*

fluid (**फ़्लुइड**) noun
तरल जो बह सके, anything that is able to flow. *Though mercury is a metal, but it is ~.*

flush (**फ़्लश**) noun
आकस्मिक तेज बहाव, sudden flow of water. *The sweeper ~ed the toilets.*

fly (**फ़्लाई**) noun
मक्खी, gnat, उड़ना move through. *~ from Delhi to Bombay.*

foam (**फ़ोम**) noun
झाग fomentation. *~ on a glass of beer.*

focus (**फ़ोकस**) noun
किरण, बिन्दु a point where rays meet. *Bring the object in ~ if you want to shoot a good picture.*

foe (**फ़ो**) noun
शत्रु, दुश्मन, enemy. *We always have less friends and many ~s.*

fold (**फ़ोल्ड**) verb
मोड़ना, पर्त करना, bend, अन्त हो जाना, *The business finally ~ed up last week.*

follow (**फ़ौलो**) verb
पीछे चलना, अनुसरण करना, pursue. *You run first and I will ~ you.*

fond (**फ़ोंड**) adjective
प्रेमी, स्नेहपूर्ण, अत्यनुरागी affecti-

onate. *To be ~ of dogs.*

food (फूड) noun
खाद्य पदार्थ, भोजन, eatables. *I want some ~ and water.*

fool (फूल) noun
बेवकूफ़, मूर्ख, a silly or stupid man. *He ~ed around.*

foot (फुट) noun
पाँव, पैर, end of the leg, तली bottom. *His ~ got injured when he fell down.*

for (फ़ौर) preposition
के लिए, वास्ते, indicating destination. *I am going out ~ four days.*

force (फ़ोर्स) noun
ताकत, शक्ति, strength, power of body and mind, विवश करना oblige, compel. *He was ~d to land.*

fore (फ़ोर) adjective
आगे का, पूर्ववर्ती, toward the front. *He has come to the ~ as a union leader.*

forecast (फ़ोरकास्ट) verb
पूर्वानुमान करना, predict. *It will rain, was his ~.*

forehead (फ़ोरहैड) noun
ललाट, मस्तक, part of the head above eyes. *His ~ shows that he is intelligent.*

foreign (फ़ॉरिन) noun
विदेश, परराष्ट्रीय, another country. *His duty is in ~ service.*

forest (फ़ॉरेस्ट) noun
वन, जंगल, कानन a large tract of land with trees and bushes. *There is a dense ~ in the way to Bilaspur.*

forever (फ़ॉरएवर) adverb
सदैव, अविरल, always, at all times. *He went on speaking as if ~.*

forgery (फ़ोर्जरी) noun
जालसाजी, कूट रचना, something forged. *Monika did ~ for making her passport.*

forget (फ़ॉरगेट) verb
भूल जाना, चूकना, याद न रहना, fail to keep in memory. *Forgive and ~.*

forgive (फ़ॉरगिव) verb
क्षमा कर देना, दया दिखाना, absolve. *I ~ his rudeness.*

forgo (फ़ॉरगो) verb
छोड़ना, त्यागना, give up, abstain. *You must ~ pleasures in order to study hard.*

form (फ़ॉर्म) noun
आकृति, शक्ल बनाना, shape, develop. *His job was to ~ boys into men.*

formal (फ़ौर्मल) adjective
औपचारिक, conventional. *He paid me a ~ visit.*

former (फ़ॉर्मर) adjective
पिछले वक्त का, of an earlier period. *The ~ proposal was preferred to the latter.*

formula (फ़ॉर्मूला) noun
सिद्वान्त, नियम, चिह्नों तथा चित्रों की सहायता से सारणीकरण, statement

of rules through signs. *What is the ~ for area of a circle?*

fort (**फ़ोर्ट**) noun
किला, fortified place. *Rana Pratap's ~ is in Kundalgarh.*

fortune (**फ़ौर्चून**) noun
भाग्य, तकदीर, किस्मत, fate, luck, chance. *He went to Bombay to try his ~.*

forty (**फ़ौर्टी**) noun
40, चालिस XL is the symbol of this number. *A sleeper bus carries ~ passengers.*

forward (**फ़ौरवर्ड**) adverb
आगे की ओर, toward the front. *Let us move ~.*

foul (**फ़ाउल**) verb
दूषित करना, न्यायविरुद्ध, खेल नियम का उल्लंघन. *It looked like a corner when he kicked it, but it went ~.*

fragile (**फ़्रेजाइल**) adjective.
भंगुर, नाजुक, easily broken. *Glassware is ~.*

frame (**फ़्रेम**) noun
तस्वीर का चौखटा, border of wood etc. around a picture, बनाना to make. *Sobs shook her ~.*

frank (**फ़्रैंक**) adjective
स्पष्टवादी, unreserved in speech. *A ~ smile.*

fraud (**फ़्रॉड**) noun
छल, कपट, घोखा, criminal deception. *Get money by ~.*

free (**फ़्री**) verb
मुक्त करना, स्वतंत्र, set at liberty. *A ~ nation.*

freeze (**फ़्रीज़**) verb
जमना, be so that water turns into ice. *Water ~s at 0ºC.*

friction (**फ़्रिक्शन**) noun
घर्षण, rubbing of surfaces. *~ between two stones can create fire.*

friend (**फ़्रैंड**) noun
मित्र, दोस्त, person attached by affection. *He is a ~ of the poor.*

frock (**फ़्रॉक**) noun
कुरती, dress of a girl. *The little girl wore a ~.*

from (**फ़्रॉम**) preposition.
से, जहाँ से शुरुआत की, starting point. *Travel ~ Kolkata to Nagpur.*

front (**फ़्रन्ट**) noun
सामना, मुख, चेहरा, face. *The ~ of a building.*

fruit (**फ़्रुट**) noun
फल, product of tree, परिणाम outcome, आय profit. *Apple is a sweet ~.*

fry (**फ़्राई**) verb
तलना, पकना, पकाना, cook. *~ some rice to eat.*

fuel (**फ्युअल**) noun
ईंधन, लकड़ी, कोयला, तेल, combustible matter. *Fill up the car tank with ~.*

full (**फुल**) adjective
भरा हुआ, परिपूर्ण, completely filled. *My car tank is ~.*

fun (फ़न) noun
मज़ाक, तमाशा, खेल amusement. *Let's have ~.*

function (फ़ंक्शन) noun
कार्य, उत्सव, kind of action, public ceremony. *There is a three days' annual ~ in the school.*

funny (फ़नी) adjective
मज़ेदार, हास्यास्पद, providing fun. *The picture is quite ~.*

furnish (फ़र्निश) verb
सामानों से घर सजाना, to equip with what is necessary. *~ this room properly. He was allotted a full ~ed house at govt. cost.*

furniture (फ़र्नीचर) noun
मेज़, कुर्सी, सोफ़ा, tables, chairs, etc. with which a house, office, shop is furnished.

further (फ़र्दर) adverb
अधिक दूर, at a greater distance *Don't go ~.*

fuse (फ्यूज़) noun
विद्युत धारा के मुख्य तार का गलना जिससे विद्युत-सर्किट टूट जाता है, पिघलना, पिघलाना, a protective device in electric circuit. *Equip the plug with a ~.*

fusion (फ्यूज़न) noun
गलन, द्रवण, process of melting, विलय, संयोजन, विलयीकरण, to unite. *H. bomb works on ~ reaction.*

fuss (फ़स) noun
कोलाहल, बेकार का हंगामा, किसी व्यक्ति को परेशान करना, झमेला, useless bustle, excessively busy with trifles. *She is a ~y girl.*

future (फ्यूचर) adjective
भविष्य, time after the present. *The ~ is uncertain.*

□□□□

G

g
मुद्रण में प्रयुक्त लघु अक्षर

g
लेखन में प्रयुक्त लघु अक्षर

मूल उच्चारण **जी**

ग ज प्रयोग में उच्चारण ज्यादातर 'ग', शुक्र है।

अंग्रेजी वर्णमाला का सातवाँ अक्षर

gain (गेन) noun
लाभ, नफ़ा, profit, advantage. *~ed at the top of class.*

gallery (गैलरी) noun
कला दीर्घा, art centre.

gamble (गैम्बल) verb
जुआ खेलना, शर्त लगाना, try to win money by playing games. *He ~d away a lot of money in one night.*

game (गेम) noun
क्रीडा, खेल, play, sport. *Asian ~s.*

gang (गैंग) noun
दल, गिरोह, group. *A ~ of robbers.*

gaol (जेल) noun
कारागार, जेल, jail. *He spent three years in ~.*

gap (गैप) noun
दरार, खाली स्थान, fence. *A ~ in the wall.*

garden (गार्डन) noun
उद्यान, बगीचा, *A kitchen ~.*

garland (गारलैंड) noun
माला. *To decorate with a ~.*

garment (गारमैन्ट) noun
वस्त्र। *readymade ~s.*

gas (गैस) noun
गैस, airlike substance. *Air is a mixture of ~es.*

gate (गेट) noun
फाटक, द्वार, प्रवेश द्वार, way to pass. *~ way*

gather (गैदर) verb
एकत्रित करना, संग्रह करना. *He soon ~ed a crowd around him.*

gave (गेव) verb
दिया. *She ~ me a bouquet.*

gay (गे) adjective
प्रसन्नचित्त, cheerful. *The ~ voice of young children.*

gender (जैन्डर) noun
लिंग. *The feminine ~ . The neuter ~ .*

general (जनरल) adjective
सामान्य, of most people or things. *~ election, ~ knowledge. Army ~ store.*

genius (जीनियस) noun
विद्वान, प्रतिभाशाली, extra brilliant. *He is a ~ in mathematics.*

gentle (जेन्टिल) adjective
भद्र, सज्जन, kind, amiable. *The cow is a ~ animal.*

gerund (जीरण्ड) noun
क्रिया में ing लगी हुई संज्ञा. *He is fond of walking.*

get (गैट) verb
लेना, हो जाना, become. *~ him before he escapes.*

girl (गर्ल) noun
बालिका, कन्या, लड़की, female child. *My wife and I have two ~s.*

give (गिव) verb
देना, सुपुर्द करना hand over. *~ him a birthday present.*

glad (ग्लैड) adjective
प्रसन्न, pleased. *I am ~ to meet you.*

global (ग्लोबल) adjective
विश्वव्यापी, worldwide. *It is my dream of ~ peace.*

glory (ग्लोरी) adjective
ख्याति, नेकनामी, high fame, परमेश्वर का गुणगान, adoration of God, exaltation. *The ~ of sunset is blissful.*

glove (ग्लव) noun
दस्ताना. *We must wear ~ s in the winter.*

glow (ग्लो) verb
चमकना, shine. *The face of a girl ~s when young.*

go (गो) verb
जाना, चलना, move, pass. *I must ~ to bring the book.*

goal (गोल) noun
गोल, लक्ष्य, target. *The ball headed towards the ~.*

goat (गोट) noun
बकरा animal with horns. *Milk of ~s.*

god (गौड) noun
देवता, deity. *Cupid is the ~ of love.*

God (गौड) noun
परमात्मा, खुदा, अल्लाह, Supreme Being.

gold (गोल्ड) noun
स्वर्ण, सोना. *Ring of ~.*

gold medal (गोल्ड मेडल) noun
सोने का तमगा. *He was awarded a ~ when he topped the competition.*

good (गुड) adjective
उत्तम, अच्छा, गुणी। *This car has ~ brakes.*

gorgeous (गौरजियस) adjective
भव्य, splendid. *His dress was simply ~.*

gossip (गॉसिप) noun
गपशप, general talk. *Some people are fond of ~.*

government (गवर्नमैंट) noun
हुकूमत, शासन, *What we need is a strong ~.*

grade (ग्रेड) noun
दर्जा, वर्ग, श्रेणी, value, quality. *He passed with a good ~.*

grain (ग्रेन) noun
अन्न, दाना, कण, the seeds of wheat, rice, etc. *You should take the promise with a ~ of salt.*

grammar (ग्रामर) noun
व्याकरण, *A thorough knowledge of ~ is essential to master a language.*

grand (ग्रैंड) adjective
प्रभावशाली, शानदार, very impressive. *The function was a ~ success.*

grant (ग्रान्ट) verb
मंजूर करना, देना, allow, consent, to give. *I ~ his honesty. He was ~ed leave.*

grass (ग्रास) noun
घास, दूब, thin green leaves that grow on the earth.

gratitute (ग्रेटिट्यूड) noun
आभार, कृतज्ञता, एहसान thankfulness. *I express my ~ for helping me.*

grave (ग्रेव) noun
कब्र, समाधि, *The ~s of the dead.* गंभीर, महत्वपूर्ण. *A ~ mistake.*

great (ग्रेट) adjective
महान, बड़ा, विशाल, *Take ~ care of your health.*

green (ग्रीन) adjective.
हरा. *Shades of ~ and blue.*

greet (ग्रीट) verb
स्वागत करना *Always ~ your friends with a smile.*

grief (ग्रीफ) noun
शोक, गहन दुःख, deep sorrow. *He was stricken with ~.*

grind (ग्राइन्ड) verb
पीसना। crush to make powder. *~ the corn.*

grip (ग्रिप) verb
कस कर पकड़ना, पकड़, seize firmly. *The ailing child ~ed its mother's hand.*

ground (ग्राउन्ड) noun
ज़मीन, भूमि, earth. *The matter covered a lot of ~.*

grow (ग्रो) verb
बड़ा होना, पनपना *A full ~n elephant is very large.*

guess (गैस) verb
अंदाज़ लगाना, कल्पना करना, suppose. *Can you ~ my age? ~papers are available in the market.*

guest (गैस्ट) noun
मेहमान, अतिथि, *Are you expecting ~s at dinner tonight?*

guidance (गाइडैन्स) noun
मार्गदर्शन, निर्देशन. *Under his ~.*

guilt (गिल्ट) noun
अपराध, कसूर, crime, sin. *The ~ of the accused was in doubt.*

gulf (गल्फ़) noun
खाड़ी a deep wide chasm in the sea, अंतर, difference. *There is a big ~ between the generations.*

gum (गम) noun
मसूढ़ा, गोंद. *Children like chewing ~.*

gun (गन) noun
बन्दूक, तोप, cannon, carbine, pistol. *A few terrorists were ~ned down at the spot.*

gutter (गटर) noun
परनाला, मोरी. *Please take out the child out of the ~.*

gym (जिम) noun
short for gymnasium. व्यायामशाला, अखाड़ा. *Young boys go to ~ for bodybuilding.*

□□□□

H

h मुद्रण में प्रयुक्त लघु अक्षर

h लेखन में प्रयुक्त लघु अक्षर

मूल उच्चारण **एच**

ह प्रयोग में उच्चारण केवल एक

अंग्रेजी वर्णमाला का आठवाँ अक्षर

habit (हैबिट) noun
आदत, something one often does. *He has the ~ of reading novels.*

had (हैड) verb
past tense of has and have, रखता था. *He ~ a big house.*

hair (हेअर) noun
बाल, केश, long, thin, dark things that grow on the head. *Brush your ~.*

half (हाफ़) noun
आधा, one of two equal parts of something. *He wrote only ~ of the story.*

hall (हॉल) noun
बड़ा कमरा, large room. *Schools must have ~s.*

halt (हाल्ट) verb
यात्रा के बीच में रुकना, a short stop on a march. *He had a ~ for tea in a hotel.*

hammer (हैमर) noun
हथौड़ा, tool with heavy head. *He ~ed nails into the wood.*

hand (हैन्ड) noun
हाथ, हस्त, part of the human arm beyond wrist. *His ~s were in the coat pockets.*

handicap (हैन्डीकेप) noun
बाधा, रास्ते का रोड़ा, disadvantage. *Poor eyesight is a ~ for a student.*

handicapped (हैन्डीकैप्ड) adjective
विकलांग, मंदबुद्धि, crippled, mentally deficient. *There are separate schools for the ~.*

handle (हैन्डल) noun
मूठ, हत्था, हाथ से पकड़ना, a part by which something is held by hand. *Wash your hands before you ~ edibles.*

handsome (हैंडसम) noun
सुन्दर, खूबसूरत, उदार, पर्याप्त

goodlooking, generous, enough. *Rs. 501 is quite a ~ birthday present.*

hang (हैंग) verb
लटकाना, लटकना, to support. *~ it on the wall.*

hanger (हैंगर) noun
जिस पर कोई वस्तु लटकाई जाती है, a frame used for hanging.

haphazard (हैंपहैज़र्ड) adjective
बेसिलसिलेवार, उलटा-सीधा, without plan. *He dealt with the enquiry in a ~ way.*

happen (हैपन) verb
होना, घटित होना, to take place, come about. *How did the accident ~?*

happy (हैपी) adjective
सुखी, भाग्यशाली, pleased, lucky. *He is ~ after his marriage.*

harass (हैरस) verb
परेशान करना, पीड़ित करना, to torment, disturb persistently. *He was ~ed by the problems of a large family.*

hard (हार्ड) adjective
सख्त, ठोस, कठोर, firm, solid, a difficult problem. *Racing made the boys ~.*

hardly (हार्डली) adverb
मुश्किल से, scarcely. *He is ~ fifty.*

hare (हेयर) noun
खारगोश, खरहा fast running animal with long ears. *There was a race between a ~ and a tortoise.*

harm (हार्म) noun
हानि, क्षति, नुकसान पहुँचाना, damage, injury. *There is no ~ in doing so now.*

harsh (हार्श) adjective
रूखा, कठोर, rough, unpleasant. *~ are the colours of this painting.*

has (हैज़) verb
past tense of have, Ist person singular. *He ~ my book.*

haste (हेस्ट) noun
जल्दी, hurry. *He went off in great ~.*

hat (हैट) noun
टोप, covering of head. *He approached his boss with ~ in hand.*

hate (हेट) verb
घृणा करना, strong dislike. *She ~s talkative girls.*

have (हैव) verb
to own, to possess. होना, रखना, अधिकार में रखना, वश में रखना. *~ you got a good pen?*

haven (हैवन) noun
बन्दरगाह, आश्रयस्थल, place of safety or rest. *Terrorists will not find a safe ~ here.*

he (ही) pronoun.
वह, the other person. *~ is in the garden.*

head (हैड) noun
सिर, मस्तिष्क upper part of the body, संस्था का प्रधान. *He is a ~*

taller than his sister.

heal (हील) noun
घाव पुरना, भरना curing of wounds. *The wound will take time to ~.*

health (हैल्थ) noun
स्वास्थ्य, general condition of the body. *She is in delicate ~.*

hear (हिअर) verb
सुनना, listen. *Deaf people cannot ~.*

heart (हार्ट) noun
दिल, हृदय, muscular organ which keeps the blood in circulation. स्नेहकेन्द्र, प्रेम का केन्द्र *In your ~ you know that I am your friend.*

heat (हीट) noun
गर्मी, ऊष्मा, ताप, the degree of hotness, गरम करना. *Switch the ~ing system on.*

heaven (हैवन) noun
स्वर्ग, देवलोक the abode of gods. *Thank ~s, you were not injured.*

heavy (हैवी) adjective
वजनी, भारी, of great weight, *Air is ~ with moisture.*

hectic (हैक्टिक) adjective
सतत, लगातार, सरगर्मी से भरा, intense, with agitation. *The period preceding the trip was ~ and exhausting.*

heed (हीड) verb
ध्यान देना, pay attention to, ख्याल करना, take notice of. *Pay ~ to the warning.*

height (हाइट) adjective
ऊँचाई, चरम सीमा, measurement from bottom to top. *The ~ of fashion.*

heir (हेयर) noun
वारिस, उत्तराधिकारी, successor. *The eldest son is usually the ~ to a king.*

hell (हैल) noun
नरक, घोर यातना, the abode of evil spirits, क्रोध प्रकट करना. *What the ~ you want me to do?*

helmet (हैल्मेट) noun
शिरस्त्राण, लौह टोप, a protective head covering. *The ~ is compulsory for a motorcyclist.*

help (हैल्प) noun
सहायता, मदद, to do something for somebody. *You must ~ your old parents.*

hen (हैन) noun
मुर्गी, female of cock.

hence (हैन्स) adverb
यहाँ से, अब से, इस कारण from here, from now, for this reason. *He was late ~ he was not allowed to enter the class.*

henna (हेना) noun
मेंहदी, हिना, shrub producing red-brown dye. *He dyes his hair with ~.*

her (हर) pronoun
उस स्त्री को, objective case of she. *Give ~ two books to read.*

herb (हर्ब) noun
शाक, lowgrowing plant. जड़ी-बूटी. *~s are used in medicines and cosmetics.*

here (हियर) adverb
यहाँ, at this place. *~ is your ball.*

hero (हीरो) noun
वीर, नायक, brave, courageous, noble man. *Dhayan Chand was the ~ of Indian hockey in his days.*

heroin (हैरोइन) noun
मादक पदार्थ, narcotic drug derived from morphine. *~ is used as drug.*

heroine (हीरोइन) noun
वीरांगना, गरिमायुक्त नारी, नायिका *Portia is the ~ of the Merchant of Venice.*

herself (हरसैल्फ) pronoun
स्वयं उसका, अपना *She hurt ~.*

hide (हाइड) verb
छिपना, छिपाना, to prevent from being seen. *The future is hidden from us.*

hi-fi (हाइ-फाई) noun
short of high fidelity, ऐसा यंत्र जो बिल्कुल समान ध्वनि उत्पन्न करे. *His Sanyo transistor was ~.*

high (हाई) adjective
ऊँचा, उच्च, extending far upwards. *There was an aeroplane ~ in the sky.*

hijack (हाइजैक) verb
रास्ते में ले उड़ना, चुरा लेना, अपने कब्जे में कर लेना, to steal in transit. *The B.J.P. has managed to ~ the temple movement from the clutches of V.H.P.*

hill (हिल) noun
पहाड़ी, natural elevation from the earth's surface. *Nainital is a good ~ station.*

hind (हाइन्ड) adjective
पिछला, the back part. *The ~ legs of a cow.*

hint (हिन्ट) noun
संकेत, इशारा, इशारा देना, indirect indication. *The teacher gave some ~s about the question paper.*

hip (हिप) noun
नितम्ब, कूल्हा, fleshy part of the thigh.

hire (हायर) verb
किराए पर लेना, to take the services for wages. *He ~d a car for going to picnic.*

his (हिज़) adjective, pronoun
उसका, belonging to. *He hurt ~ leg.*

history (हिस्ट्री) noun
इतिहास, branch of knowledge. *Their prominence was ~ical.*

hit (हिट) verb
बल लगाकर मारना, प्रहार *He ~ the man on his head.*

ho (हो) interjection
अरे, अहा, expressing surprise

or admiration, also 'oh'. ~, *he is ill!*

hobby (**हौबी**) noun
शौक, शग़ल, अभिरुचि, an activity of interest. *Philately is her ~.*

hoist (**हॉइस्ट**) verb
ऊपर उठाना, किसी यंत्र से ऊपर उठाना, to lift up, फहराना *On 15th August our flag is ~ed everywhere in India.*

hold (**होल्ड**) verb
मज़बूती से पकड़ना, keep fast, grasp. *The mother was ~ing her baby's hand.*

hold on (**होल्ड ऑन**) verb
खतरे के समय डटे रहना to stand firm at the time of danger. *You should ~ for another hour.*

hold (**होल्ड**) noun
पकड़, रोक, power to hold. *The receptionist put me on ~.*

hole (**होल**) noun
छेद, विवर, a pit, hollow place. *The road is full of ~s.*

holiday (**होलिडे**) noun
अवकाश, छुट्टी *Sunday is a ~.*

hollow (**हौलो**) adjective.
पोला, असत्य, थोथा, अवतल, गड्ढेदार, छिद्र, not solid, false. *My friend settled abroad and left a ~ in my life.*

holy (**होली**) adjective
पवित्र, ईश्वर की सेवा में समर्पित, धार्मिक, sacred, devoted to the service of God. *Varanasi is a ~ place.*

home (**होम**) noun
घर, गृह, निवास, स्वदेश, परिवार, place where one lives. *After retirement I shall make my ~ in the country.*

honest (**ऑनेस्ट**) adjective
सच्चा, भला, ईमानदार, upright. *I don't ~ly know.*

honey (**हनी**) noun
शहद, मधु, nectar, प्रेयसी, दिल की रानी, sweetheart. *You look great tonight, ~.*

honorary (**आनरेरी**) adjective
सम्मानसूचक, बगैर वेतन के, given for honour only, without usual duties. *The university presented Dr. Nelson Mandela with an ~ degree.*

honour (**औनर**) noun
सम्मान, सम्मान करना, प्रतिष्ठा, respect, esteem. *Sachin is an ~ to Indian cricket.*

hook (**हुक**) noun
काँटा, कुन्दा, a curved metal piece to hang or hold something. *The telephone is off the ~, place it properly.*

hoot (**हूट**) noun
उल्लू की बोली, cry of an owl, सभा से उखाड़ना, scorn. *The crowd ~ed out the speaker.*

hop (**हॉप**) verb
कूदना, उछलना, फुदकना jump, यात्रा करना, उत्तेजित करना. *The frog ~ped all over the ground and disappeared.*

hope (होप) noun
आशा, उम्मीद, feeling of trust and confidence. *There is not much ~ of recovery.*

horn (हॉर्न) noun
सींग hardpointed, curved out growths on the head of cattle. *An ox has two thick long ~s.* तुरही, भौंपू *A motor ~.*

horror (हौरर) noun
आंतक, भय, extreme fear or dislike. *She was struck with ~ on seeing the snake. This is a ~ film, you'll be frightened to see it.*

horse (हॉर्स) noun
घोड़ा, अश्व, stallion, तुरंग. *~ power equals to 745.7 watts. He is interested in ~ riding.*

hospitable (हॉस्पिटेबल) adjective
सत्कार करने वाला, आतिथ्यकारी, treating guests generously, hospitality. *He is an ~ man.*

hospital (हॉस्पिटल) noun
अस्पताल, चिकित्सालय, place for treatment. *My sister is a ~ nurse.*

host (होस्ट) noun
मेज़बान, person who receives and entertains guests. *His father acted as ~ at the dinner party.*

hostel (हॉस्टल) noun
छात्रावास, place for boarding and lodging of students. *He is not residing in the ~.*

hot (हॉट) adjective
गरम, तप्त, being at high temperature. *Today, it is very ~.*

hotel (होटल) noun
होटल, लोगों के ठहरने की जगह, place where rooms and food are provided. *I stayed in a ~ on my way to Nagpur.*

house (हाउस) noun
घर, गृह, घर में ठहराना. *We can ~ you and your friends.*

how (हाऊ) adverb
कैसे, किस प्रकार, in what way. *~ did you escape?*

huge (ह्यूज) adjective
विशाल, very large. *The blue whale is a ~ animal.*

human (ह्यूमन) adjective
मानवीय, मानवोचित of man, mankind. *Selfishness is ~ nature.* human being, नर, नारी, जन, मानव, man, woman, child, person.

humble (हम्बल) adjective
विनीत, नम्र, modest. *He is ~ with his elders.*

humour (ह्यूमर) noun
मज़ाक, amusement. *He is a very ~ous person.*

hunger (हंगर) noun
भूख, क्षुधा, desire for food, लालसा, strong craving. *The factory workers have gone on a ~ strike.*

hunt **(हंट)** noun
शिकार, आखेट, chase animals to kill them. *Crowded shops are happy ~ing ground for pickpockets.*

hurry **(हरी)** noun
जल्दबाजी, eager, haste. *There is no need for ~.*

hurt **(हर्ट)** verb
चोट पहुँचाना, घायल करना, to damage, to cause bodily injury. *He ~ his forehead when he fell.*

husband **(हज़बैंड)** noun
स्वामी, पति, a man to whom a woman is married. *Her ~ is a doctor.*

hyper **(हाईपर)** prefix
उपसर्ग, अधिक, ज्यादा, प्रचुर, above, over, excess. ~ *sensitive.*

hyphen **(हाईफ़न)** noun
ऐसा चिह्न जो दो शब्दों को जोड़ने के लिए लगाया जाता है. (-) sign used to join two words together, e.g., ex-wife, Anglo-French.

hypocrisy **(हिपक्रेसी)** noun
दिखावा, ढोंग, पाखंड, दम्भ, insincerity.

□□□□

I

I i

मुद्रण में प्रयुक्त दीर्घ तथा लघु अक्षर

𝒥i

लिखने में प्रयुक्त दीर्घ तथा लघु अक्षर

मूल उच्चारण **आइ**

इ आ प्रयोग में उच्चारण ज्यादातर 'इ'

अंग्रेजी वर्णमाला का नवाँ अक्षर और तीसरा स्वर – इसे नवाँ स्थान क्यों दिया गया?

I (आई) pronoun
मैं, used to refer himself. *Ramu said, ~ want to go now.*

ice (आइस) noun
बर्फ, frozen water. *The ~ is thick enough for skating.*

icon (आईकौन) adjective
प्रतिमा, प्रतीक, मूर्ति, चित्र, an image, a representation. *He has become an ~ because his deeds are very good.*

idea (आईडिया) noun
भाव, विचार, thought, picture in mind. *This essay gives you a good ~ of life in ancient India.*

Ideal (आइडियल) adjective
आदर्श, पूर्ण, satisfying, one's idea of what is perfect. *~ism has no place in politics.*

Identical (आइडेन्टिकल) adjective
वही, वैसा ही, समरूप, the same, exactly alike. *These triangles are ~.*

idle (आइडिल) adjective
बेकार, आलसी, not working or active. *We spent many ~ hours during the holidays.*

if (इफ) conjunction
यदि, अगर, on condition that. *I will go there even ~ it tires me.*

ignore (इग्नोर) verb
ध्यान न देना, उपेक्षा करना, take no notice of. *He ~d the advice of his elders.*

i.e. (आई.ई.)
id est का संक्षेप, that is to say. अर्थात्, यानी, *Hot drinks, ~, tea and coffee.*

ill (इल) adjective
बीमार, अस्वस्थ, not well, sick. *He is ~ these days.*

illegal (इल्लीगल) adjective
गैरकानूनी, contrary to law. *Child labour is ~.*

illustrate (इलस्ट्रेट) verb
चित्रित करना, उदाहरण आदि की मदद से समझाना, to draw sketches to explain by examples. *I ~ to make comprehension easy.*

image (इमेज) noun
छवि, प्रतिमा, प्रतिरूप, mental picture, statue, likeness. *I have this ~ of you as always being cheerful.*

imagine (इमेजिन) verb
कल्पना करना, अनुमान लगाना, suppose, assume. *We can't ~ life without electricity.*

imitate (इमिटेट) verb
नकल करना, अनुकरण करना, to copy behaviour. *One should ~ the great and good.*

immediate (इमीजिएट) adjective
निकटतम, आसन्न, nearest. *Mr. Telang is my ~ neighbour.*

impair (इम्पेअर) verb
नुकसान, क्षति पहुँचाना, to damage, to injure. *His hearing was ~ed by an accident.*

impart (इम्पार्ट) verb
प्रदान करना, देना, to disclose, to relate, tell. *I won't ~ any secret information to you.*

impatient (इम्पेशेन्ट) adjective
उतावला, अधीर, eagerly desirous. *They were ~ to start on a holiday trip.*

import (इम्पोर्ट) verb
आयात करना, to buy from a foreign country. *Our country has ~ed wheat this year.*

important (इम्पौर्टैन्ट) adjective
आवश्यक, महत्वपूर्ण, significant. *He is an ~ person in the office.*

impossible (इम्पौसिबिल) adjective
असम्भव, नामुमकिन, not possible. *It is ~ to live with him.*

impress (इम्प्रैस) verb
प्रभावित करना, छाप डालना, to persuade. *His speech made a strong ~ion on his audience.*

imprison (इम्प्रिज़न) verb
कैद करना, बंदी बनाना, to put in prison. *She felt ~ed in her own home.*

improve (इमप्रूव) verb
सुधारना, सँवारना, to make better in quality. *Try to ~ your health.*

impure (इम्प्योर) adjective
गंदा, मैला, दूषित, अपवित्र, dirty. *Drinking water must not be ~.*

in (इन) adverb
अन्दर, भीतर, inwards, *Please come~.* within. *Smoking is not allowed ~ the cinema hall.*

inaugurate (इनऑगुरेट) verb
उद्घाटन करना *The Chief Minister ~d the science exhibition.*

incense (इनसैन्स) noun
सुगंधित धूप fragrant substance, perfume. *We used to burn ~ sticks in honour of the deity.*

inch (इन्च) noun
एक फुट का बारहवां भाग 2.54 cm. *They could'nt move an ~ because the road was jammed by crowds.*

include (इनक्लूड) verb
शामिल करना, मिला लेना, to bring in, *The shopkeeper ~d the local taxes also with the price.*

income (इन्कम) noun
आय, आमदनी, money earned. *I don't pay any ~ tax as my ~ is not taxable.*

incomplete (इन्कम्पलीट) adjective
अपूर्ण, अघूरा, असमाप्त, not complete. *Your work is still ~.*

incorrect (इनकरैक्ट) adjective
गलत, not correct. *This sentence is grammatically ~.*

increase (इनक्रीज) verb
बढ़ना, बढ़ाना, to make greater. *The driver ~d the speed of the car.*

indecent (इनडीसैन्ट) adjective
अनुचित, अशोभनीय, अश्लील, vulgar, unseemly, obscene. *Young boys and girls play ~ scenes in public places.*

indefinite (इनडैफ़िनिट) adjective.
अनिश्चित, असीमित, not clearly defined. *He has ~ amount of wealth.*

independence (इन्डिपैन्डेन्स) adjective
स्वतंत्रता, आज़ादी, freedom. *He wants ~ from his parents.*

indirect (इनडायरैक्ट) adjective
टेढ़ा, अप्रत्यक्ष, not straight. *He told me to help ~ly.*

indulge (इनडल्ज) verb
तुष्ट करना, इच्छा के वशीभूत हो जाना, *Sweets after dinner were served, but I did not ~.*

infant (इनफ़ैन्ट) noun
शिशु, छोटा बच्चा, a child who can't even walk. *The new candidate is a political ~.*

inform (इन्फॉर्म) verb
सूचना, जानकारी देना, to impart information. *Have you ~ed them of your arrival?*

informal (इन्फ़ॉर्मल) adjective
अनौपचारिक, irregular. *The officer asked ~ly to purchase vegetables to his clerk.*

inhale (इन्हेल) verb
साँस लेना, breathe in. *Smokers who ~ cigarettes are likely to be addicted to nicotine.*

initial (इनिशल) adjective
प्रारम्भिक, शुरू की. *She came ~ly to spend a few days, but in the end she stayed for a month.* first letters of one's name as MKG (Mohandas Karamchand Gandhi), छोटे हस्ताक्षर

injure (**इनजर**) verb
चोट, हानि पहुँचाना, अपकार करना, impair, to cause damage, घायल करना. *Many people died and were ~d in the accident.*

injustice (**इनजस्टिस**) noun
अन्याय, नाइंसाफी, lack of justice. *In saying this you do her an ~.*

innocent (**इन्नोसैन्ट**) adjective
निर्दोष, blameless, harmless. *He is quite ~.*

input (**इनपुट**) noun
निवेश, आदान, data put in. *An ~ of energy is essential for electrical instruments.*

inquiry (**इनक्वाइरी**) noun
पूछताछ, जाँच, query. *There had been an ~ about Bofors deal.*

insecure (**इनसिक्योर**) adjective
अरक्षित, कमजोर, not safe, without protection. *Being alone in the house, she felt ~.*

insert (**इनसर्ट**) verb
डालना, फँसाना, घुसेड़ना, to put, fit. *~ a new chapter in the book.*

inside (**इनसाइड**) noun
अन्दर, भीतर, in the room or something. *During the curfew people remained ~ their houses.*

insight (**इनसाइट**) noun
कुशाग्रबुद्धि, सूझबूझ, intuition. *An able leader must have ~ into political matters.*

insoluble (**इनसौल्युबल**) adjective
अघुलनशील, अविलेय, incapable of forming a solution. *Vitamin D is ~ in water.*

inspect (**इन्सपैक्ट**) verb
मुआयना करना, सावधानी से देखना, examine carefully. *The auditors ~ed the account.*

institute (**इन्सटीट्यूट**) noun
संस्थान organization. *The engineering ~ of Roorkee.*

instruct (**इन्सट्रक्ट**) verb
बताना, निर्देष देना, to teach, शिक्षा देना. *Mr Baghel is Director of Public ~ion.*

insult (**इन्सल्ट**) verb
अपमान करना, तिरस्कार, to hurt a person's dignity. *That book is an ~ to one's intelligence.*

integration (**इन्टिग्रेशन**) noun
एकता, एकीकरण, bringing together. *Moral education is necessary for national ~.*

intellectual (**इण्टेलैक्चुअल**) adjective
बौद्धिक, प्रतिभासम्पन्न, मनीषी, विद्वान, of the intellect. *Dr. Radhakrishnan was a great ~.*

intelligent (**इण्टैलीजेन्ट**) adjective
मेधावी, होशियार, wise, prudent. *An ~ student is disciplined also.*

interest (**इन्टरैस्ट**) noun
रुचि *He takes great ~ in politics.*

ब्याज *I lent him Rs. 500 at 9% ~.*

Internal (इनटर्नल) adjective
भीतरी, आन्तरिक, अन्दरूनी, inside. *The ~ politics of the country is very dirty.*

interval (इनटरवल) noun
अन्तरावकाश, अन्तराल recess, विराम, विश्राम, *Two friends are meeting after an ~ of 15 years.*

interview (इन्टरव्यू) noun
साक्षात्कार, भेंट, नौकरी आदि की मौखिक परीक्षा, *The C.M. refused any ~ to the press.*

introduce (इन्ट्रोड्यूस) verb
परिचय कराना, जान पहचान कराना *The new students were ~d to one another.* प्रवेश कराना, शामिल करना. *~ a tube into the wound.*

invalid (इनवैलिड) noun
अमान्य not valid, दुर्बल, असमर्थ *He has become ~ for life.*

invest (इन्वैस्ट) verb
पूँजी लगाना, पैसा लगाना, put money in. *He ~ed Rs. 10,000 in Indira Bonds.*

invitation (इन्विटेशन) noun
निमंत्रण, न्यौता, the act of inviting. *Display of toys in window cases is an ~ to the children to purchase them.*

IOU (आई ओ यू) noun
विनिमय ऋण पत्र (= I owe you). *He gave an ~ to his creditor.*

iron (आयरन) noun
लोहा, a metal कपड़े पर इस्त्री करना, बहुत मजबूत, *He has an ~ constitution.*

irregular (इररैग्युलर) adjective
अनियमित, गलत, contrary to rules. *His attendance in the school is ~.*

irritate (इरिटेट) verb
नाराज करना, गुस्सा दिलाना, चिढ़ाना, exite, make angry. *It ~s me to have to shout to be heard.*

is (इज़) verb
है, a form to be used with he, she, it or with singular nouns.

issue (इश्यू) verb
देना, बाँटना, वाद-विवाद का विषय, distribute, problem. *~ warm clothing to the troops.*

it (इट) pronoun
यह, वह. *~ is a new watch. ~ is raining.*

itch (इच) noun
खुजली, खाज, प्रबल इच्छा, तरसना, skin causing desire to scratch. *He is suffering from ~. They have an ~ for money.*

its (इट्स) adjective
निर्धारक के रूप में प्रयोग possessive form of 'it'. *The table has lost ~ shine.*

□□□□

J

j
मुद्रण में प्रयुक्त लघु अक्षर

j
लिखने में प्रयुक्त लघु अक्षर

मूल उच्चारण **जे**

ज प्रयोग में उच्चारण सिर्फ एक

अंग्रेजी वर्णमाला का दसवाँ अक्षर

jack (जैक) noun
भारी बोझ उठाने का यंत्र, ताश के पत्तों का गुलाम. *~ up the car and change the damaged wheel. ~ of hearts.*

jacket (जैकिट) noun
मिरजई, small coat with sleeves. *Political leaders generally wear ~s.*

jaggery (जैगरी) noun
गुड़, शक्कर, raw sugar.

jail (जेल) noun
कारागर, बंदीगृह, prison. *That man was in ~ for three months in a cheating case.*

jam (जैम) noun
मुरब्बा, sweet pickle. *He spread some strawberry ~ on the bread.* दबाना, कुचलना, squeeze यातायात ठप्प हो जाना. *The traffic has been ~med.* रेडियो प्रसारण में गड़बड़ करना, *~mers are used in jails for jamming mobile telephone signals.*

January (जैन्युअरी) noun
वर्ष का प्रथम माह, जनवरी, first month of year. *In northern India ~ is the coolest month.*

jar (जार) noun
कर्कश ध्वनि, harsh sound, झन्नाहट. *We felt a ~ring jerk when the engine was coupled to the train.* मर्तबान। tall vessel with wide mouth. *A ~ of coffee.* मेल न खाना. *Your opinion ~s with mine.*

jasmine (जैसमिन) noun
चमेली, a shrub with white or yellow flowers. *There is a wreath of ~ flowers for the deity.*

jaundice (जॉनडिस) noun
पीलिया, कामला रोग, disease caused by an excess of bile in the blood. *He suffered with ~ and was admitted in the hospital.*

jaw (जौ) noun
जबड़ा, bone structure having teeth,

jealous (जैलस) adjective
डाह करनेवाला, ईर्ष्यालु, कुढ़ना, one resentful against a person. *I am tired of all these ~ies and quarrels.*

jeans (जीन्स) noun
मोटी सूती पतलून, trousers of strong cotton to wear. *She was wearing a pair of tight blue ~s.*

job (जौब) noun
काम धंधा, नौकरी, piece of work. *He got a part-time ~ as a gardener.*

join (जौइन) verb
मिलाना, जोड़ना, एकीकरण करना, unite. *I will ~ you in five minutes.*

joke (जोक) noun
हँसी मजाक, दिल्लगी करना, amusement. *I am only ~ing.*

joy (जौय) noun
खुशी, प्रसन्नता, उल्लास, हर्ष, deep pleasure. *We heard with ~ the news of your appointment.*

judge (जज) noun
न्यायाधीश, person who decides a case in court of law. न्याय करना, निर्णय देना. *Will you be a ~ at the Fancy Dress show next month?*

jug (जग) noun
जग, बड़ा पानी का टोंटीदार बर्तन, deep vessel with a handle. *Place a water ~ on the dining table.*

juice (जूस) noun
रस, the liquid from fruit or vegetables. *Pineapple ~ is his favourite.*

july (जुलाई) noun
पाँचवा महीना, fifth month of the year. *Schools open from first ~.*

jump (जम्प) noun
कूद, उछाल, *Long ~. High ~.* मूल्यवृद्धि *The prices have suddenly ~ed.* कूदना, फलांगना, लांघना *The horse ~ed all the fences.*

jungle (जंगल) noun
वन, forest. *Cut a path through the ~.*

junior (जूनियर) adjective
स्तर में छोटा, उम्र में छोटा, younger, lower in rank. *He is my ~ in age by three years.*

just (जस्ट) adjective
ठीक, सही, उचित, fair. *Be ~ to everybody.* बिल्कुल, अभी-अभी *It is ~ four o'clock.*

juvenile (जुवेनाइल) noun
छोटा बच्चा, छोटा जानवर, किशोर व्यक्ति (लड़का, लड़की) very young. *You are young but acting like a ~.*

□□□□

K

k
मुद्रण में प्रयुक्त लघु अक्षर

k
लिखने में प्रयुक्त लघु अक्षर

मूल उच्चारण के

क न
प्रयोग में उच्चारण ज्यादातर 'क' n मिलाकर (kn) न

अंग्रेजी वर्णमाला का ग्यारहवाँ अक्षर

keen (कीन) adjective.
तेज़, sharp, उत्सुक, eager, तीक्ष्ण, sensitive *He is very ~ about going to hill stations.*

keep (कीप) verb
रखना, सम्हाल कर रखना, have something. नजरबन्द रखना ~ *in custody*, सम्पर्क रखना, गुप्त रखना secret. *He ~s my cow when I am out.*

kerchief (करचिफ़) noun
सिर पर बाँधने का रूमाल, cloth used by woman as a head covering.

kerosene (कैरोसीन) noun
मिट्टी का तेल, a distil of petroleum.

ketchup (कैचप) noun
खुशबूदार स्वादिष्ट चटनी, flavoured sauce of tomato or mushroom. *Eat the pizza with ~.*

key (की) noun
चाबी, ताली, कुंजी, metal instrument to move the bolt of a lock. टाइपराइटर या कम्प्यूटर के अक्षर, letters of typewriter or a computer. *Use the ~ to open the gate.*

kick (किक) verb
लात मारना, दुलत्ती, ठोकर, to strike with foot. *The bruise was caused by a ~.* जोश, excitement. *He gets his ~s by playing football.* कार की गति बढ़ाना। *He ~ed his car to high gear.*

kid (किड) noun
बकरी का बच्चा, young goat. बच्चा, शिशु, young child. *A young ~ was playing in the park.*

kid (किड) verb
चिढ़ाना, हँसी उड़ाना, बेवकूफ़ बनाना *She is always ~ded for her accent.*

kidnap (किडनैप) verb
अपहरण करना, छल से या जबरदस्ती उठा ले जाना carry off somebody by force or fraud. *Keep an eye on ~pers.*

kidney (किडनी) noun
गुर्दा, वृक्क, a pair of organ in abdomen to secrete urine. *She expired of chronic ~ failure.*

kill (किल) verb
जान से मारना, नष्ट करना, put to death. *His response ~ed our hope.*

kind (काइन्ड) adjective
दयालु, मेहरबान, having sympathy or love. *It was very ~ of you to help us in our time of need.* प्रकार, किस्म, type. *Verbs are of two ~s.*

king (किंग) noun
राजा, नृप, a male ruler. *The age of ~s is now over.*

kiss (किस) verb
चूमना, चुम्बन लेना, love given with lips. *The baby gave me a ~.*

kitchen (किचन) noun
रसोई घर, पाकशाला, cooking room. *Take your meal on the ~ table.*

kite (काइट) noun
पतंग, चील, bird of pray of the hawk family. *The ~ snatched away a loaf of bread from the child's hand. The young boy was flying a ~.*

knee (नी) noun
घुटना, घुटनों पर झुकना, joint between thigh and leg. *The company was almost brought to ~s by the long strike.*

knife (नाइफ) noun
चाकू sharp-edged blade with handle. छुरा, छुरी *She will be under the ~ for removal of her tumour.*

knit (निट) verb
जोड़ना, गाँठ लगाना, बुनना, to join closely and firmly. *He ~ted his theory with the ideas of others.*

knob (नौब) noun
गोलाकार उभार, घुंडी, roundshaped projecting part. *Press the ~ to switch the set on.*

knock (नॉक) noun
चोट, प्रहार, आघात, दरवाजा खटखटाना, a rap. *I hear a ~ at the door.* घूँसा, blow with the fist. *The ~ knocked me flat.*

knot (नौट) noun
गाँठ, twine, loop. *Tie a ~ in the string.*

know (नो) verb
जानना, have in mind. *Do you ~ him?*

knowledge (नौलिज) noun
जानकारी, ज्ञान, acquaintance with facts. *A baby has no ~ of good and evil.*

❑❑❑❑

L

l
मुद्रण में प्रयुक्त लघु अक्षर

l
लेखन में प्रयुक्त लघु अक्षर

मूल उच्चारण **एल**

ल प्रयोग में उच्चारण एक ही है

अंग्रेजी वर्णमाला का बारहवाँ अक्षर

lab (लैब) noun
प्रयोगशाला, short for laboratory. *In science ~ students perform experiments.*

label (लेबल) noun
चिप्पी, नामपट्टी, किसी वस्तु पर लगाने वाला कागज़, धातु का टुकड़ा जिस पर वस्तु का संक्षिप्त विवरण होता है, a piece of paper or metal marked for fixing something to indicate the nature of ownership, destination, etc. *Put ~s on your luggage.*

labour (लेबर) noun
कार्य, परिश्रम (शारीरिक या मानसिक), hard work (physical or mental). *Human ~ is one of the factors in production.*

lac (लैक) noun
लाख, lakh, लाक्षा, sealing wax

lace (लेस) noun
जाली, लेस, फ़ीता netlike ornamental fabric strip, जूते का फ़ीता। *The sky is ~d with red at sunset.*

lad (लैड) noun
छोकरा, बालक, नवयुवक, boy, young man. *The ~ jumped the fencing and ran away to the street.*

lady (लेडी) noun
महिला, स्त्री, पत्नी, भले घर की औरत, a polite word for woman. *If your ~ship will step this way, please.*

lake (लेक) noun
झील, सरोवर, large area of water enclosed by land. *~ Victoria is a great lake.*

lamb (लैम्ब) noun
मेमना, young of sheep. *He is such a ~, you should not speak harshly to him.*

lame (लेम) adjective
लँगडा, लूला, unable to walk, असंतोषजनक *This is a ~ excuse for not attending the meeting*

असहाय, अयोग्य, inefficient.

lamp (लैम्प) noun
लैम्प, प्रकाश देने वाला यन्त्र, a thing that gives light, kerosene, electric lamp, gas lamp. *Switch on the ~.*

land (लैन्ड) noun
ज़मीन, भूमि, solid part of earth's surface, देश, country. *How much ~ do you own?*

lane (लेन) noun
गली, संकीर्ण मार्ग, पगडंडी, a narrow way, track, channel, course. *There are six ~s on the running track.*

language (लैंग्वेज) noun
भाषा, जुबान, words people speak, human speech, manners of expression. *Music has been called the universal ~.*

lap (लैप) noun
गोद, आँचल, मनुष्य की जाँघों का अगला भाग, upper part of the thighs. *The mother had the baby on her ~.*

lapse (लैप्स) noun
चूक, भूल, slip of memory, अन्तराल, अन्त, समाप्ति, लापरवाही के कारण किसी सुविधा का अन्त, the termination of right through neglect. *The allotment given by the government ~d, as the financial year ends.*

large (लाजं) adjective
बड़ा, विशाल, लंबा चौड़ा, of considerable size. *This family needs a ~ house.*

last (लास्ट) adjective
अंतिम, आखिरी, फिसड्डी, that comes after all, to continue. *We have enough food to ~ for a week.*

late (लेट) adjective
देर से, विलम्ब से, after the right time. *The Taj Express is ~ by ten minutes.*

lateral (लेटरल) adjective
बाजू का, पार्श्विक, बगल का, directed to the side. *His house is situated in the ~ of the temple.*

latrine (लैट्रीन) noun
संडास, शौचगृह, pit to receive urine and excrement.

laugh (लाफ़) verb
हँसना, खिलखिलाना, हँसी उड़ाना, उपहास करना, express emotions as pleasure. *Everybody ~ed at her witty jokes.*

launch (लौन्च) verb
किसी नए व्यवसाय, कार्य आदि का प्रारम्भ, to start something, get going. *The company ~ed its new model of car in the market.*

laundry (लौन्ड्री) noun
कपड़े घोने एवं इस्त्री करने का स्थान, where clothes are washed and pressed. *Send these shirts to the ~.*

law (लॉ) noun
कानून, विधि, विधान, rule made by authority for correct conduct of life. *Taking salad*

with the dinner was an absolute ~ of the family.

lawyer (लॉयर) noun
वकील, कानूनदां, a person who practices law. *Don't sign the paper until you have consulted your ~.*

lay (ले) verb
बिछाना, सही स्थिति में रखना, put in a certain position. *Who will ~ the carpet?* लेटा (past tense of lie) *He ~ on a cot and fell asleep.*

layer (लेयर) noun
स्तर, पर्त, तह, material spread over a surface. *There is a ~ of dust on this table.*

lazy (लेज़ी) adjective
सुस्त, कामचोर, indolent. *He is a ~ fellow.*

lead (लीड) noun
जस्ता, a metal, मार्गदर्शन करना, guide, आगे होना, ahead. *Who is ~ing?*

leader (लीडर) noun
नेता, नायक, मुखिया, person who leads. *He bears the qualities of ~ship.*

leaf (लीफ) noun
पत्ती, पत्ता, पत्र, पंखुड़ी, lateral outgrowth of stem or branch. कागज, पन्ना. *The ~ of banana is very long. Sweets covered with silver ~.*

leak (लीक) noun
दरार, crack. *There is a ~ in the garden hose,* चूना, चुपके से सूचना देना, to escape by leakage. *The news of the Israeli minister in India was ~ed.*

lean (लीन) adjective
कृश, दुबला, पतला, क्षीणकाय, thin, lacking in fullness. *She is very ~ and thin.*

leap (लीप) verb
कूदना, छलांग मारना, jump. *For him the marriage was a ~ in the dark.*

learn (लर्न) verb
सीखना, शिक्षा प्राप्त करना, acquire knowledge. *We ~ in the schools.*

least (लीस्ट) adjective
न्यूनतम, कम से कम, सबसे छोटा, smallest. *I have not even the ~ knowledge of their divorce.*

leather (लैदर) noun
चमड़ा, चर्म, tanned skin. *Winter wears are made from Angora ~.*

leave (लीव) verb
चले जाना, छोड़ना, प्रस्थान करना, to go away from. *When the train will ~ the station?* छुट्टी, अवकाश holiday.

ledger (लेजर) noun
बहीखाता, लेखाबही, book in which accounts are kept in business. *His account is on page 25 of the ~.*

left (लैफ्ट) verb
past tense of leave. छोड़ दिया, त्याग दिया, bereave बायाँ, opposite of right. *Your ~ hand is weak.*

leg (**लैग**) noun
टाँग, लात, the part from thigh to foot. *He lost his left ~ in an accident.*

legal (**लीगल**) adjective
वैधानिक, कानून के अनुसार, *Your acts are not ~.*

legible (**लेजीबल**) adjective
स्पष्ट, सुपाठ्य. *His writing is neat and ~.*

leisure (**लेज़र**) noun
अवकाश, फुरसत, spare time. *During the examinations students have no ~.*

length (**लैन्थ**) noun
लंबाई, distance between two places. *The ~ of this room is six metres.*

lens (**लैंस**) noun
चश्मा, कैमरा, दूरबीन आदि में प्रयुक्त काँच, a transparent material with one or more curved surfaces for spectacles, camera, telescope, etc. *She uses contact ~es.*

less (**लैस**) adjective & adverb.
थोडा, कम मात्रा में, to a smaller extent. *His essay was ~ than perfect.*

lesson (**लैसन**) noun
सबक, पाठ, उदाहरण, चेतावनी, something to be learnt. *Let his failure be a ~ to all of you.*

let (**लैट**) verb
करने देना, allow, permit. *Please ~ me see, what happens.*

letter (**लैटर**)
अक्षर *There are 26 ~s in English.* पत्र, लिखित संदेश. *In reply to your ~ I have to say...*

level (**लैवल**) adjective
समतल, सपाट, flat surface, समता, साम्य, status, rank. *Keep company with people of your own ~.*

lever (**लीवर**) noun
टेकन, उत्तोलक, a bar used to lift heavy objects, माध्यम, साधन *Please move this ~ to change gear.*

levy (**लेवी**) verb
कर लगाना, वसूल करना *A departure tax is levied on all travellers.*

liability (**लाइबिलिटी**) noun
बाध्यता, दायित्व, obligation, responsibility. *The ~ of the firm exceed Rs. Ten lakhs.*

liar (**लायर**) noun
झूठा, असत्य बोलने वाला, person who tells lies. *Nobody believes a ~.*

liberal (**लिबरल**) adjective
उदार, दयालु, generous, broadminded. *You will find him very ~.*

library (**लाइब्रेरी**) noun
पुस्तकालय, पुस्तकों का संग्रह, collection of literary materials. *Collect necessary material for your thesis from the ~.*

license (**लाइसेंस**) noun
शासन से मिलने वाली विशेष अनुमति, अनुज्ञा पत्र, लाइसेंस *He has a ~ to work as a guide.*

lid (**लिड**) noun
ढकना, ढक्कन, cover of the top of something. *The ~ of a jar.*

lie (**लाई**) verb
असत्य, झूठ बोलना, false statement. *You are lying.*

lie (**लाई**) verb
लेटना, विश्राम करना, be at rest. *Do not ~ in the bed till late in the morning.*

life (**लाइफ़**) noun
जीवन, जिन्दगी, period from birth to death. *There is no ~ on the moon.*

lift (**लिफ्ट**) **verb**
ऊँचा करना, ऊँचा उठाना, to raise to a higher position. *The stone is too heavy for me to ~.*

light (**लाइट**) noun
प्रकाश, रोशनी करना, जलाना, not dark, provided with light. *Sun is the main source of ~.* कम वजनी, हल्का. *As ~ as feather.*

like (**लाइक**) adjective
समान, सदृश, similar. *He looks ~ his mother.* एक जैसी वस्तु, उसके समान, of the same kind, sort. *I hate extremists and their ~s.* पसन्द करना, have a taste for. *Do you ~ meat?*

lily (**लिली**) noun
कुमुदिनी (फूल), pretty flowers. *He has planted various kinds of lilies in his garden.*

lime (**लाइम**) noun
चूना, white powder used to paint walls. *Before Diwali we paint our house walls with ~.* नींबू, citrus fruit. *~ contains a good quantity of Vitamin C.*

limit (**लिमिट**) noun
सीमा, हद, सिरा, छोर, boundary, the most that is possible. *His greed has no ~.*

line (**लाइन**) noun
रेखा, रस्सी, धागा, a long mark, piece of string. *Hang the clothes on ~ to be dry. Draw a straight ~.*

link (**लिंक**) noun
कड़ी, जंजीर, loop of a chain, सम्पर्क, बंधन, मिलाना, जोड़ना *The new bridge will ~ the island to the mainland.*

lion (**लायन**) noun
शेर, सिंह, केसरी, flesheating animal. *~s are found in Africa and S. Asia.*

lip (**लिप**) noun
होंठ, ओष्ठ, fleshy edge of mouth. *I heard it from his own ~s.*

liquid (**लिक्विड**) noun
द्रव, तरल पदार्थ, substance like water or oil, fluid. *Don't add too much ~ to the mixture.*

list (**लिस्ट**) noun
सूची, फेहरिस्त, तालिका, names of persons or things written on

a paper. *Make a ~ of the things to be purchased.*

listen (लिसन) verb
सुनना, hearing. *Don't ~ to him.*

litre (लीटर) noun
द्रव मापने की इकाई, 1000 ml. *A ~ milk.*

little (लिटिल) adjective
छोटा, नन्हा, थोड़ा, not big, small, short. *Shall we go for a ~ walk?*

live (लिव) verb
जिन्दा रहना, जीवित वस्तु, having life, जिन्दा, ~ *cartridge,* रहना, to stay. *He ~s in a flat.*

liver (लिवर) noun
जिगर, यकृत, कलेजा a large, red-brown organ in the body. *This patient is suffering from ~ trouble.*

load (लोड) noun
बोझ, माल, burden. *A truck with a full ~ of water melons.*

loaf (लोफ) noun
पावरोटी, डबलरोटी का टुकड़ा, a portion of bread or cake. *We had ~ with butter in the breakfast,* निवाला, ग्रास, कौर, moulded mass of food. *Half a ~ is better than no bread.* आवारा घूमना, निरुद्देश्य घूमना, waste time idly, saunter lazily. *They ~ ed for hours along the sea beach.*

loan (लोन) noun
ऋण, उधार, कर्ज money somebody lends. *He requested me for a ~ of two thousand rupees.*

local (लोकल) adjective
स्थानीय, pertaining to a particular place. *She is a ~ girl from this area.*

locality (लोकेलिटी) noun
स्थान, जगह, नगर, इलाका, मौका, घटनास्थल, a particular place. *Your house is in a good ~.*

lock (लौक) noun
सिर के बालों का गुच्छा, a tress or portion of hair, लट, *The scanty ~ of the pretty doll.* ताला bolt. *This ~ is of 8 levers.*

locker (लॉकर) noun
लॉकर, बैकों में कीमती सामान रखने की अलमारी, *Hire a ~ to keep your jewellery in the custody of a bank.*

locket (लॉकेट) noun
लॉकेट, pendant. *He wears a ~ in his chain.*

lodge (लॉज) verb
ठहरने की जगह, *The flood victims were ~d in tents.*

lone (लोन) adjective
अकेला, एकाकी, alone, single, isolated. *His house is in a ~ place.*

long (लौंग) adjective
लंबा, बड़ा, दीर्घ, measuring from end to end. *Amazon is the ~est river in the world.*

look (लुक) verb
देखना, to see, निगाह डालना ~ *before*

you leap.

loop (**लूप**) verb
गाँठ, फन्दा, छल्ला, a knot, fastening to join.

loose (**लूज़**) adjective
ढीला, free, not tied up. *Your brother's coat is ~ on your body.*

lose (**लूज़**) verb
खो देना, वंचित होना, गँवाना, not be able to find something without possession. *Keep it carefully, don't ~ it again.*

loss (**लौस**) noun
क्षति, हानि, act of losing. *Goods were sold at a ~.*

lot (**लौट**) noun
सम्पूर्ण सख्या या मात्रा, the whole number or quantity. *The whole ~ of fans is defective.*

lotus (**लोटस**) noun
पद्‌म, कमल, वारिज, नीरज, पंकज, जलज, a beautiful white flower projecting above the water. *Lord Brahma sits in the ~ position.*

loud (**लाउड**) adjective
ऊँचा, शोर करनेवाला, causing great noise. *Don't speak so ~ly.*

love (**लव**) noun
स्नेह, प्रेम, warm, kind feeling. *Parents ~ their children.*

low (**लो**) noun
नीचा, निम्न स्तर, not high. *The rupee has fallen to a new ~ against the dollar.*

loyal (**लॉयल**) adjective
वफ़ादार, कर्तव्यनिष्ठ, निष्ठावान, विश्वासपात्र, faithful to sovereign, fidel. *Rajputs are known for their ~ty.*

luck (**लक**) noun
भाग्य, किस्मत, fortune. *Good ~ in your examinations.*

luggage (**लगेज**) noun
यात्री का सामान, baggage. *You have four pieces of ~ with you.*

lunch (**लन्च**) noun
दोपहर का भोजन, mid-day meal. *He takes his ~ in the office.*

lung (**लंग**) noun
फेफड़ा, फुफ्फुस, breathing organs. *His right ~ is not functioning well.*

lustre (**लस्टर**) noun
चमक, कान्ति, brightness, finish *~ of pearls.*

luxury (**लक्ज़री**) noun
विलासिता, आनन्द, *He lives in ~.*

lyricist (**लिरिसिस्ट**) noun
गीतों के बोल लिखने वाला, songwriter.

□□□□

M

m
मुद्रण में प्रयुक्त लघु अक्षर

मूल उच्चारण **एम**

m
लिखने में प्रयुक्त लघु अक्षर

म प्रयोग में उच्चारण एक ही, धन्यवाद!

अंग्रेजी वर्णमाला का तेरहवाँ अक्षर

machine (मशीन) noun
उपकरण, यंत्र, कल, a device that modifies motion. *The tailors use sewing ~s.*

mad (मैड) adjective
उन्मत्त, विक्षिप्त, पागल, insane, mentally ill. *She was ~ at her husband for coming very late at night.*

madam (मैडम) noun
महोदया, भद्र महिला, courteous form of address to a woman. *~, please take your seat.*

made (मेड) adjective
बनाया, निर्मित, produced, making in a particular way. *He is a self~ man.*

magic (मैजिक) noun
मंत्र, जादू, witchcraft, sorcery. *He pulled a pigeon out of the hat by ~.*

magistrate (मैजिस्ट्रेट) noun
न्याय करने वाला अधिकारी, a civil officer charged with the administration of law.

magnet (मैगनेट) noun
चुंबक, a metal piece that attracts iron. *He succumbed to the ~ism of her smile.*

magnify (मैगनिफ़ाई) verb
बढ़ाना, आवर्धन करना, make something larger. *A microscope is a good magnifier.*

maid (मेड) noun
कुँवारी, अविवाहित लड़की, कन्या, maiden. *Engage a ~ for housework.*

mail (मेल) noun
पत्र, पार्सल, डाक भेजना, letter, packages. *~ this letter by air.*

main (मेन) adjective
प्रमुख, महत्वपूर्ण, chief, most important, खास *Chandni Chowk is the ~ market of the old city.*

maintain (मेन्टेन) noun
मरम्मत, देखरेख, रखरखाव, चालू रखना, continue, keep up. *He has to ~ a big family.*

major (मेजर) noun
वयस्क, बालिग, a person of full legal age. *He is 21, he is a ~.*

make (मेक) verb
बनाना, तैयार करना, अस्तित्व में आना *She will ~ tea for everybody.*

malaria (मलेरिया) noun
मच्छरों द्वारा काटने से होने वाला ज्वर, मलेरिया, जूड़ी, fever caused by biting infected anapheles. *Take quinine and get rid of ~.*

male (मेल) noun
नर, पुरुष, मर्द, opp. of female. *There are four ~ members in the family.*

mall (माल) noun
छायादार मार्ग, ठंडी सड़क, a shady public promenade. माल रोड, खरीदारी के लिए ढका हुआ स्थान *Vishal is a fine ~ in Faridabad.*

mammal (मैमल) noun
स्तनधारी जीव, animals who drink, milk from their mother's body while young.

man (मैन) noun
मनुष्य, आदमी, पुरुष, adult male. *He is a ~ of 46.*

manage (मैनेज) verb
व्यवस्था करना, काबू में रखना, control, take care of. *How can he ~ with such an income?*

manager (मैनेजर) noun
व्यवस्थापक, प्रबंधक, a person controlling a business. *My father is an excellent ~.*

mango (मैंगो) noun
आम, रसाल, fruit. *Green ~es are not sweet.*

manipulate (मैनीपुलेट) verb
चतुराई से काम करना, handle, manage esp. with skill. *A clever politician knows how to ~ public opinion.*

mankind (मैनकाइन्ड) noun
मनुष्य मात्र, मनुष्य जाति, the human race or species. *Bicycle is an invention for the benefit of ~.*

manner (मैनर) noun
किसी काम के करने या होने का तरीका या ढंग, way in which a thing happens. *This is not the proper ~ of behaving with elders.* शिष्टाचार social behaviour. *He has rough ~s.*

many (मैनी) adjective
बहुत से, अनेक, in large numbers, numerous. *~ people want to go now.*

map (मैप) noun
मानचित्र, नक्शा, representation on paper of a country. *Whole cities were wiped off the ~.*

marble (मार्बल) noun
संगमर्मर, hard limestone. *The Taj Mahal is made of white ~.*

March (मार्च) noun
अँग्रेजी वर्ष का तीसरा महीना, third month of the year. आगे बढ़ना,

चलना go forward. *They ~ed and demanded an apology.*

mare (मेयर) noun
घोड़ी, गधी, she horse or donkey.*~'s nest.*

margin (मार्जिन) noun
सिरा, छोर, इलाका, blank space of a written page. *The left hand ~ is being used for noting the question number.*

mark (मार्क) noun
चिह्न, निशान, धब्बा, line, cut, spot. *Why have you made these ~s on my new book?*

market (मार्केट) noun
बाज़ार, हाट, where selling or buying goods is done. *Is there any ~ for meat in Varanasi?*

maroon (मरून) noun
dark red to purplish red colour, गहरा लाल या नीला लाल रंग। *This carpet is ~.*

marriage (मैरिज) noun
शादी, विवाह, निकाह, to take somebody as one's husband or wife. *On the day of his ~ he was thirty.*

marvel (मार्वल) noun
आश्चर्य, अचम्भा, wonderful example, अति उत्तम. *He is a ~ of society.*

mash (मैश) noun
घुली हुई वस्तु, पानी में उबाला अनाज, grain cooked in water. *~ the fruit up so the baby can eat it.* कुचले हुए, पिसे हुए beaten, crushed.

mask (मास्क) noun
मुखौटा, बनावटी वेश, pretense. *The robbers were wearing ~s.*

mass (मास) noun
ढेर, बहुसंख्या, heap, large number. *The ~es have become politically conscious.*

master (मास्टर) noun
स्वामी, मालिक, employer, ruler. *That dog is devoted to his ~.*

mat (मैट) noun
चटाई, floor cover, *Spread a ~ and sit comfortably.*

match (मैच) noun
दियासलाई, माचिस, a piece of wood which makes fire when rubbed. *Strike a ~ to light the candle.* मुकाबला, खेल contest, game. *There was a ~ between England and India.*

mate (मेट) noun
साथी, friend. *He is my class ~.* पति, पत्नी में से एक *He has been a faithful ~ to her.*

material (मेटीरिअल) adjective
भौतिक, वस्तुपरक, of matter. *Don't conceal the ~ facts of the case.*

matter (मैटर) noun
विषय, कार्य, मामला, बात, something one talks about or does, *The subject ~ of your essay is very poor.*

mature (**मैच्योर**) adjective
परिपक्व, पकाना, वयस्क, विकसित, perfected. *His experiences in the city ~d him.*

maxi (**मैक्सी**) noun
औरतों का नीचे तक का लबादा, woman's ankle-length skirt.

maze (**मेज़**) noun
भूल भुलैया, confusing network. *He is in a ~ since his embezzlement has come to light.*

meal (**मील**) noun
भोजन, lunch or supper. *He had the first ~ of the day.*

mean (**मीन**) adjective
तुच्छ, नीच प्रवृत्ति का, ignoble, low, बीच का, औसत, in middle position. *You must find a ~ between frankness and rudeness.*

measure (**मेज़र**) noun
माप, मात्रा, परिमाण, नापना, unit of size, quantity, degree. *Meter is a ~ of length.*

medicine (**मेडीसिन**) noun
औषिधि, दवा, drug. *You have headache, take some ~.*

medium (**मीडियम**) noun
साधन, माध्यम, मध्यस्थिति, agency, means. *Newpapers are proper advertising ~.*

meet (**मीट**) verb
मिलना, आमना-सामना होना, come face to face. *We often ~ each other.*

melody (**मैलोडी**) noun
मधुर संगीत, लय, सुर, sweet music. *He is a master of ~.*

melt (**मैल्ट**) verb
गलना, गलाना, पिघलाना, become liquid due to heat. *The hot sun ~ed the ice.*

member (**मैम्बर**) noun
सदस्य, each of the persons comprising a group. *He is a ~ of sports club.*

memento (**मेमेन्टो**) noun
यादगार, निशानी, स्मारक, something that serves as reminder.

memo (**मेमो**) noun
ज्ञापन, स्मृति पत्र, short of memorandum a note written about something.

memory (**मेमोरी**) noun
स्मरणशक्ति, याददाश्त, स्मृति, remembrance. *The Taj was constructed in the ~ of Mumtaz Mahal.*

mend (**मैन्ड**) verb
मरम्मत करना, repair, set right, दुरुस्त करना. *Mutual talk may ~ matters.*

mental (**मैन्टल**) adjective
मानसिक relating to mind. *The boy is ~ly retarded.*

mention (**मैन्शन**) noun
उल्लेख, ज़िक्र, चर्चा, कथन, incidental reference *Did the concert get a ~ in the papers?*

menu (**मैन्यू**) noun
भोजन की तालिका, list of dishes

available in hotels. *What is on the ~ tonight?*

mercy (मर्सी) noun
दया, क्षमा, pity, clemency. *Shylock showed no ~ to Antonio.*

merge (मर्ज) verb
एक में मिलना, लीन होना, become one, विलय, *The two companies are considering ~r.*

merit (मैरिट) noun
श्रेष्ठता, विशिष्टता, गुण, खूबी, excellence, worth. *He was selected for the post on ~.*

met (मैट) verb
मुलाकात हुई, मिलें *We ~ at the railway station.*

mice (माइस) noun
चूहे, plural of mouse.

middle (मिडिल) noun
मध्य का, बीच वाला, मध्य, part which is equidistant. *He was standing in the ~ of the road.*

might (माइट) noun
शक्ति, ताकत, बल, power, strength, past tense of may आज्ञा मांगने के लिए उपयुक्त शब्द।

mild (माइल्ड) adjective
मृदु, मंद, शांत, soft, gentle, pleasant. *The weather is ~ today.*

milk (मिल्क) noun
दुग्ध, दूध, white secretion from the mammary glands of mammals. *It is no use crying over spilt ~.*

million (मिलियन) noun
दस लाख, 10,00,000

mind (माइन्ड) noun
दिमाग, ध्यान, a faculty of brain, memory, remembrance. *Keep something in ~.*

mine (माइन) noun
मेरा, मेरी, belonging to me. *He is a close friend of ~.* खदान, सुरंग खोदना, *Coal is ~d in Jharia.*

minus (माइनस) adjective
घटाना, opp. of plus, less, subtraction. *The child could not ~ 20 from 125.*

mischief (मिसचिफ़) noun
शैतानी, अपकार, हानि, क्षति, शरारत, injury, damage. *Provocative speeches may cause great ~.*

miser (माइज़र) noun
कंजूस, कृपण, stingy person. *A ~ can't enjoy the pleasures of life.*

miss (मिस) verb
कुमारी unmarried girl. *~ Marina.* चूकना, छोड़ देना, fail to hit, catch, see. *He ~ed the train.*

mist (मिस्ट) noun
कोहरा, धुंध, fog, haziness. *Forgotten in the ~ of time.*

mistake (मिस्टेक) noun
भूल, गलती, error, fault. *We all make ~s.*

mister (मिस्टर) noun
(abbr. Mr.) महाशय, श्रीमान

Hello! ~ John, where are you going?

misuse (**मिसयूज़**) verb
दुरुपयोग करना, use wrongly. *He is misusing his powers.*

mix (**मिक्स**) verb
मिलाना, सम्पर्क में आना, mingle, blend. *~ a little milk in the flour.*

mob (**मौब**) noun
भीड़, crowd. *The police fired to disperse the ~.*

mobile (**मोबाइल**) adjective
चलताफिरता, मोटर गाड़ी, movable, गतिशीलता, मोबाइल फ़ोन, *He has a ~ phone.*

mode (**मोड**) noun
ढंग, तरीका, पद्वति, manner of doing. *He is much concerned to keep up with the prevailing ~.*

model (**मौडल**) noun
नमूना, ढाँचा, प्रतिरूप, आदर्श, example, specimen, plan, pattern. *A wooden ~ of Taj.*

modern (**मॉडर्न**) adjective
आधुनिक, अर्वाचीन, of recent time, new and uptodate. *People should adopt ~ ways of living.*

modify (**मौडिफ़ाई**) verb
सही करना, विकसित करना, to correct, make changes. *The new government has modified the structure of education.*

moist (**मॉइस्ट**) adjective
नम, गीला, wet. *Her eyes were ~ at her son's illness.*

molar (**मोलर**) noun
दाँत, डाढ, teeth used for grinding food.

moment (**मोमेन्ट**) noun
पल, क्षण, very brief period of time. *Just a ~ please.*

monarch (**मौनर्क**) noun
बादशाह, राजा, सुल्तान, supreme ruler of state. प्रभावशाली व्यक्ति *He is the ~ of national shipping.*

Monday (**मनडे**) noun
सोमवार, the second day of the week.

money (**मनी**) noun
पैसा, धन, मुद्रा, coins to buy things, paper money. *This article is not worth the ~ you paid for it.*

monitor (**मौनिटर**) noun
कक्षा का मानिटर, pupil to look after the boys in the absence of the teacher. *Who is the ~ of the class?*

monk (**मौंक**) noun
साधु, सन्यासी, योगी, sage. *He is leading the life of a ~.*

monkey (**मंकी**) noun
बन्दर, वानर, नटखट बालक, an animal with long tail, mischievous boy.

monopoly (**मोनोपली**) noun
सर्वाधिकार, एकाधिकार, exclusive control of a commodity. *The government has a ~ in drugs.*

month (**मन्थ**) noun
माह, महीना, 30 days. *This is the ~ of March.*

mood (**मूड**) noun
चित्तवृत्ति, मिजाज़, state of mind. *He always remains in a jovial ~.*

moon (**मून**) noun
चंद्रमा, चाँद, earth's natural satellite, at a distance of 238857 miles. diameter 2160 miles. *Tonight is full ~ night.*

moped (**मोपेड**) noun
पैडल तथा पैट्रोल से चलने वाली मोटर साईकिल, lowpowered motorized bicycle.

moral (**मौरल**) adjective
नैतिक, सदाचार, सद्विचार सम्बंधी, concerned with the rules of right conduct, ethical. *He bears a good ~ character.*

morale (**मौरेल**) noun
मनोदशा, मनोबल, हौसला, mental condition with respect of cheerfulness, confidence, zeal, etc.

more (**मोर**) adjective
अधिक (संख्या, परिमाण, गुण), greater in number, quantity, quality, extent or degree. *I would like to have some ~ tea.*

mortuary (**मोर्चुएरी**) noun
मुर्दाघर, शवगृह a funeral home.

mosaic (**मोज़ेइक**) noun
पच्चीकारी, चित्रकारी design made of inlaid work. *The ~ work in Taj is beyond words.*

most (**मोस्ट**) adjective
सर्वाधिक, अधिकतम in greatest degree. *~ politicians pretend to be what they are not.*

mother (**मदर**) noun
माँ, माता, जननी female parent. *~, may I help you in lifting your box?*

motif (**मोटिफ़**) noun
अभिप्राय, कलाकृति, आकर्षक डिज़ाइन pattern, *There is an eagle ~ on the curtain.*

motion (**मोशन**) noun
गति, हरकत the act of moving, *The train is in ~.* मलत्याग act of emptying the bowels.

motive (**मोटिव**) adjective
कारण, उद्देश्य a reason for doing something. *There is always a ~ behind every crime.*

motor (**मोटर**) adjective
मोटर, गति प्रदान करने वाला यंत्र engine for propelling vehicles.

mount (**माउन्ट**) verb
किसी के ऊपर चढ़ना *~ the horse carefully.* ऊपर चलना, go up, climb. *The cost of small items is ~ing.*

mourn **(मोर्न)** noun
विलाप करना, शोक करना, दुःखी होना। *~ the death of a leader.*

mouth **(माउथ)** noun
मुख, मुँह, organs inside the lips. किसी बर्तन, गुफा का मुँह *A lion was seen sitting at the ~ of the cave.*

move **(मूव)** verb
चलाना, हटाना, चाल, गति, change of place or position. *Don't jump out of a train when it is on the ~.*

movie **(मूवी)** noun
चलचित्र, motion picture. *Spend the evening at the ~.*

much **(मच)** adjective
बहुत अधिक, ज्यादा, large quantity. *He ate too ~ at the dinner.*

mud **(मड)** noun
गीली मिट्टी, कीचड़, पंक, soft wet earth. *The rain turns dust into ~.*

mug **(मग)** noun
मग्गा, मग, drinking vessel with a handle. *Give me a ~ of water.*

mulberry **(मलबरी)** noun
शहतूत, tree on which silk-worm feeds its fruit.

mule **(म्यूल)** noun
खाच्चर, the offspring of a donkey and horse. *~ is used for carrying load.*

multi **(मल्टी)** prefix
used in the sense of much or many. अधिक अथवा बहुत का उपसर्ग, जैसे, multicoloured.

murder **(मर्डर)** noun
हत्या, कत्ल, वध, killing. *He was found guilty of ~.*

muscle **(मसल)** noun
माँसपेशी, muscular tissues for movement. *He is a wrestler, his ~s are strong.*

museum **(म्यूज़ियम)** noun
संग्रहालय, अजायबघर, place where objects of permanent value are kept and displayed.

music **(म्यूज़िक)** noun
संगीत, गीत, सुरीला शब्द. *~ must be made a compulsory subject for girls.*

must **(मस्ट)** verb
बाध्य होना, अवश्य होना, आवश्यक है, होगा, पड़ेगा, जरूरी है. to be bound, ought to, should, inevitable, certain. *You ~ give an application if you want leave.*

mustard **(मस्टर्ड)** noun
राई, सरसों, black or white seeds from which oil is extracted.

mute **(म्यूट)** adjective
शान्त, चुप, making no sound, dumb. गूँगा, मूक, *She is ~ since her birth.*

mutual **(म्युचुअल)** adjective
दोनों ओर का, पारस्परिक, in common. *Solve your differences ~ly.*

myself (**माईसैल्फ़**) pronoun
अपने आप, स्वतः. *I repaired it ~.*

mystery (**मिस्टरी**) noun
रहस्य, छिपी हुई बात, something which is hidden. *The crime remained an unsolved ~.*

myth (**मिथ**) noun
कल्पित कथा, legendary story. *His relation of whom he boasts is only a ~.*

❑❑❑❑

N

n
मुद्रण में प्रयुक्त लघु अक्षर

n
लिखने में प्रयुक्त लघु अक्षर

मूल उच्चारण **एन**

न प्रयोग में उच्चारण

अंग्रेजी वर्णमाला का चौदहवाँ अक्षर

nail (नेल) noun
नाखून, नख, horny plate at the lips of fingers or toes. *Her ~s are dyed with ~ polish.* कील, मेख, चोबा, काँटा. *The carpenter couldn't hammer the ~ properly.*

naked (नेकिड) adjective
वस्त्रहीन, नग्न, uncovered. *The child was ~ after the bath.*

name (नेम) noun
नाम, words by which a person or thing is called. *His ~ is Sharad.*

nap (नैप) noun
झपकी लेना, ऊँघना, short sleep. *He was found ~ping in the class.*

nappy (नैपी) noun
बच्चों को पहनाई जाने वाली चड्ढी, towelling cloth for babies. *A disposable ~.*

narcotic (नारकोटिक) noun
मूर्च्छा देने या सुन्न करने वालीऔषधि, substance that blunts the senses. *Teenagers are getting addicted to ~s in many countries.*

narrate (नैरेट) verb
वर्णन करना, कहना, to tell something. *~ the story of Alibaba and forty thieves.*

narrow (नैरो) adjective
तंग, संकरा, संकुचित, limited. *He has a ~ circle of friends.*

nasty (नेस्टी) adjective
गंदा, अरुचिकर, filthy, unclean. *The sea got ~ after we left the port.*

nation (नेशन) noun
राष्ट्र, जाति, people belonging to a particular territory. *India is our ~.*

native (नेटिव) noun
देशवासी, countryman. *They*

held a meeting of ~s of Japan.

natural (**नेचुरल**) adjective
प्रकृति से संबंधित, concerned with nature.

nature (**नेचर**) noun
प्रकृति, निसर्ग, the whole universe, the visible creation. *It is the ~ of a bird to fly.*

naughty (**नौटी**) adjective
शैतान, उपद्रवी, नटखट, unruly, disobedient. *Some children are ~ by nature.*

nausea (**नौसिआ**) noun
मिचली, उबकाई, वमन, vomit. *During early pregnancy most women suffer from ~.*

navy (**नेवी**) noun
नौसैना, नौशक्ति, entire fleet of ships of a nation. *Indian ~ is strong enough to guard its coasts.*

near (**निअर**) adjective.
समीप, निकट, पास, not far, close. *My house is quite ~.*

nearly (**निअरली**) adverb
लगभग, करीब-करीब, almost. *It is ~ 4 o'clock but you are not ready.*

neat (**नीट**) adjective
साफ़-सुथरा, स्वच्छ, tidy, clean. *He satisfied his opponent by a ~ answer.*

necessary (**नैसेसरी**) adjective
आवश्यक, जरूरी, essential, imperative. *Food is ~ for life.*

neck (**नैक**) noun
गर्दन, ग्रीवा, part joining the head to trunk. *We broke our ~s to get there on time.*

nectar (**नैक्टर**) noun
अमृत, elixir, पराग, मधुरपेय, मकरन्द, honey. *Water is the ~ of life.*

need (**नीड**) verb
आवश्यकता होना, जरूरत, requirement, necessity. *Do you ~ money?*

needle (**नीडल**) noun
सुई, सुआ, instrument for sewing. *~ is used for sewing and darning.*

negative (**निगेटिव**) adjective
नकारात्मक, निषेधात्मक, implying denial. *He replied my questions in the ~.*

neglect (**नैगलैक्ट**) verb
उपेक्षा करना, भूल जाना, to omit, to treat carelessly. *The playground was in a state of ~.*

negligent (**नैगलिजेंट**) adjective
लापरवाह, असावधान. *The factory workers are ~.*

neighbour (**नेबर**) noun
पड़ोसी, पासवाला, a person who lives near you. *Be sweet with your ~s.*

neither (**नीदर**) adverb
दोनों मे कोई भी नहीं, not one. *I like ~ of you.*

nephew (**नेफ़्यू**) noun
भतीजा, भांजा, son of brother or sister.

nerve (**नर्व**) noun
तंत्रिका, body fibre. *He has ~s of iron.*

nest (**नैस्ट**) noun
घोंसला, a birdhouse. *The sparrows are ~ing under the eaves.*

net (**नैट**) noun
जाल, फन्दा, twine, snare, fishing nets. वास्तविक, असली, *~ price. ~ profit.*

neuter (**न्यूटर**) adjective
नपुंसक लिंग, neither masculine nor feminine. *Tables, chairs etc. are of ~ gender.*

never (**नेवर**) adverb
कभी नही, not ever. *I have ~ been abroad.*

new (**न्यू**) adjective
नया, ताजा, नवीन, of recent origin. *What is the ~est fashion these days?*

news (**न्यूज**) noun
संदेश, समाचार, information, findings. *I was glad to read the ~ of your success.*

next (**नैक्स्ट**) adjective
अगला, समीप का, nearest. *The ~ edition will be out ~ year.*

nice (**नाइस**) adjective
अच्छा, उत्तम, सुहावना, pleasant, agreeable. *She is a ~ girl.*

nickname (**निकनेम**) noun
छोटा या संक्षिप्त नाम, चिढ़ाने का नाम, name substituted as in ridicule or familiarity. *He was ~d because he was so taller.*

night (**नाइट**) noun
रात्रि, अन्धकार, period between sunset to sunrise. *During the ~ we sleep.*

nil (**निल**) noun
कुछ नहीं, शून्य, nothing. *He is ~ in instrumental music.*

nip (**निप**) verb
काटना, चिकोटी भरना, सख्ती से दबाना, to pinch, squeeze, bite. *A crab ~ped me while I was swimming.*

no (**नो**) adjective
नहीं, कोई भी नहीं, not any. *I have ~ good book on grammar.*

Noble Prize (**नोबेल प्राइज़**)
साहित्य, विज्ञान, चिकित्सा विज्ञान, अर्थशास्त्र, शान्ति, के लिए दिए जाने वाला पुरस्कार, group of prizes awarded annully by Nobel Foundation (Sweden) for outstanding achievements in Physics, Chemistry, Medicine, Economics, Peace, etc.

noble (**नोबल**) adjective
उदार, कुलीन, उत्तम, of high birth,

exalted. *He bears a ~ moral character.*

nod **(नौड)** verb
स्वीकृति में सिर हिलाना *He sat ~ding by the fire.*

no way **(नो वे)** adverb
बिलकुल नहीं, किसी भी प्रकार नहीं, not at all. *There is ~ you can do it.*

noise **(नॉइज़)** noun
शोर, हल्ला, कोलाहल, din, harsh sound. *Why do you make ~?*

nominal **(नॉमिनल)** adjective
नाममात्र का, अवास्तविक, not real. *She is only the ~ chairman.*

nominate **(नॉमिनेट)** verb
नामांकित करना, मनोनीत करना, propose, to appoint. *Mr. Martin is a ~d member of the committee.*

none **(नन)** pronoun
कोई भी नहीं, कुछ भी नहीं, not any, no one. *~ of them had the book I wanted.*

nonsense **(नौनसैन्स)** noun
सारहीन, बकवास, lacking in sense. *He is a great ~.*

noon **(नून)** noun
दोपहर, midday.

north **(नॉर्थ)** noun
उत्तर दिशा, towards left from the rising sun. *They stood facing towards the ~.*

nose **(नोज़)** noun
नाक, the organ of smell and respiration. *We smell with our ~.*

not **(नौट)** adverb
न, मत, नहीं, denial, disapproval. *You must ~ do that.*

notary **(नोटरी)** noun
लेखाप्रमाणक, legal officer authorized to witness documents, affidavits, etc. *Mr. Chauhan is performing his work as ~.*

note **(नोट)** noun
टिप्पणी, short record. *You must practise to speak without ~s for debating competitions.*

nothing **(नथिंग)** pronoun
कुछ नहीं, not anything. *There is ~ to say.*

notice **(नोटिस)** noun
सूचना, लिखित चेतावनी, intimation, written warning. *Give the tenant a month's ~ to vacate the house.*

notion **(नोशन)** noun
राय, विचार, मत, idea, opinion. *His head is full of absurd ~s.*

noun **(नाउन)** noun
संज्ञा, naming word. *A ~ is the name of a person, place or thing.*

nourish **(नरिश)** verb
पालन करना, to nurture. *Most plants are ~ed by water, drawn up by their roots.*

novel **(नौवल)** noun
नया, नए ढंग का, उत्तम, उपन्यास,

The ~s of Charles Dickens are worth reading.

now (नाउ) adverb
अभी, at the present time. *Where are you going ~?*

now-a-days (नाउ-अ-डेज़) adverb
इन दिनों, आजकल, in present times. *I am very busy ~ due to my examination.*

nowhere (नोव्हेअर)
कहीं भी नहीं, not anywhere. *The necklace was ~ to be found.*

nude (न्यूड) adjective
नंगा, naked, वस्त्रहीन, नग्नता, नंगापन *Nudity among wild tribes exists even today.*

nuisance (न्यूसेंस) noun
कष्टदायक, बाधा, offensive, troublesome. *Loudspeakers are a great ~.*

null (नल) adjective
शून्य, सारहीन, अक्षम, invalid, nil. *The contract is ~ and void.*

numb (नम्ब) adjective
सुन्न, चेतनारहित, जड़वत्, without feeling, stunned, paralyzed. *My fingers became ~ due to cold.*

number (नम्बर) noun
संख्या, गिनती, arithmetical figures. *A large ~ of people came to see the flower show.*

nun (नन) noun
साध्वी, ladies living in convent under solemn vows of poverty, chastity, obedience.

nurse (नर्स) noun
धाय, परिचारिका, a person trained to help doctors. *The young mother learned, she would be unable to ~.*

nut (नट) noun
काष्ठफल, नारियल, बादाम, सुपारी, *He cracked the large ~ against the wall.*

nutrient (न्युट्रिएन्ट) noun.
पौष्टिक आहार, providing nourishment. *Glucose is a ~.*

nylon (नाइलौन) noun
नाइलौन, synthetic fibre used for hosiery.

□□□□

O

O
मुद्रण में प्रयुक्त लघु अक्षर

o
लिखने में प्रयुक्त लघु अक्षर

मूल उच्चारण **ओ**

ओ
औ
अ
आ
ऑ

प्रयोग में उच्चारण एक ही वर्ण के पाँच - ज्यादा क्यों नहीं?

अंग्रेजी वर्णमाला का पन्द्रहवाँ अक्षर तथा चौथा स्वर – बहुत दूर लाकर पटका!

---

oak (ओक) noun
बलूत का पेड़, a large forest tree. *Under the ~ tree.*

oasis (ओसिस) noun
मरुद्यान, नखलिस्तान, fertile green area in desert. *Caravans stayed in the ~ for rest and relaxation.*

oat (ओट) noun
जई, a coarse grain. *~ is a horse cereal.*

oath (ओथ) noun
शपथ, vow. *Be on ~.*

obedient (ओबीडिएन्ट) adjective
आज्ञाकारी, one who obey's faithful. *Circus elephants are very ~.*

obey (ओबे) verb
आज्ञा पालन करना, do what one is asked to do. *~ one's elders.*

obituary (ओबिचुएरी) noun
मृत्यु समाचार, pertaining to the recording of a death. *The ~ page of newspapers.*

object (ऑबजैक्ट) noun
वस्तु चीज, anything that is visible, उद्देश्य, aim. *With the ~ of earning fame.* विरोध करना, to oppose, protest, disapprove. *I ~ to your statement.*

obligate (औब्लिगेट) verb
वचनबद्ध करना, to bind a person to do something. *He felt ~d to help.*

obligation (औबलीगेशन) noun
अहसान, अनुग्रह, आभार, a favour. *His ~s on me are many.*

oblige (औबलाइज) verb
बाध्य करना, compel. *The law ~s you to follow the rules of the country.*

oblique (ऑबलीक) adjective
तिरछा, ढालू, sloping, slanting.

He gave ~ remarks about his honesty.

observe (आबजर्व) verb
ध्यान देना, ध्यान से देखना, see, perceive, watch carefully. *He ~s much but speaks little.*

obstacle (औबस्टेकल) noun
बाधा, रुकावट, अड़चन, hindrance. *~to success.*

obtain (ऑब्टेन) verb
लेना, पाना, प्राप्त करना, उपलब्ध करना, get, acquire. *Where can I ~ a copy of the latest edition of this book?*

obvious (औबवियस) adjective
स्पष्ट, सरल, clear, plain. *His fault is ~.*

occasion (अकेज़न) noun
अवसर, मौका, समय, a particular time, suitable, right time. *This is not an ~ for laughter.*

occupant (औक्युपेन्ट) noun
ज़मीन जायदाद का कब्जेदार, a person who occupies a house, land, room or position. *He is the next ~.*

occur (अकर) verb
घटना, घटित होना, to take place, to happen. *The accident ~red last night.*

ocean (ओशन) noun
महासागर, the vast body of salt water which covers ¾ of earth's surface. *The Indian ~ lies to the south of India.*

o' clock (अ' क्लौक) adverb
घड़ी के अनुसार, of the clock. *Our school begins at 7 ~.*

odd (औड) adjective
अंक जो दो से विभक्त न हो, विषम अंक, 1,3,5,7 etc., number not even, अजीब, विचित्र, strange. *He wears rather ~ clothes.*

odour (ओडर) noun
गंध, बास, सुबास, smell, pleasant or unpleasant, ख्याति, प्रसिद्धि, शोहरत, repute. *To be in good ~ with somebody.*

of (ऑव) preposition
का, के, की, a word that shows who or what has something. *He is a man ~ noble family.*

off (ऑफ) adjective
दूर, अच्छा न लगने वाला, away from the place. *We got ~ the bus.* समाप्त, ended. *The worker strike is ~.* अलग, पृथक्, down from, away from. *Keep ~ the long grass.*

off-day (ऑफ डे) noun
छुट्टी का दिन, holiday. *Saturday is always an ~ for me.*

offence (ऑफैंस) noun
अपराध, crime. *He has been charged with a serious ~.*

offer (ऑफ़र) verb
प्रदान करना, देना, to give. *He ~ed to help me.* प्रस्ताव, अर्पण, प्रस्तुत धनराशि. *I have had an ~ of Rs.4 lakh for a car.*

office (ऑफ़िस) noun
कार्यालय, दफ्तर, room or rooms used for work or business purposes. *This is the Principal's ~.*

officer (आफ़िसर) noun
अधिकारी, अफसर, holder of an office. *An ~ in the army.*

offset (ऑफ़सैट) verb
बराबर करना, कमी पूरी करना, compensate for. *The doctors ~ their small salaries by doing private practice.*

offshoot (ऑफ़शूट) noun
उपशाखा, प्रशाखा, a branch, *An ~ of the branch.*

offside (ऑफ़साइड) noun
खेल में नियमविरुद्ध किसी खिलाड़ी की स्थिति *The forwards are all ~.*

offspring (ऑफ़स्प्रिंग) noun
संतान, संतति, children, young of any parent. *His ~s are all slightly mad.*

often (ऑफ़न) adverb
अनेक बार, अक्सर, several times, frequently. *I have ~ asked you not to go there.*

oh (ओह) interjection
अरे, हाय, denoting suspense, surprise, sorrow, fear.
~ James, will you eat some mangoes?

oil (ऑयल) noun
तेल, रोग़न, liquid obtained from plants, animals, earth. *Don't burn the midnight ~, it will tell upon your health. ~ one's bicycle.*

ointment (औइन्टमेन्ट) noun
मलहम, उबटन, medicinal paste. *Eye ~. Pennicillin ~.*

okay (ओके) adjective
adverb.
बिल्कुल ठीक, स्वीकृत, सहमत होना, to agree. *She got the doctor's ~ to play again.*

old (ओल्ड) adjective
वृद्ध, बूढ़ा, आयु, advanced in age. *He is thirty years ~. ~ people can't run fast.*

omit (ओमिट) verb
छोड़ देना, भूल जाना, leave out. *To ~ a passage from the text.*

on (औन) adverb
चालू, उन्नतिसूचक, read on, go on, take on, etc., expressing continued activity. *She danced ~ for four hours without stopping.* ऊपर की सतह पर, upper surface of.

once (वन्स) adverb
एक बार, at one time. *~ there was a king.*

one (वन) adjective
एक, प्रथम, one time. *Twenty ~. ~sided judgment.* कोई एक, anyone. *He is not ~ of my friends. The Holy ~ (God). They don't love ~ another. ~*

always cannot keep good health.

only (ओनली) adjective
केवल, एकमात्र, sole, mere. *They were the ~ visitors there.*

onset (ऑनसैट) noun
प्रारंभ, a beginning. *The ~ of maturity*, जोर का आक्रमण, धावा, a violent attack. *The ~ of winter.*

onward (ऑनवर्ड) noun
आगे बढ़ना, अग्रगामी, forward, *~ march.*

opaque (ओपेक) adjective
अपारदर्शक, not to be seen through. *Cardboard is ~.*

open (ओपन) adjective
खुला हुआ, not closed, not shut. *Don't leave the door ~.*

opinion (ओपिनियन) noun
view, thinking, belief. *What is your ~ on the new pattern of education?*

opponent (अपोनेन्ट) noun
विरोधी, शत्रु, adversary. *A member of the ~ team.*

opportunity (औपरचुनिटी) noun
सुअवसर, मौका, favourable occasion. *I have no ~ to discuss the matter with her.*

opposite (अपोजिट) adjective
सामने वाला, प्रतिकूल, facing, placed in front. *The house ~ to mine is Smith's.*

optimism (औप्टमिज़्म) noun
आशावाद. *In ~ lies the secret of joy.*

option (औप्शन) noun
विकल्प, choice. *Do you have any ~ in this matter?*

or (और) conjunction
अथवा, या, अन्यथा, वरना, one of the two, otherwise, else. *Drive faster ~ you will be late.*

oral (ओरल) adjective
मौखिक, ज़बानी, spoken or verbal. *An ~ test.* मुख से लेने वाली वस्तु *An ~ contraceptive.*

orange (औरेंज) noun
संतरा, a juicy fruit. *Are green ~s sweet?*

order (ऑर्डर) noun
वस्तुओं का सही क्रम, proper sequence. *Names were written in alphabetical ~ in the attendance register.* आदेश देना, to command. *The teacher ~ed the naughty boy to leave the classroom.*

ordinary (और्डिनरी) adjective
साधारण, सामान्य, normal, usual *For all ~ purposes.*

organ (और्गन) noun
शारीरिक अंग, parts of the body. *Body has many ~s.*

organize (औरगेनाइज़) verb
आयोजन करना, संगठन बनाना, to systematize. *~ the function.*

orient (ओरिएन्ट) noun
पूर्वीय देश, वातावरण के अनुकूल बनाना, countries of the east, to change. *To ~ one's ideas to*

new conditions.

origin (ओरिजिन) noun
स्रोत, उद्गम, मूल उत्पत्ति, source, starting point. *The ~ of a river.*

original (ओरिजिनल) adjective
मौलिक, सर्वप्रथम, first, earliest. *The ~ plan. The ~ tribe.*

originate (ओरिजिनेट) verb
शुरू करना या होना, आरम्भ करना, to cause, to begin. *The riots ~d in rivalry between two neighbours.*

ornament (ऑर्नामैन्ट) noun
अंलकार, आभूषण, गहना, that which adorns beauty. *~s of gold and silver.*

orthodox (ऑर्थडोक्स) adjective
परम्परागत, conforming to religious beliefs. *~ behaviour.*

other (अदर) adjective
दूसरा, second. *Here are two pens, one of them is mine, the ~ is my father's.*

otherwise (अदरवाइज़) adverb
अलग ढंग से, in another manner. *I cannot act ~.* अन्यथा, नहीं तो, in other respect. *The interest is low, ~ the investment is safe.*

our (अवर) adjective
हमारा, belonging to us. *This is ~ share of food.*

out (आउट) adjective
बाहर, not within. *He has gone ~.* स्थिति का बोधक, to indicate movement. *She looked ~ of the window.* चले जाओ, चलो, *Begone! ~ you go.* किसी से बचने का साधन. *He joined a fraternity because he was afraid of becoming an ~cast.* सर्वविदित हो जाना, to become public. *The truth will come ~.*

outdoors (आउटडोर्स) noun
घर के बाहर, खुले मैदान में, outside a house. *He is not really an ~ type.*

outlook (आउटलुक) noun
दृष्टिकोण, mental attitude. *What is your ~ in this matter.*

output (आउटपुट) noun
उपज, पैदावार, उत्पादन, production. *The ~ of a coal mine.*

outsider (आउटसाइडर) noun
बाहरी व्यक्ति, जो व्यक्ति किसी संस्था का सदस्य न हो, a person not member of a group. *Women feel like ~s in that club.* विदेशी, a stranger. *He is an ~.*

oval (ओवल) adjective
अण्डाकार, eggshaped. *The playing field is a large ~.*

ovary (ओवरी) noun
अंडाशय, female reproductive gland where ova develop.

oven (ओवेन) noun
भट्टी, चूल्हा, furnace for cooking food. *Bread is baked in an ~.*

over (ओवर) adverb
ऊपर, resting on the surface.

He turned ~ in bed.Spread cloth ~ the table. क्रिकेट, छः बॉल फेंका जाना, six balls bowled in succession by a bowler. *Maiden ~ by Kapil.* बाहरी, ऊपर, outside. across. *~ coat. ~ all.*

overcome (ओवरकम) verb
जीतना, win over. conquer. *~ difficulties by patience and hard work.*

overflow (ओवरफ्लो) verb
उमड़ना, लबालब भर जाना, flow over. *Rivers ~ in the rains.*

overhaul (ओवरहॉल) verb
जाँच पड़ताल, ठीक - ठीक करना examine carefully to make repairs.

overlap (ओवरलैप) verb
किसी हद तक दूसरे को ढंकना, partly cover, to lapover. *His activities and mine ~.*

overlook (ओवरलुक) verb
ध्यान न देना, अवहेलना करना, pay no attention to, to ignore. *~ one's fault.*

overrule (ओवररूल) verb
रद्द कर देना, reject. *The High Court ~d the decision of the lower court in the appeal.*

overtime (ओवरटाइम) noun
कार्य के निधारित समय से अधिक समय, work after regular hours. *You will be paid extra wages for ~.*

overweight (ओवरवेट) noun
अधिक भार, excess weight. *The tyre burst due to ~.*

owe (ओ) verb
किसी का ऋणी होना, be in debt to somebody. *I ~ him a lot of money.*

owl (आउल) noun
उल्लू, a nocturnal bird.

own (ओन) adjective
अपना, हमारा, अपना मानना, personal. *This is my ~ house.*

ox (औक्स) noun
बैल, गाय, animal of bovine family.

oxygen (औक्सीजन)
प्राण वायु, vitality giving gas.

□□□□

P

p
मुद्रण में प्रयुक्त
लघु अक्षर

p
लिखने में प्रयुक्त
लघु अक्षर

मूल उच्चारण **पी**

प / फ प्रयोग में उच्चारण – h के साथ फ

अंग्रेजी वर्णमाला का सोलहवाँ अक्षर

pa (पा) noun
पापा, papa.

pace (पेस) noun
कदम, डग, चरण, a step. *He was so weak he could not keep ~ with us.*

pacify (पैसिफ़ाई) verb
शान्त करना, संतुष्ट करना, to calm, to quieten. *To ~ an angry man.*

pack (पैक) noun
पोटली, गठरी, a bundle, a bale. *The tramp carried his belongings in a ~ on his back.* 52 ताशों की गड्डी, a set of 52 playing cards.

pack (पैक) verb
गट्ठर बनाना, to form into. *~ your luggage.*

package (पैकेज) noun
एकमुश्त सौदा, complete deal. *Ministers are trying to put a ~ that will end the dispute.*

packet (पैकिट) noun
पुलन्दा, small bundle. *A ~ of books.*

packing (पैकिंग) verb
बन्डल बनाना, process of making a bundle.

pact (पैक्ट) noun
समझौता, संधि, agreement, contract. *A new peace ~.*

pad (पैड) noun
गद्दीदार वस्तु, cushionlike mass. *A ~ed bra.*

paddle (पैडिल) noun
चप्पू, डण्डा, long piece of wood with a flat end, used to move a boat in water. *We ~ed up the canal.*

padlock (पैडलॉक) noun
बड़ा ताला जो फाटक इत्यादि पर लगाया जाता है, a lock that is used on gates and bicycles.

page (पेज) noun
पृष्ठ, सफ़ा, one side of paper.

This book has 40 ~s.

pager (पेजर) noun
संदेश संबंधी उपकरण, a radio device with a bleeper. *Every police man on patrolling duty is provided with a ~.*

pail (पेल) noun
बाल्टी, डोल, a bucket. *A ~ full of water.*

pain (पेन) noun
शरीरिक कष्ट, दर्द, ache, bodily suffering. *Prisoners were forbidden to approach the fence under the ~ of death.*

pains (पेन्स) noun
तकलीफ, प्रयत्न, कोशिश, trouble, effort. *The hotel spared no ~ to make our stay comfortable.*

paint (पेन्ट) noun, verb
रंग, रोगन, रंग से तस्वीर बनाना, to coat, decorate with. *The ads ~ the resort as a winter wonderland.*

pair (पेयर) noun
जोड़ा, जोड़ी, युग्म, युगल, a set of two things. *A ~ of musicians such as Laxmikant Pyarelal.*

palace (पैलेस) noun
महल, प्रासाद, आलीशान भवन, grand building, राजमहल, *Buckingham ~.*

palate (पैलेट) noun
तालू, the roof of mouth, स्वाद, taste. *I have a ~ for mangoes.*

pale (पेल) adjective
रंगविहीन, कांतिहीन, फीका, तेजहीन, dim, lacking intensity of colour. *She has a ~ complexion.*

pale (पेल) verb
पीला पड़ जाना, निस्तेज हो जाना, महत्व घट जाना, lose colour, to decrease in relative importance. *Her beauty ~s besides her mother's.*

palm (पाम) noun
हथेली, करतल, the surface of the hand, रिश्वत देना, *I had to grease the overseer's ~ to get my house plan sanctioned.* पूर्ण नियंत्रण होना, किसी को अपनी मुट्ठी में रखाना. *He had all the employees in the ~ of his hand.*

palm (पाम) noun
खजूर, ताड़वृक्ष, a tropical branchless tree. *The date ~. The coconut ~.*

palmist (पामिस्ट) noun
हस्तरेखा शास्त्री, a person who tells future by palm lines. *Saint Germain was a great ~.*

palsy (पैलसी) noun
पक्षाघात, लकवा, paralysis. *He suffered with cerebral ~ on the right side of his body.*

pamper (पैम्पर) verb
बहुत लाड़ प्यार करना, लाड़ प्यार से बिगाड़ देना, to treat with excessive care. *To ~ a child.*

pamphlet (पैम्फ़लैट) noun
नए विषयों पर छोटी पुस्तिका, a

booklet on current topics. An unbound printed work. *A ~ to advertise a new book.*

pan (पैन) noun
तसला, कड़ाही, a shallow vessel. *A dust ~. A bed ~.*

panel (पैनल) noun
किवाड़ या छत का पल्ला, a distinct portion of wall, door, पंचों का समुदाय, *A ~ of experts meeting to discuss Indian foreign policy.*

panic (पैनिक) noun
आतंक, दहशत, a sudden overwhelming fear. *There is great ~ due to Hindu-Muslim riots.*

pantaloon (पैन्टेलून) noun
पतलून, पैंट, a pair of trousers, a baggy. *He was in white ~ and a blue shirt.*

panther (पैंथर) noun
तेंदुआ, leopard.

panties (पैन्टीज़) noun
निकर, knicker, तंग जांघिया (औरतों और लड़कियों के पहनने का) short drawers worn by women or girls.

pantry (पैन्ट्री) noun
रसोई का कमरा, kitchen. *In long run trains there exists a ~ car.*

papa (पापा) noun
पिता, father. *~, please give me a toffee.*

papaya (पपाया) noun
पपीता, yellow melonlike fruit. *He is very fond of eating ~.*

paper (पेपर) noun
कागज, substance used for writing, printing, wrapping or packing things. *This book is made of ~. Quality ~.*

paper (पेपर) verb
दीवार पर कागज़ चिपकाना, put wallpaper on. *She is ~ing the drawing room.*

par (पार) noun
समता, बराबरी, state of being equal. *The gains and losses are on a ~.*

parade (परेड) verb
प्रदर्शन करना, कायदे से चलकर किसी चीज़ को दिखाना, to walk in order to display something. *She ~d up and down in her new dress.*

paradise (पैराडाइज़) noun
स्वर्ग, heaven, पूर्ण शान्ति एवं सुख का स्थान, place of perfect peace and happiness.

paraffin (पैराफिन) noun
मोम, wax, परिष्कृत मिट्टी का तेल. *A ~ lamp, stove.*

paragraph (पैराग्राफ) noun
गद्यांश, अनुच्छेद, a distinct portion of written or printed matter usually with an indentation of new line. *The ~ is easy to understand.*

paraphrase (पैराफ्रेज़) verb
व्याख्या करना, अनुवाद, भावार्थ, to express in other words. *This is not the correct ~ of his speech.*

parasite **(पैरासाइट)** noun
परजीवी, पराश्रयी, an animal or plant that lives on another to get its food. *Louse is a ~.*

pardon **(पार्डन)** noun
क्षमा, माफ़ी, forgiveness. *I beg your ~ for coming late.*

parent **(पेरेन्ट)** noun
माता-पिता, father-mother, ancestor. *He lives with his ~.*

park **(पार्क)** noun
वाटिका, उद्यान, बगीचा, a place of public recreation. मोटर गाड़ी आदि खड़ी करने का स्थान, parking place for motor cars, etc. *Can I ~ my car here?*

parliament **(पार्लियामेंट)** noun
संसद, कानून बनाने वाली सर्वोच्च सभा, supreme lawmaking assembly. *Member of ~.*

parlour **(पार्लर)** noun
किसी कार्य विशेष के लिए बनाया स्थान, भवन या कमरा, a room or apartment for certain professions. *Ice cream ~. Beauty ~.*

parole **(पैरोल)** noun
कैद की अवधि से सशर्त छुटकारा, वायदे पर रिहा किया हुआ बन्दी, conditional release of prisoner prior to the end of imprisonment. *Released on ~.*

parrot **(पैरट)** noun
तोता, शुक, सुग्गा, bird of beautiful plumage, taught to repeat words.

part **(पार्ट)** noun
भाग, अंश, a fragment, piece, section, fraction. *Learn the poem in ~s.*

part **(पार्ट)** verb
अलग करना, विभाजित करना, to separate, divide. *The policeman ~ed the two fighters.*

partial **(पार्शल)** adjective
अधूरा, आंशिक, incomplete, पक्षपाती, biased. *His selection to the post is an outcome of ~ity.*

participate **(पार्टीसिपेट)** verb
सम्मिलित होना, to take part. *I shall surely ~ in my friend's birthday party.*

particle **(पार्टिकिल)** noun
कण, लेशमात्र, small bit, piece. *There is not a ~ of truth in her story.*

particular **(पार्टीकुलर)** adjective
विशिष्ट, खास, special. *You took no ~ interest in my case.*

partition **(पार्टीशन)** noun
दीवार, बड़े कमरे को छोटे कमरे में विभाजित करने वाला पर्दा, a division into parts. *~ of India in 1947.*

partner **(पार्टनर)** noun
साझीदार, भागीदार, associate. *They are ~s in a firm.*

party **(पार्टी)** noun
दल, पक्ष, पक्षकार, group. *He was a ~ to the crime.*

pass (पास) noun
सफलता, प्रवेश पत्र, success. *You need to ~ the exam to enter the college.*

passage (पैसेज) noun
मार्ग, रास्ता, the route. *Book his ~ to Moscow,* अनुच्छेद, a section of written work. *A difficult ~ for explanation.*

passion (पैशन) noun
प्रबल स्नेह, घृणा अथवा क्रोध की भावना, strong feeling of love, hate or anger. *A ~ for music.*

past (पास्ट) adjective
भूतकाल, जो बीत गया, over and gone. *It was a bad time, but it's all ~ now.*

paste (पेस्ट) noun
कोई चीज़ चिपकाने हेतु गोंद, लेई, गाढ़ा गीला पदार्थ, any material in a soft mass to stick. *Tooth ~. ~ up a notice.*

pat (पैट) adverb
सही वक्त पर, at the right moment. *~ came the answer.* हथेली से स्नेहपूर्वक थपथपाना, tap gently with open hand. *She ~ted the baby to sleep.*

patch (पैच) noun
पैबन्द, थेगड़ी, चिप्पी, a piece sewed on a garment. *A ~ on the inner tube of tyre. ~ up the hole in this pair of trousers.*

patience (पेशेन्स) noun
धैर्य, सहिष्णुता, endurance. *To work with ~.*

patient (पेशेन्ट) adjective
सहनशील, सन्तोषी, tolerant. *Be ~ with the unruly child,* बीमार, मरीज, sick, ill, *I have been a ~ of Dr. Gupta for many years.*

patriot (पैट्रिअट) noun
देशप्रेमी, देशभक्त, a person who loves his country with devotion. *Rana Pratap and Shivaji were great ~s.*

patrol (पैट्रोल) verb
रक्षार्थ गश्त करना, पहरा देना. *The Border Security Force ~s these areas regularly.*

patron (पैट्रन) noun
संरक्षक, आश्रयदाता, हितैषी, a promoter, a protector, a supporter, संस्थापक, शुभचिंतक, हितैषी, benefactor. *A ~ of scholars.*

pattern (पैटर्न) noun
उदाहरण, नमूना, ढांचा, example, model, sample. *His life is a ~ of modesty.*

pause (पॉज़) noun
विश्राम, विराम, ठहराव, a brief stop, wait, hesitate. *He ~d at the bank of the river for a moment.*

pavilion (पविलियन) noun
शामियाना, मंडप, open building used for shelter.

pay (पे) noun
वेतन, तनख्वाह, money paid for regular service. *Draw one's ~ at the end of the month.*

pay (पे) verb
खर्च करना, चुकाना, to defray cost

or expense. *I had to ~ his hotel bills.*

pea (पी) noun
मटर, a legume, *Pisum sativum* seeds.

peace (पीस) noun
शांति, अमनचैन, freedom from war and disorder. *~ has been restored in the city.*

peak (पीक) verb
चोटी, ऊपर पहुँचना, the highest point. *Land prices have ~ed.*

peanut (पीनट) noun
मूँगफली, seeds of legume *Arachis hypogea.*

pear (पियर) noun
नाशपाती, fleshy sweet fruit.

pearl (पर्ल) noun
मोती, silvery white gem. *A bracelet of ~s.*

peasant (पीज़ेन्ट) noun
किसान, कृषक, खेतिहर, engaged in agricultural labour, farmer. *He is a ~.*

peculiar (पिक्युलियर) adjective
विचित्र, अजीब, strange, uncommon. *He is a man of ~ nature.*

pedestrian (पिडेस्ट्रियन) noun
पादचारी, पैदल चलनेवाला, walker. *~s should make use of footpath to avoid accidents.*

peel (पील) verb
छिलका उतारना, take off the skin or bark. *Would you ~ for me a banana?*

pen (पैन) noun
लेखनी, कलम, an instrument for writing with ink. *Fountain ~. Ball-point ~.*

penal (पेनल) adjective
दंड संबंधी, relating to punish - ment by law. *~ code.*

penalty (पैनल्टी) noun
किसी अपराध के कारण दंड, जुर्माना, punishment. *The ~ for damaging public property.*

pending (पैंडिंग) preposition
अपूर्ण, अधूरा, फैसला न होने तक, while awaiting, *~ litigation.*

penetrate (पैनिट्रेट) verb
घुसना, आरपार करना. *A sharp nail ~ d my toe.*

penis (पेनिस) noun
लिंग, पुरूष की जननेन्द्रिय, the male organ of urination and copulation.

pension (पेंशन) noun
अवकाशप्राप्त कर्मचारी को दी जाने वाली वृत्ति, पेंशन, regular payment made after retirement. *Old age ~.*

peon (पिअन) **noun**
चपरासी, attendant, अर्दली, orderly

people (पीपुल) noun
लोग, जन, persons in general. *The ~ in my neighbourhood are very selfish.*

per (पर) preposition
प्रति, प्रत्येक के लिए, for each. *~ day. ~ hour.*

per cent **(परसैंट)** noun
प्रतिशत, rate for hundred. *Only a small ~age of people are literate.*

percept **(परसैप्ट)** noun
मन की उपज, कल्पना, product of perceiving. समझने योग्य. *Example is better than ~.*

perfect **(परफ़ैक्ट)** adjective
पूर्ण, आदर्श, दोषरहित, flawless, of highest quality. *God alone is ~. A ~ friend.*

perform **(परफॉर्म)** verb
पूर्ण करना, सम्पन्न करना, to carry out, execute. *Try to ~ your duties well.*

perfume **(परफ्यूम)** noun
इत्र, सुगंध, sweet odour, scent. *The ~ of the flowers.*

period **(पीरिअड)** noun
काल, अवधि, specific length of time. *A physics ~ of 40 minutes.*

periphery **(पेरीफ़ेरी)** noun
परिधि, बाहरी सीमा, external boundary. *They have always been at the ~ of the movement.*

permanent **(परमानैन्ट)** adjective
स्थायी, lasting, not temporary. *Is this your ~ address?*

permit **(परमिट)** verb
आज्ञा या अनुमति देना, allow, to give permission. *Would you please ~ me to smoke here?*

persist **(परसिस्ट)** verb
आग्रह करना, दृढ़ रहना, to persevere, to stand firm. *He ~s to work in his company.*

person **(पर्सन)** noun
व्यक्ति (पुरूष या स्त्री), man, woman. *Who is that ~?*

personal **(पर्सनल)** adjective
निजी, व्यक्तिगत, private, of a person. *My ~ property.*

personality **(पर्सनेलिटी)** adjective
व्यक्तित्व, quality of being of a person. *She has a very strong ~.*

persuade **(परसुएड)** verb
समझाना, कायल करना, convince. *How to ~ you that I am sincere?*

perturb **(परटर्ब)** verb
व्यग्र करना, व्याकुल करना, disturb, disquiet, agitate. *The sad news of my friend's death ~ed me greatly.*

pessimism **(पैसीमिज़्म)** noun
निराशावाद, tendency to look at the dark side of things. *His ~ has the effect of depressing everyone.*

pet **(पैट)** noun
पालतू पशु, tamed animal, person treated as a favourite. *He is the teacher's ~ student.*

petition **(पिटिशन)** noun
प्रार्थना, अनुरोध, प्रार्थनापत्र, request, prayer, formal appeal. *A ~ for*

aid.

petrol (**पैट्रोल**) noun
पैट्रोल, inflammable refined mineral oil.

petticoat (**पैटीकोट**) noun
घाघरा, साया, पैटीकोट, a woman's underskirts.

pharmacy (**फ़ार्मेसी**) noun
औषधालय, डिसपेंसरी, औषधि बेचने की दुकान, preparation and dispensing of medicines and drugs, dispensary.

phenomena (**फ़िनोमेना**) noun
दृश्यमान वस्तु, तथ्य या परिस्थिति, a fact, occurrence, *To study the ~ of nature.*

phone (**फ़ोन**) noun
फ़ोन करना, टेलीफ़ोन यंत्र, a telephone receiver. *Why waste time, ~ him to come here soon.*

photo (**फ़ोटो**) noun
प्रकाश चित्र, photograph. *The children took ~s of the park.*

photostat (**फ़ोटोस्टैट**) noun
हस्तलिपि चित्र, दस्तावेजों की प्रतिलिपि बनाने का कैमरा, फ़ोटो प्रतिलिपि, a copy made with this camera. *This is the ~ of an examination paper.*

phrase (**फ्रेज़**) noun
शब्द–समुदाय, वाक्यखंड, मुहावरा, group of words. *A neatly ~d greeting.*

physical (**फ़िजिकल**) adjective
भौतिक, शारीरिक, कायिक, of the body. *Walking is the best ~ exercise.*

physician (**फिज़िशियन**) noun
वैद्य, हकीम, चिकित्सक, डॉक्टर, a person legally qualified to practice medicine.

pick (**पिक**) verb
चुनना, चुना गया व्यक्ति या पदार्थ, choice, selection. *He is our ~ for president.*

pick (**पिक**) noun
कुदाली, गैंती, small sharp instrument. *A tooth ~.*

pickle (**पिकल**) noun
अचार, मुरब्बा, something preserved in brine or marinade. *The dish was accompanied by a variety of tasty ~s.*

picnic (**पिकनिक**) noun
सैर सपाटा, लघुयात्रा एवं वहाँ साथ में मिलकर खाना पीना, pleasure trip. an outing. *Let's go for a ~.*

picture (**पिक्चर**)
चित्र, तस्वीर, प्रतिकृति, photograph, painting, drawing, sketch. *What a fine ~!*

piece (**पीस**) noun
खंड, टुकड़ा, part or bit, fragment. *A ~ of bread.*

pig (**पिग**) noun
सुअर, swine. *Don't be such a ~.*

pigeon (**पिजन**) noun
कपोत, कबूतर, bird of dove family.

pill (पिल) noun
गोली, टिकिया, वटी, medicine in the form of a little ball. *Take one ~ each time.*

pillar (पिलर) noun
स्तम्भ, खम्भा, upright column.

pillow (पिलो) noun
सिरहाना, तकिया, cotton stuffed cloth case.

pilot (पाइलट) noun
माँझी, मल्लाह, विमानचालक, one who steers an airplane. *He is a ~ officer.*

pin (पिन) noun
आलपिन, पिन, pointed slender piece.

pink (पिंक) noun
हल्का लाल या गुलाबी रंग, light red. *Dressed in ~.*

pipe (पाइप) noun
नली, tube. *Water ~. Drain ~.*

pit (गड्ढा) noun
गड्ढा, गर्त, hole. *He fell into a large ~.*

pitch (पिच) noun
डामर, कोलतार, coaltar. ऊँची या नीची गाढ़ना, आवाज़ , the high or low of sound to fix, central part of the cricket field, the area between the wicket.

pity (पिटी) noun
दया, रहम, sympathy. *I asked him to have ~ on the poor old man.*

place (प्लेस) noun
स्थान, जगह, रखना, to put in a particular space. *~ these books on the table.*

placement (प्लेसमेंट) noun
स्थान निर्धारण, location. *~ of job.*

plain (प्लेन) adjective
देखने, सुनने, समझने में आसान, easy to see, hear or understand. *~ language.*

plain (प्लेन) noun
समतल भूमि, मैदान, *The Gangetic ~s.*

plan (प्लान) noun
ढाँचा, नक्शा, मानचित्र, योजना, a design. *What are your ~s for the holidays?*

plane (प्लेन) noun
हवाई जहाज, aeroplane. *I will travel by ~ to Mumbai.*

planet (प्लैनिट) noun
ग्रह, सूर्य की परिक्रमा करने वाला, बुध, शुक्र, पृथ्वी, मंगल, गुरु, शनि, यूरेनस, नेपच्यून, प्लूटो, Mercury, Venus, Earth, Mars, Jupiter, Saturn, Neptune, Pluto. *~ s of the Sun.*

plant (प्लान्ट) noun
पेड़ पौधे, *A rose ~.*

plaster (प्लास्टर) noun
दीवार पर लगाने का पलस्तर, to be coated on the walls.

plastic (प्लास्टिक) noun
कोमल, लचीला, ढालने योग्य, easily shaped or moulded. *Clay is a ~ substance.* कृत्रिम लचीले पदार्थ, plastic.

plate (प्लेट) noun
तश्तरी, flat dish. *A ~ of nuts.*

platform (प्लेटफ़ॉर्म) noun
चबूतरा, मंच, स्टेज, *A railway ~.*

play (प्ले) noun
मनोरंजन, क्रीड़ा, amusement, recreation. *The students are at ~ in their free period.*

play (प्ले) verb
खेलना, आनन्द उठाना, to enjoy. *Let them go out and ~.*

pleasant (प्लैज़न्ट) adjective
सुहावना, आनन्ददायक, affording pleasure. *A ~ morning.*

please (प्लीज) verb
खुश करना, कृपा करके, मेहरबानी करके, polite request. *~ sit down.*

pleasure (प्लैज़र) noun
प्रसन्नता, खुशी, feeling of happiness or satisfaction. *It gave me a lot of ~ to hear of your success.*

plenty (प्लैन्टी) noun
बहुतायत, प्रचुरता, abundance. *There was food and drink in ~.*

plinth (प्लिन्थ) **noun**
मकान की कुर्सी, आधार, base of a building.

plot (प्लॉट) noun
ज़मीन का टुकड़ा, piece of ground. मानचित्र पर निशान लगाना. षड्यंत्र रचना, *A ~ of land. A ~ to overthrow the government.*

pluck (प्लक) verb
तोड़ना, to pull off. *The gardener objected to ~ing flowers.*

plus (प्लस) preposition
धन, जमा, addition to. *Four ~ six is ten.*

pocket (पौकिटं) noun
जेब, खीसा, a small bag with dress. *~ in a shirt, coat, pant, waistcoat, etc.*

poem (पोइम) noun
कविता, काव्य, composition in verse, poetry. *A small ~.*

point (पॉइन्ट) noun
नुकीला बिन्दु, dot. *The ~ of a pin, knife, pencil, etc.* सिरा, छोर, sharp end.

point (पॉइन्ट) verb
इशारा करना, संकेत करना। *The hour hand ~s to ten.*

poison (पॉइज़न) noun
विष, जहर, substance to destroy life, impair health. *Socrates was given a cup of ~ to drink.*

pole (पोल) noun
ध्रुव, North ~. South ~. लट्ठा, खम्भा, shaft.

police (पुलिस) **noun**
रक्षक दल, पुलिसबल *The members of ~ force.*

polish (पॉलिश) verb
पॉलिश करना, चमकाना, चिकना करना, to make smooth and glossy, सभ्य, शिष्ट, नम्र बनाना, to refine, to make elegant. *A ~ed gentleman.*

polite (पोलाइट) adjective
शिष्ट, सभ्य, नम्र, सुशील, polished, refined. *He was known for his ~ness.*

politics (पॉलिटिक्स) noun
राजनीति, the art or science of political government. *The Mandal reforms became embroiled in ~.*

pollute (पॉल्यूट) verb
गंदा करना, मलिन करना, दूषित करना, to destroy purity. *Rivers are ~d with chemical wastes from factories.*

pool (पूल) noun
गड्ढा, पोखर, a small body of still water, to collect. एकत्र करना

poor (पुअर) adjective
निर्धन, गरीब, दरिद्र, कंगाल, having little or no money. *A ~ family living on welfare.* बेचारा, unfortunate, कम, थोड़ा, अभाव, deficient. *Most of us live on ~ food.* अकुशल, दुबला पतला, दोषपूर्ण, त्रुटिपूर्ण *~ soil.*

popular (पौपुलर) adjective
लोकप्रिय, *A ~ preacher. ~ science. ~ medicine. ~ music.*

population (पौपुलेशन) noun
जनसखंया, number of people living in a place. *The ~ of Agra is more than a million.*

pore (पोर) noun
छिद्र, tiny opening. *Sweat passes through ~s.*

portable (पोर्टेबल) adjective
वहनीय, जो आसानी से ले जाया जा सके, conveyed easily. *A ~ typewriter.*

portion (पोर्शन) noun
अंश, भाग, खंड, हिस्सा. *Let me read a ~ of the manuscript.*

position (पोजीशन) noun
स्थिति, स्थान, जगह, स्थल, हालत, proper place. *Sit in a comfortable ~.*

positive (पॉज़िटिव) adjective
निश्चित, पक्का, सन्देहरहित, स्पष्ट, definite, sure, *Give him some ~ advice.*

possible (पॉसिबिल) adjective
संभव, that can be done. *Return home as soon as ~.*

post (पोस्ट) noun
स्थान, डाक, place, the way of sending and getting letters. *The soldiers are at their ~s,* दौड़ समाप्ति का खंभा, *To be beaten at the ~.*

postal (पोस्टल) adjective
डाक सम्बंधी, of the post. *~ expenses, ~ rates.*

poster (पोस्टर) noun
इश्तहार, विज्ञापन, संबंधित मुद्रित कागज, bill posted in a public place. *Cinema ~. Advertisement ~s.*

posting (पोस्टिंग) noun
नियुक्ति, पदस्थापन, तैनाती, assignment to a post. *~ order.*

post-mortem (पोस्ट-मौर्टम) noun
शव-परीक्षा, medical examination after death. *The dead bodies were sent for ~.*

pot (पौट) noun
धातु या मिट्टी का बर्तन, vessel, *A ~ of water, a flower ~. Give me a ~ of milk.*

potato (पोटैटो) noun
आलू, edible stem, आलू का पौधा, potato plant.

pouch (पाउच) noun
छोटी थैली, बटुआ, a small bag. *A tobacco ~. A water ~.*

pound (पाउन्ड) noun
ब्रिटिश मुद्रा और वज़न, British currency and weight.

pour (पोर) verb
उँडेलना, बरसना, to rain in torrents. *~ a jug of water into the bucket.*

poverty (पौवर्टी) noun
गरीबी, दरिद्रता, निर्धनता, state of being poor. *Born in ~, live in ~, die in ~.*

powder (पाउडर) noun
चूरा, पाउडर, any solid substance finely crushed. *Face ~. Baking ~. The use of ~ puff saves wastage of ~.*

power (पॉवर) noun
शक्ति, ऊर्जा, strength, energy. *I have enough muscle ~ Electric ~, Horse ~.*

practical (प्रैक्टीकल)
प्रायोगिक, व्यावहारिक, that can be put into practice, workable. *~ examination. A suggestion with little ~ value.*

practice (प्रैक्टिस) noun
आदत, नियम, अभ्यास, habitual action. *Latecoming has become his ~. Dowry has come into ~.*

praise (प्रेज़) verb
तारीफ, प्रशंसा, सराहना करना, बड़ाई करना, to speak highly, to applaud. गुणगान करना. *~ an honest man.* परमात्मा के गुणगान करना, give honour to God. *We ~ the almighty for all that he has done for us.*

pray (प्रे) verb
स्तुति करना, आराधना करना, to beseech earnestly. *The farmers are ~ing for rain.*

prayer (प्रेअर) noun
प्रभु से प्रार्थना, उपासना, वन्दना, आराधना, act of praying to God. worship, hymn. *To kneel down in ~.*

precaution (प्रिकौशन) noun
सावधानी, पूर्वप्रबंध, caution employed beforehand. *~ against fire. Take the raincoat just as a ~.*

precious (प्रैशस) adjective
मूल्यवान, कीमती, costly, valuable. *Life is ~. We had ~ moments together.*

precis (प्रेसिज़) noun
सारांश, संक्षिप्त विवरण, an abstract, a concise summary. *A ~ is usually one third of the original.*

predict (प्रिडिक्ट) verb
भविष्यवाणी करना, forecast, to tell in advance. *It is impossible to ~ who will win.*

preface (प्रिफ़ेस) noun
प्राक्कथन, प्रस्तावना, भूमिका, author's preliminary remarks at the beginning of the book. *Write a ~ to the book.*

prefect (प्रीफ़ैक्ट) noun
अधिनायक, मॉनिटर, शासक, authority. *~s in a college.*

prefer (प्रिफ़र) verb
अधिक पसन्द करना, ज्यादा अच्छा लगना, like better, choose rather than. *I ~ coffee to tea. I ~ walking to cycling.*

prefix (प्रीफ़िक्स) noun
उपसर्ग, word or syllable placed before a word to alter its meaning. *En is the ~ in endanger. Non is the ~ in nonsense.*

pregnant (प्रैगनेन्ट) adjective
गर्भवती, गर्भिणी, a female having a child in her womb.

prejudice (प्रैजुडिस) noun
पूर्वधारणा, पूर्वाग्रह, an opinion formed in the mind beforehand. *She has a ~ against me.*

premier (प्रीमिअर) adjective
प्रथम, प्रधान, first in position. *A ~ concern of Tatas.* प्रधानमंत्री का पद. *He was offered the ~ship.*

premiere (प्रीमिअर) noun
नाटक या फ़िल्म का प्रथम प्रदर्शन, first public performance of a play or film. *~ of a new foreign film.*

preparation (प्रैपरेशन) noun
तैयारी, प्रबंध, आयोजन, उपक्रम, preparing. *The furniture is in ~.*

prepare (प्रिपेयर) verb
तैयार करना, साधन जुटाना, to make ready, to get ready. *~ the meal. ~ for a journey.*

preposition (प्रिपोजिशन)
संबंधवाचक शब्द, word placed usually before a noun or pronoun to mark some relation, e.g., on, of, into, in spite of.

prescribe (प्रिसक्राइब) verb
औषध-निर्देश देना, to order the use of a medicine. *The doctor has ~d these tablets for me.*

prescription (प्रिसक्रिपशन) noun
डाक्टर का नुस्खा, medicines suggested by a doctor to a patient. *The doctor gave me a ~ of painkillers.*

presence (प्रेज़ेन्स) noun
उपस्थिति, किसी स्थान पर किसी के रहने की क्रिया, state of being present at a place. *Your ~ is*

requested at the dinner.

present **(प्रिज़ेन्ट)** adjective
उपस्थित, being in the place. *He was ~ at the wedding.*

present **(प्रिज़ेन्ट)** noun
उपहार, भेंट, तोहफा, a gift. *I shall send you a nice ~ on Diwali.*

present **(प्रिज़ेन्ट)** verb
सामने रखना, प्रदर्शन करना, to put before. *Please ~ my cheque next week at the bank.*

preserve **(प्रिज़र्व)** verb
बचाना, सुरक्षा करना, to save from injury or decay. *Wax polish ~s wood and leather. ~ one's eyesight.*

preside **(प्रिसाइड)** verb
अध्यक्ष होना, to occupy place of authority. *The manager ~s at the meeting of the school governing body.*

president **(प्रैसिडेन्ट)** noun
सभापति, प्रधान, अध्यक्ष, head of assembly, meeting, society. *The ~ of debating society.*

press **(प्रेस)** noun
दबाव, smooth or creased effect caused by pressing or ironing. *Your suit is out of ~.* दबाने की मशीन, छापाखाना, मुद्रणालय, an establishment for printing books, papers, etc., समाचार पत्र समूह, newspaper group.

press **(प्रेस)** verb
दबाना, to push against. *~ the door to open.*

pressure **(प्रेशर)** noun
दाब, भार, the exertion of force upon a surface by an object, air or fluid, etc. *Atmospheric ~.*

prestige **(प्रैस्टिज)** noun
गौरव, प्रतिष्ठा, reputation, achievement. *A question of one's ~.*

presume **(प्रिज़्यूम)** verb
मान लेना, to assume to be correct. *He ~d it to be true.*

pretend **(प्रिटैंड)** verb
बहाना बनाना, स्वांग करना, ढोंग करना, to feign. *He is ~ing to be ill.*

pretty **(प्रैटी)** adjective
सुन्दर, मनोहर, handsome. *The baby looks ~ in this frock.*

prevent **(प्रिवैन्ट)** verb
रोकना, बाधा डालना, stop, hinder. *Who ~ed you from going there?*

previous **(प्रीवियस)** adjective.
पहले से, पिछला, former, preceding. *You have been ~ly warned to be more cautious.*

prey **(प्रे)** noun
शिकार, आखेट, animal hunted for food. *The kite was eating its ~.*

price **(प्राइस)** noun
मूल्य, कीमत, दाम, भाव, amount of money for which something is sold or bought. *~ of gold is rising rapidly.*

prick (प्रिक) verb
किसी चीज में छोटा छेद या निशान बनाना, चुभाना, make a small hole in something, cause pain to. *~ holes in a paper. ~ one's finger with a pin.*

pride (प्राइड) noun
अभिमान, अहंकार, arrogance, excessive self-esteem, गौरव का स्रोत, *The ~ of youth. The soldiers are their country's ~.*

priest (प्रीस्ट) noun
पादरी, पुरोहित, पुजारी, a clergyman, a religious minister.

primary (प्राइमरी) adjective
प्राथमिक, प्रथम, *A ~ school,* असली, मौलिक, मूलभूत, *A ~ part.* मुख्य रूप से *The building was ~ly meant for library.*

prince (प्रिन्स) noun
राजकुमार, शहज़ादा, the son of a king.

principal (प्रिंसिपल) adjective
प्रधान, प्रमुख, most important. *Rice is the ~ food of Bengal.* प्रथम, सर्वोच्च, सर्वश्रेष्ठ. *The Ganges is one of the ~ rivers of Asia.* स्कूल का संचालक, प्राचार्य. *I must consult my ~ before agreeing to your proposal.*

principle (प्रिंसपिल) noun
सिद्वान्त, आधारभूत तथ्य, मूल तत्व, fundamentals. *The basic ~s of morality. They have agreed to the proposal in ~ but still we have to negotiate the terms.*

print (प्रिन्ट) verb
छापना, मुद्रित करना, to publish. *~ 2000 copies of the catalogue. The ~ed matter can be easily read.*

prison (प्रिज़न) noun
जेल, कारागार, a jail.

prisoner (प्रिज़नर) noun
कैदी, बंदी, a person in jail.

privacy (प्राइवेसी) noun
गोपनीयता, secrecy. *They were wedded in ~.*

private (प्राइवेट) adjective
व्यक्तिगत, निजी, अपना, गुप्त, रहस्यपूर्ण, गैरसरकारी, *A ~ message, A ~ school to prepare students for competitions.*

prize (प्राइज़) noun
पारितोषिक, पुरस्कार, इनाम, a reward for superiority. *A ~ for regular attendance.*

pro (प्रो) prefix
उपसर्ग, supporting, पूर्व, अग्र, आदि अर्थवादी उपसर्ग, provision, prologue, proceed, produce, protract, etc.

probability (प्रोबेबिलिटी) noun
संभावना, अनुमान, event that may happen. *There is little ~ of his regaining health. A probable winner in long jump.*

problem (प्रॉब्लम) noun
समस्या, question to be solved. *The main ~ is age limit. Presenting ~s.*

proceed (प्रोसीड) verb
आगे बढ़ना, जारी रखना, to go ahead, to continue. *Please ~ with your work.*

process (प्रोसेस) noun
काम करने/होने का ढंग, actions to do something. *The ~ of blood circulation in the body.* कार्यरीति, प्रक्रिया, *Loading the cargo is a slow ~.*

produce (प्रोड्यूस) noun, verb
पैदावार, उत्पत्ति, उपज, उत्पादन करना, manufacture, grow, make. *~ silk goods. ~ heavy crops. ~ more food.*

profit (प्रौफ़िट) noun
लाभ, सुविधा, प्राप्ति, gain, advantage, benefit. *Gross ~ of a firm. Net ~ of a company.*

proforma (प्रोफ़ोर्मा)
फ़ॉर्म, क्रमिक, रीति के अनुसार, as a matter of form.

programme (प्रोग्राम) noun
कार्यक्रम, a plan. *A ~ on T.V.*

progress (प्रोग्रेस) noun
विकास, उन्नति, प्रगति, तरक्की, developmental activity. *The walkers made slow ~ up the rocky path.*

project (प्रोजैक्ट) noun
योजना, plans. *~ of a new dam.*

prolong (प्रोलौंग) verb
समय बढ़ाना, लम्बा करना, make longer, *~ed journey. ~ed discussion.*

promise (प्रौमिस) noun
वचन, प्रतिज्ञा, वायदा, an assurance. *He gave me a solemn ~ to help me in need.*

promote (प्रमोट) verb
तरक्की देना, उच्च पद देना, give higher position. *He was ~d to the rank of sergeant. To ~ world peace.*

prompt (प्रौम्प्ट) adjective
फुर्ती से किया गया, जल्दी, शीघ्र, done at once, quick. *A ~ reply to a letter.* परदे के पीछे से एक्टर को शब्द बताते जाना, words spoken to help an actor.

pronunciation (प्रोनन्सिएशन) noun
उच्चारण, act of pronouncing. *Your ~ is clear.*

proof (प्रूफ़) noun
प्रमाण, सबूत, evidence. *Is there any ~ of your presence in the meeting?* दुर्भेद्य, जिस पर किसी चीज़ का असर न हो, *Water~. Fire~, Sound~, Bullet~* . प्रेस द्वारा भेजा गया प्रूफ़, *Pass the ~s for the press.*

proper (प्रौपर) adjective
सही, ठीक, उचित, right, correct, suitable. *Do the ~ thing at the time. Not a ~ thing to do in the public.*

property (प्रॉपर्टी) noun
सम्पत्ति, जायदाद, things owned, possession. *A man of ~.* गुण, विशेषता, खूबी. *Paraffin has the ~ of dissolving grease.*

proportion (प्रपोर्शन) noun
अनुपात, relation of two things with regard to their magnitude. *The ~ of income to expenditure. The room is wide in ~ to its height.*

propose (प्रपोज) verb
प्रस्ताव रखना, विचारार्थ कोई बात रखाना, put forward for consideration, discussion or adoption. *You should ~ this resolution at the general meeting. I ~ to go there next week.*

proprietor (प्रोप्राइटर) noun
स्वामी, मालिक, owner esp. of a business firm. *The net profit of a business goes to its ~.*

pros and cons (प्रॉस एन्ड कॉन्स) noun
समर्थन और विपक्ष में तर्क, arguments in favour and against. *Consider well the ~ of the case.*

prose (प्रोज़) noun
गद्य, language not in verse form. *A writer of Hindi ~.*

prospect (प्रौस्पेक्ट) noun
आसार, सम्भावना, आशा, उम्मीद, *This job has excellent ~s. What ~s exist after completing the course?*

prospectus (प्रॉसपैक्टस) noun
स्कूल कॉलिज आदि की विवरणिका, a descriptive booklet giving the main objects and plans of an institution. *A college ~. The ~ of a limited company.*

prostitute (प्रौस्टिट्यूट) noun
वेश्या, रंडी, गणिका, whore, a woman who offers herself for sexual intercourse for money. *She ~d herself in order to support her children.*

protect (प्रोटैक्ट) verb
सुरक्षित रखना, keep safe. *You need woollen clothes to ~ you against the cold.*

protest (प्रोटेस्ट) verb
विरोध प्रदर्शित करना, विरोध, express objection. *He ~ed that he had never seen the criminal before.*

proud (प्राउड) adjective
अभिमानी, अंहकारी, घमंडी, having a high opinion of one's own dignity, importance or superiority. *He is ~ to belong to a rich family.*

prove (प्रूव) verb
सिद्ध करना, प्रमाणित करना, साबित करना, supply proof of. *Can you ~ what you say?*

provide (प्रोवाइड) verb
प्रबंध करना, जुटाना, पहले से ही तैयारी करना, to make due preparations beforehand, ~ *good education to children.*

province (प्रौविन्स) noun
प्रान्त, सूबा, प्रदेश, a large administrative unit of a country or empire. *The ~ of*

Uttar Pradesh.

prudent (प्रूडेंट) adjective
चतुर, बुद्धिमान, careful, wise, *A ~ wife, In a ~ manner.*

pub (पब) noun
शराबघर, short form of public house. *Go to ~ for a drink.*

public (पब्लिक) adjective
जो सबका हो, सार्वजनिक, जनता, connected with people in general. *~ property.*

publish (पब्लिश) verb
पुस्तकों का प्रकाशन करना, सार्वजनिक सूचना देना, to make public. *Will you ~ my books?*

pull (पुल) noun
खिंचाव, act of drawing. *Give a ~ to the rope.* खींचना, draw. *The dentist ~ed out his tooth.*

pulse (पल्स) noun
नाड़ी, नब्ज़, throbbing of the arteries. *~ rate.*

pulse (पल्स) noun
दाल, edible seeds of leguminous plants, peas, beans, lentils.

pump (पम्प) noun
पम्प, machine for forcing liquid or gas into, out of or through something. *Petrol ~. ~ air into the tube.*

punctual (पंक्चुअल) adjective
समय का पाबन्द, not late, prompt. *Be ~ in payment of taxes. ~ity is a noble quality.*

punish (पनिश) verb
दण्ड देना, सजा देना, to subject to pain, loss, confinement, death, etc., as a penalty for some offense. *To ~ a thief.*

punishment (पनिशमेन्ट) noun
दण्ड, सज़ा, to make someone suffer for wrongdoing.

pup (पप) noun
पिल्ला, जानवरों का छोटा बच्चा, a young dog, a young of various other animals. *A mother dog and her ~.*

pupil (प्यूपिल) noun
शिष्य, विद्यार्थी, a person usually learning in school. *Newly admitted ~s.*

pupil (प्यूपिल) noun
आँख की पुतली, circular opening in the centre of the iris of the eye that regulates the amount of light passing to the retina.

puppet (पपेट) noun
गुड़िया, a small doll, किसी के हाथ की कठपुतली, *A ~ government. A ~ ruler.*

purchase (परचेज़) verb
खरीदना, to buy. *~ a good pen.*

purchase (परचेज़) noun
क्रय, खरीद, action of buying. *The receipt is the proof of ~.*

pure (प्यूर) adjective
शुद्ध, खालिस, unmixed, unadulterated. *~ gold. ~ air. ~ water.*

purple (पर्पल) noun
बैंगनी, नीलारुण, red and blue mixed together.

purpose (परपज़्) noun
अभिप्राय, इरादा, मंशा, उद्देश्य, intention. *What is the ~ of the law?*

purse (पर्स) noun
बटुआ, थैली रुपया-पैसा रखने के लिए, small bag for keeping money.

pursue (परसू) verb
पीछा करना, शिकार करना, to follow, to chase. *~ a robber*, कार्य जारी रखना. *~ one's studies.*

pus (पस) noun
मवाद, पीप, produced by suppuration and found in abscesses. *The doctor lanced the boil to let the ~ out.*

push (पुश) verb
धकेलना, धक्का, thrust. *He ~ed the door hard and opened it.*

put (पुट) verb
to set, to place. रखना, स्थापित करना. *He ~ the inkpot on the desk.* सुपुर्द करना, entrust. *I shall ~ the matter into the hands of my soldiers.*

put off (पुट ऑफ) verb
उतारना, to lay aside. *He ~ his shoes before going into the house.*

put on (पुट औन) verb
पहनना, to wear, *~ clothes, turban, shoes, spectacles, etc.*

put-out (पुट आउट) verb
बुझा देना, to extinguish. *To ~ the lamp.*

put up (पुट अप) verb
प्रस्ताव रखना, to propose. *She was ~ for the position of secretary.*

puzzle (पज़ल) noun
पहेली, कठिन प्रश्न, problem difficult to answer, समस्या, *A crossword ~.*

pyre (पायर) noun
चिता, मुर्दा जलाने के लिए लकड़ियों का ढेर, large pile of wood for burning a dead body.

□□□□

Q

q मुद्रण में प्रयुक्त लघु अक्षर

q लिखने में प्रयुक्त लघु अक्षर

मूल उच्चारण **क्यू**

प्रयोग में उच्चारण – **क** क्या k से सब काम नहीं चल सकता था?

अंग्रेजी वर्णमाला का सत्रहवाँ अक्षर

quack (क्वैक) noun
बत्तख की आवाज, sound of duck. *Ducks ~.*

quack (क्वैक) noun
नीम हकीम, अनाड़ी डाक्टर, charlaton. *He is not a qualified doctor. He is simply a ~.*

quadrangle (क्वाड्रेंगल) noun
चतुष्कोण, चतुर्भुज, खुला मैदान, आँगन, plane figure of four sides, an open yard in this shape.

qualification (क्वालिफ़िकेशन) noun
योग्यता, अर्हता, संशोधन, सीमा, a quality, accomplishment. *He has the required ~s for the job.*

quality (क्वालिटी) noun
गुण, विशेषता, high degree of goodness, *A man of good qualities.* सामान्य विशेषता, general excellence. *Our company is more concerned with ~.*

quantity (क्वानटिटी) noun
परिमाण, मात्रा, amount, extent. *How much ~ of sugar do you need?*

quarrel (क्वैरिल) noun
झगड़ा, विवाद, लड़ना, angry dispute or altercation. *They ended their ~ and became friends.*

quarter (क्वार्टर) noun
चौथा भाग, fourth part. *A ~ of an hour.* किसी भी घंटे के 15 मिनट पूर्व या बाद में, *A ~ to four (3.45),* 25 सेंट. *It will cost you two ~s.* निवास स्थान, accomodation. *Where have you rented a ~ for yourself?*

quash (क्वैश) verb
कुचलना, दबाना, crush, subdue, खारिज करना, to annul. *To ~ a rebellion.*

queen (क्वीन) noun
मलिका, सम्राज्ञी, wife of a king. ~

Elizabeth of England.

question (क्वेश्चन) noun
सवाल, प्रश्न, *~ no. 4 in the examination paper was quite difficult. It was simply a ~ of time.*

queue (क्यू) noun
लम्बी कतार, a file or line. *Stand in a ~.*

quiet (क्वाइट) adjective
शान्त, निश्चल, calm, tranquil. *A ~ person.*

quintal (क्विन्टल) noun
एक सौ किलोग्राम का वजन, 100 kg. *A ~ of wheat.*

quit (क्विट) verb
छोड़ जाना, चले जाना, to depart, to leave. *The Britishers were asked to ~ India in 1942.*

quite (क्वाइट) adverb
बिलकुल, सर्वथा, completely, altogether. *I ~ agree with you on this point.*

quiz (क्विज़) verb
जाँच करने के लिए प्रश्न पूछना, to ask questions as a test of knowledge. *Take part in the ~.*

quota (कोटा) noun
निर्धारित अंश, fixed proportion. *He completed his ~ of work for the day and left.*

quotation (कोटेशन) noun
उद्वरण, abstract. *~ from the Bible.*

quote (कोट) verb
उद्धृत करना, हवाला देना, दाम बताना, to cite, to refer to. *~ a section of the code.*

Q.E.D.
quod erat demonstrandum, यही सिद्ध करना था, it was to be proved.

❑❑❑❑

R

r मुद्रण में प्रयुक्त लघु अक्षर

मूल उच्चारण **आर**

r लिखने में प्रयुक्त लघु अक्षर

र प्रयोग में उच्चारण एक ही है, दो क्यों नहीं?

अँग्रेजी वर्णमाला का अठारहवाँ अक्षर

rabbit (रैबिट) noun
खरगोश, शशक, small burrowing animal of hare family.

rabbies (रैबीज़) noun
पागल कुत्ते के काटने से होने वाला रोग, an acute infectious viral disease of the nervous system transmitted by the saliva of infected animal esp. dogs, causing hydrophobia.

race (रेस) verb
दौड़ लगाना, चाल में प्रतियोगिता, contest of speed. *100 metre ~ ; Slow cycle ~.*

race (रेस) noun
कुल, वंश, a group of persons related by common descent. *Aryan ~. Dravidian ~. The Mongoloid ~.*

rack (रैक) noun
चारा या सामान रखने का टाँड, frame for holding things. *A luggage ~. A book ~. A hat ~.*

racket (रैकिट) noun
बेइमानी से धन कमाने में लगे व्यक्ति, earning money by extortion, fraud. गलत पेशा, धन्धा. *A person engaged in many ~s.* टैनिस या बैडमिन्टन खेलने का बल्ला, *To strike the ball with a ~.*

radar (रैडार) noun
रेडियों तंरगों द्वारा ठोस पिन्डों की अन्तरिक्ष में उपस्थिति जानने का यंत्र. *To locate an aircraft by ~.*

radiate (रेडियेट) verb
विकिरण होना, to emit rays, *A stove that ~s warmth. A woman who ~s happiness.*

radical (रैडिकल) adjective
बिलकुल भिन्न, very different. *A ~ difference. A ~ change in foreign policy.*

rag (रैग) noun
चिथड़ा, फटे पुराने वस्त्र, torn, old and dirty cloths. *I use a ~ to clean the floor.*

rage (रेज) noun
क्रोध, उन्माद, violent anger. *He was trembling with ~.*

raid (रेड) noun
हमला, धावा, an invasion. *Killed in an air ~.* दबिश, पुलिस की कार्यवाही. *Police carried out a ~ on the hideouts of the criminals.* छापा मारना, आक्रमण करना. *A security guard was killed in the bank ~.*

rail (रेल) noun
लोहे की पटरी जिस पर रेलगाड़ी चलती है, one of a pair of steel that provides running surfaces for wheels of locomotives and railroad cars. *Travel by ~.*

railway (रेलवे) noun
रेलमार्ग जिस पर गाड़ियाँ दौड़ती हैं rail-track. *A network of ~.*

rain (रेन) noun
वर्षा, मेघ, water falling from clouds. *The farmers want ~.*

rain (रेन) verb
वर्षा होना, गिरना, to fall as rain. *It ~ed heavily last night.*

rainbow (रेनबो) noun
इन्द्रधनुष, an arc of prismatic colours appearing in the sky after rains.' *A ~ pattern.*

raise (रेज़) verb
खड़ा करना, lift up. *~ this man from his knees.*

raisin (रेज़िन) noun
किशमिश, मुनक्का, dried sweet grapes.

rally (रैली) verb
एकत्र करना, to collect. *The party ~ied in support of the Prime Minister at the Boat Club.* जनसमूह, a large gathering. *The public ~ was well attended.*

ramp (रैम्प) noun
ढलान, गतिशील नसैनी, सीढ़ी, sloping surface, a path that goes to a higher or lower place.

random (रैन्डम) adjective
बेतरतीब, बिना सोचे समझे, occurring without aim. *The ~ selection of members.*

range (रेन्ज) verb
कतार में लगाना, arrange in a row. *The scouts ~ themselves along the route of the procession.* विस्तार, distance one can see.

rank (रैंक) noun
श्रेणी, किसी विशेष श्रेणी में आना, occupy a particular place or position. *He ~s well as head of the classmates in mathematics. The D.M. being out of station the A.D.M. is the ~ing officer.*

ransom (रैन्सम) noun
फिरौती, मुक्ति के लिए माँगा गया धन, the redemption of kidnapped person. *A large ~ for a kidnapped child.*

rape (रेप) verb
बलात्कार करना, किसी लड़की या औरत से उसकी इच्छा के विरुद्ध संभोग करना, to force a girl or woman to have sex against

her will. *He was sentenced to jail for committing a ~.*

rare (रेअर) adjective
दुर्लभ, अनूठा, असाधारण, uncommon, unusual. *A ~ book. A ~ incident. A ~ word. We had a ~ time last week.* कम घना, विरल, not dense, thin. *~ mountain air.*

rascal (रैस्कल) noun
दुर्जन, धूर्त, बदमाश, a base, unscrupulous person. *Both the men are ~s.*

rash (रैश) adjective
उतावला, अधीर, acting too hastily. *~ driving. ~ young boy.*

rash (रैश) noun
त्वचा पर छोटी-छोटी फुसियाँ, an eruption on the skin.

rat (रैट) noun
चूहा, a long tailed rodent larger than mouse.

rate (रेट) noun
चाल, गति, speed. *Walking at the ~ of 5 km. an hour.*

rate (रेट) noun
दर, मूल्यांकन, estimated value. *They ~d him kind and hospitable.*

rather (रादर) adverb
बल्कि, preferably. *I will resign ~ than take part in such an unfair deed.*

ratify (रैटिफ़ाइ) verb
पुष्ट करना, समर्थन करना, to consent, to make valid. *~ the agreement.*

ratio (रेशिओ) noun
अनुपात, relation between two quantities determined by dividing. *The ~ between 25 and 75 is 1: 3.*

ration (राशन) noun
रसद, खाद्य-पदार्थ की निश्चित मात्रा, fixed daily allowance of food. *We will have to ~ sugar.*

rational (रैशनल) adjective
विवेकी, विचारवान, sensible, reasonable. *The patient seemed quite ~.*

raw (रॉ) adjective
कच्चा, बिना पका, uncooked, immature. *~ vegetables.* प्राकृतिक स्थिति में. *~ iron*, अदक्ष, अकुशल, unskilled, untrained. *He is a ~ hand in the factory.*

ray (रे) noun
किरण, रश्मि, narrow beam of light. *~s of the sun. Moon ~s.*

razor (रेज़र) noun
उस्तरा, ब्लेड, instrument used for shaving.

re (रि) prefix
फिर या पुनः के अर्थ में उपसर्ग, in the sense of again, e.g. reappear, redo, replay, reenter.

reach (रीच) verb
पहुँचना, arrive, stretch out. *He ~ed out his hand for the book*

but it was too far away. विस्तार, फैला होना. *My school ~es as far as the railway station.*

reaction (रिएक्शन) noun
प्रतिक्रिया, action in response. *What was his ~ to your proposal?*

read (रीड) verb
पढ़ना, to look at and apprehend the meaning of written, printed words. *Can you ~ this book?*

ready (रैडी) adjective
तैयार, तुरंत, इच्छुक, willing. *~ to work,* बने बनाये, in action. *~made clothes.*

real (रिअल) adjective
वास्तविक, actually existing. *He is the ~ manager of the institution.*

realize (रिअलाइज) verb
अनुभव करना, समझना, feel, understand. *Do you ~ your weakness?* पैसा वसूल करना. *~ one's debts,* पूरी तरह आभास होना. *~ the extent of the damage due to earthquakes.*

really (रिअली) adverb
वास्तव में, सचमुच, in reality, truly. *What do you ~ think about him as a journalist?*

ream (रीम) noun
काग़ज़ का रिम, 20 दस्ते अथवा 480 या 500 काग़ज़, measure for paper, 480 or 500 sheets.

reap (रीप) noun
फसल काटना, cut the crop. *~ the field of wheat.*

rear (रिअर) noun
पिछली पंक्ति, पिछला भाग, the back position, hinder part. *The garden is in the ~ of the house.*

reason (रीज़न) noun
कारण, हेतु, वजह, प्रयोजन, उद्देश्य, तर्कबुद्धि, ground motive, faculty of rational thought, sanity. *What is the ~ of your failure?*

rebate (रिबेट) noun
कटौती, किसी कर या ऋण में, discount, amount by which tax, debt is reduced. *A ~ of 5% for early settlement.*

rebel (रिबैल) noun
विद्रोही, राजद्रोही, person who defies authority. *The ~lious forces.*

rebirth (रिबर्थ) noun
पुर्नजन्म, renewal of life, re-incarnation, revival. *The ~ of the soul. The ~ of conservatism.*

recall (रिकौल) verb
वापस बुलाना, summon back. *~ the agent from his post.* याद आना, स्मरण होना, recollect, remember. *I don't ~ his name at present.*

recap (रिकैप) verb
संक्षेप में दोहराना, short form of recapitulate. *Let me just ~ on*

what we have diiscussed so far.

receipt (रिसीट) noun
रसीद, पावती, प्राप्ति पत्र, being received. *We got ~s for everything we bought.*

receive (रिसीव) verb
लेना, स्वीकार करना, पाना, accept, take, get. *I was warmly ~d by them.*

recent (रीसेंट) adjective
हाल का, आधुनिक, नवीन, modern, new. *~ fashion, Result ~ly declared.*

reception (रिसैप्शन) noun
प्राप्ति, स्वागत समारोह, act of receiving. *Room for the ~ of guests. A wedding ~.*

recess (रिसैस) noun
अल्पअवकाश, मध्यावकाश, temporary withdrawl from usual work. *Students enjoy during the ~ of 20 minutes.*

recessive (रिसैसिव) adjective
अप्रभावी, having tendency to recede.

recharge (रीचार्ज) verb
किसी बन्दूक या बैटरी को पुनः प्रयोग हेतु सही करना, charge again. *Ask the driver to get the battery of the car ~d.*

recipe (रेसिपी) **noun**
नुस्खा खाना बनाने का, तरकीब, directions for preparing some food.

recital (रिसाइटल) noun
किसी घटना का विवरण, गायन. *A ~ of complaints. A ~ of poems, A dance ~.*

recite (रिसाइट) verb
पाठ करना, सुनाना, say aloud from memory. *~ a few verses from Wordsworth.*

reclaim (रिक्लेम) verb
सुधार कर ठीक करना, bring back waste products to new use. *We will have to ~ new lands to grow more food.* वापस माँगना, request to return something. *You can ~ the property you had lost.*

recognize (रिकोगनाइज़) verb
पहचानना, जान लेना, to know, to identify. *I can ~ him from a distance.* मान्यता देना, acknowledge. *The new institution was not ~.*

recollect (रीकलैक्ट) verb
स्मरण करना, याद करना, remember. *I can ~ my school days even today.*

recommend (रैकमैन्ड) verb
सिफ़ारिश करना, अनुमोदन करना, speak in favour of. *I ~ that you consult a doctor. ~ this child to somebody's care.*

record (रिकॉर्ड) noun
अभिलेख, लिखित वर्णन, written account of events, facts, etc. *A ~ of road accidents. Keep a ~ of income and expenditure.*

record (रिकॉर्ड) verb
अंकित करना, लिपिबद्ध करना, set

down in writing. *The programme was ~ed in detail. ~ a speech, piece of music, a talk, a play, etc.*

recover (रिकवर) verb
फिर से पाना. get back, *~ one's health after long illness,* ठीक होना, become well. *Light diet will help you ~ from weakness.* फिर से सुधार आना, to improve. *Economy is ~ing after a period of recession.*

recreation (रिक्रिएशन) noun
मनोरंजन, खेलकूद, amusement enjoyment. *Various means of ~.*

recruit (रिक्रूट) noun
नई भर्ती, नया सदस्य, newly enlisted soldier, new member or supporter.

rectify (रैक्टीफ़ाई) verb
ठीक करना, सही करना, to set right, to correct. *To ~ an error. A good teacher is a good rectifier.*

recur (रिकर) verb
बार-बार होना, फिर से होना, to occur again. *A ~ring problem, illness, etc.*

recycle (रीसाइकिल) verb
पुरानी चीज़ों को पुनः उपयोगी बनाना, to treat used material so it can be used again *~ P.V.C., waste paper.*

red (रैड) adjective
लाल, colour of blood. *Letter boxes are of ~ colour. His baby's eyes were ~ with continuous weeping.*

redden (रैडन) verb
लाल करना, लाल होना, make or become red. *~ed with shame, anger, etc.*

reddish (रैडिश) adjective
कुछ कुछ लाल, लालिमा लिए हुए, somewhat red. *~ sky at the time of sunset. ~ hair.*

redirect (रीडिरैक्ट) verb
पुनप्रेषित करना, to change the direction or course of. *His letters were ~ed to the new address.*

redress (रिड्रैस) verb
सही करना, ठीक करना, to set right. *To ~ the employees' grievances.*

reduce (रिड्यूस) verb
कम करना, घटाना, lessen, make smaller. *~ the speed of the car, drive carefully.*

refer (रैफ़र) verb
निर्देष हेतु उच्च अधिकारी के पास भेजना, to submit to authority for consideration. *The matter has been ~ed to the committee.*

referee (रैफ़री) noun
निर्णायक, a man who controls matches, judges points in dispute. *Both the ~s in the football match were impartial.*

reference (रिफ़रैन्स) noun
संदर्भ, हवाला, mention, allusion.

Look up a ~. You are to quote our ~ when replying.

refill (रीफ़िल) noun
दुबारा भरी गई वस्तु, new filler. ~ *the empty cylinder with gas. A ~ for a ball point pen.*

refine (रिफ़ाइन) verb
शुद्ध करना, दोष दूर करना, to purify, free from impurities. ~ *your writing style.*

reflect (रिफ़्लैक्ट) verb
टकराने के बाद वापस लौटना, throw back (light, heat, sound). *The sunlight was ~ed from the water of the lake*, शीशे में प्रतिबिम्ब बनना, to give an image in a mirror.

reflection (रिफ्लेक्शन) noun
परछाई, छाया, image in mirror or water.

reform (रिफौर्म) noun
सुधार करना, अच्छा बनाना, make better, *~ a sinner. ~ yourself. ~s in educational system.*

refract (रिफ्रेक्ट) verb
आवर्तन, प्रकाश किरणों का मुड़ना, the change of direction of rays of light, sound, heat.

refresh (रिफ़्रैश) verb
ताजा करना, make fresh, to give new vigour by giving food, rest, etc. *We ~ ourselves during the recess.*

refrigerate (रिफ्रिजरेट) verb
ठंडा करना, शीत गृह में रखना, to make cool or cold. to preserve in cold storage.

refund (रिफन्ड) verb
प्राप्त किया हुआ धन वापिस लौटाना, pay back money received. ~ *the excess amount received.*

refuse (रिफ़्यूज) verb
मना करना, अस्वीकार करना, reject an offer. *I ~d him to lend my book.*

refuse (रिफ़्यूज) noun
कूड़ा, मल, rubbish, waste material. *Town ~ is dumped outside the town.*

refute (रिफ़्यूट) verb
गलत साबित करना, खंडन करना, to prove to be wrong, contradict. *My lawyer ~d all his arguments.*

regain (रिगेन) verb
पुनः प्राप्त करना, recover possession of. *To ~ one's health.*

regard (रिगार्ड) noun
सम्बन्ध, मामला, reference, an aspect, relation. *I have nothing to say in this ~.*

regard (रिगार्ड) verb
मानना, महत्व प्रदान करना, consider, attach importance to. *He ~s me with favour.*

regime (रेजीम) noun
शासन पद्धति, व्यवस्था, form of government, of administration. *A dictatorial ~.*

region (रीजन) noun
प्रदेश, क्षेत्र, part of country with or without boundaries. *The*

equatorial ~. ~al languages.

register (रजिस्टर) noun
पंजी, a book of records. *The attendance ~. Cash ~. A ~ of donors.*

register (रजिस्टर) verb
हिसाब लिखना, रजिस्टर में लिखना. *To write formally in a ~. ~ the birth of our chid. Get yourself ~ed in employment office.* पत्रादि को पंजीकृत कराकर भेजना, registry. *It is safer to ~ letters containing important documents.*

regress (रिग्रैस) verb
पीछे हटना, पीछे जाना, go backward. *~ to primitive stage.*

regret (रिग्रेट) verb
दुःखी होना, to be sorry. *I ~ my inability to help you.*

regular (रैग्युलर) adjective
नियमानुसार, नियम से, systematic, orderly. *Work should be done in a ~ manner.*

rehearse (रिहर्स) verb
प्रदर्शन के पूर्व किसी कार्यक्रम का अभ्यास करना, practise a programme for public performance. *Our teacher is rehearsing us for the Republic Day.*

reign (रेन) noun
शासन, राज्य, rule, dominion. *During the ~ of Aurangzeb.*

reject (रिजैक्ट) verb
पसन्द न करना, खारिज करना, disapprove, discard. *His first novel has been ~ed by the critics.*

rejoice (रिजौइस) verb
खुश होना, प्रसन्न होना, to feel pleasure, great joy. *They ~d at the sight of their lost kitten.*

relate (रिलेट) verb
हाल सुनाना, बतलाना, give an account of facts, tell a story. *My grandma ~ed to me the story of a clever fox.* संबंध लगाना, सम्बद्ध होना, रिश्तेदारी होना, have some family relation. *He is not ~d to me in any way.*

relation (रिलेशन) noun
सम्बंध, a connection between two things. *The ~ between doctor and patient.* रिश्तेदारी. *He invited all his ~s to his son's marriage.*

relax (रिलैक्स) verb
ढीला होना, आराम करना, विश्राम करना, *Curfew has been ~ed for four hours. He is tired, let him ~ for two hours.*

release (रिलीज) verb
मुक्त करना, छोड़ देना, set free, discharge. ब्रिकी हेतु बाज़ार में लाना. *The new edition of the book has been ~d. The ~ of a new film.*

reliable (रिलाएबिल) adjective
विश्वासी, भरोसे के लायक, dependable, trustworthy. *~ news. ~ people.*

relief (रिलीफ़) noun
पीड़ा, कष्ट आदि में आराम,

lessening of pain or anxiety. *The injection gave the patient much ~.* विश्राम, recess, relaxation. *The duty from 9 AM to 8 PM, with only one hour ~.*

religion (रिलीजन) noun
धर्म, मज़हब, concern over what exists beyond the visible world. धार्मिक भावनाओं के अनेक रूपों में से कोई, one of the variant systems of faith, e.g.; Hinduism, Islam, Christianity, Jainism, etc. जीवन का अंग. *Hockey was like a ~ for Dhyan Chand.*

relish (रैलिश) verb
स्वाद लेना, आनन्द लेना, to enjoy, to get pleasure. *Hunger is the best ~ for food.*

rely (रिलाई) verb
भरोसा करना, depend confidentially. *You may ~ on me for help.*

remain (रिमेन) verb
रुकना, बना रहना, continue to exist. *She ~ed quiet.* बाकी रह जाना, be left, still present. *If you take out 5 from 9,4 ~s. After the fire very little ~ed of the building. Much still ~s to be done.*

remand (रिमान्ड) verb
अधिक जानकारी प्राप्त करने हेतु किसी अपराधी को फिर से हिरासत में भेजा जाना, send back a criminal into custody. *He has been ~ed for four weeks.*

remark (रिमार्क) verb
टिप्पणी करना, फब्ती कसना, say something, comment. *It is unmannerly to ~ on somebody's appearance.* आलोचना करना *What are your ~s on the article?*

remedy (रैमिडी) noun
उपचार, इलाज, cure for disease. *Morning walk is the best ~ for indigestion.* ठीक करना, सुधारना, put right. *Your spelling mistakes can be remedied by practice. Remedial measures for flood.*

remember (रिमैम्बर) verb
याद करना, स्मरण करना, keep in mind, recall. *You can't even ~ her name. Just wait, I am trying to ~ the exact date of the accident.*

remind (रिमाइन्ड) verb
याद कराना, स्मरण कराना, to cause a person to remember. *May I ~ you to answer his letter. His face ~s me of his father.*

remit (रैमिट) verb
ऋण से माफ़ी देना, to exempt somebody from debt. *Loans to farmers have been ~ted.* धन भेजना, transmit money. *The money has been ~ted by money order.* क्षमा करना, पापों से मुक्त करना, (of God) forgive. *Almighty God! ~ our sins.*

remote (रिमोट) adjective
दूरवर्ती, सुदूर, far apart, distant, secluded. *~ from the subject*

under discussion. A ~ village.

remote control (रिमोट कन्ट्रोल) noun
दूरी से नियंत्रण, control of the operation from a distance by radio signals. *~ of a T.V. set.*

remove (रिमूव) verb
हटाना, अंत करना, दूसरे स्थान पर ले जाना, take to another place. *He has been ~d from his service.*

renown (रिनाउन) noun
ख्याति, नाम, कीर्ति, यश, fame, glory, reputation. *P.T. Usha of Kerala is a ~ed racer.*

rent (रैन्ट) noun
किराया, भाड़ा, money paid periodically by the tenant to the owner. *Monthly ~ of house.*

repair (रिपेयर) verb
मरम्मत करना, सुधारना, mend, restore to good condition. *The machine has become serviceable after necessary ~.*

repay (रिपे) verb
रकम वापिस करना, pay back, compensate, लौटाना. *If you lend me some money, I will ~ you next month. She ~ed the compliment with a smile.*

repel (रिपैल) verb
पीछे धकेलना, धकियाना, मना करना, drive back. *She ~led his advances. To ~ the army assault.*

repeat (रिपीट) verb
दोहराना, say or do again. *History ~s itself.*

repent (रिपैन्ट) verb
पछताना, पश्चात्ताप करना, regret, feel sorry. *He has to ~ his thoughtless act.*

replace (रिप्लेस) verb
प्रतिस्थापन करना, take the place of. लौटना, वापिस करना, व्यक्ति या वस्तु को बदल कर दूसरी वस्तु लाना *Nothing can ~ a mother's love. Coal can be ~ed by oil.*

reply (रिप्लाई) verb
उत्तर देना, जवाब देना, to answer. *I am glad for your favourable ~.*

report (रिपोर्ट) verb
सूचना देना, वर्णन करना, वर्णन, to give account of, to narrate. *He ~ed the matter to police. Annual ~ of the school.*

represent (रिप्रिज़ैन्ट) verb
प्रदर्शन करना, प्रतिनिधित्व करना, depict, show. *This painting ~s a spring. I ~ed him at the meeting.*

reproduce (रिप्रोड्यूस) verb
प्रतिलिपि बनाना, संतान उत्पन्न करना, to make a copy of, form anew. *This copier can ~ colour photographs. Bring forth offsprings, ~ one's kind.*

republic (रिपब्लिक) noun
गणराज्य, गणतंत्र, a state in which the supreme power rests in public. *~ of India.*

repute (रिप्यूट) adjective
प्रसिद्धि, नाम करना, सुविख्यात होना, to be deemed at. *He was ~ d to be millionaire.*

request (रिक्वैस्ट) noun
प्रार्थना करना, विनय के साथ माँगना, a petition, asking for something to be given. *Make a ~ for further stay.*

require (रिक्वायर) verb
चाहना, माँगना, to need, to want. *All cars ~ regular servicing.*

rescue (रैसक्यू) verb
खतरे से बचाना, save from danger. *~ the child from drowning.*

research (रिसर्च) noun
खोज, अन्वेषण, शोध, investigation.

resent (रिज़ैन्ट) verb
नाराज होना, take ill, be angry at. *He ~ed my absence.*

reserve (रिज़र्व) noun
संचित, kept for use in future. *A ~ fund. The gold ~ to cover the issue of currency notes.*

reside (रिज़ाइड) verb
बसना, रहना, dwell, live. *He ~ s in London. Political power ~s in military strength.*

resignation (रैज़िगनेशन) noun
पदत्याग, इस्तीफ़ा, leaving a job. *The Minister submitted his ~.*

resolve (रिसौल्व) verb
हल करना, to analyse, to solve, to determine. *~ into factors. ~ to do a thing. ~ the problem.*

resort (रिजौर्ट) noun
आश्रय, विश्रामगृह, final available resource to. *~ to war. Auli (in U.P) is a skiing ~.*

resource (रिसोर्स) noun
साधन, स्रोत, support, aid. *We must make the utmost use of our ~s.*

respect (रैस्पैक्ट) noun
आदर, सम्मान, esteem. *I have no ~ for cowards.*

respiration (रैस्पिरेशन) noun
श्वास क्रिया, breathing for release of energy.

respond (रैस्पौंड) verb
जवाब देना, प्रतिक्रिया करना, act in answer, to react. *I ~ed to his letter with a phone call.*

response (रेस्पौंस) **noun**
उत्तर, answer, प्रतिक्रिया, अनुक्रिया, reaction. *In ~ to your letter of enquiry. She made no ~ to my query.*

rest (रैस्ट) **noun**
आराम, repose. *Sunday is the day of ~ for many.* अवशेष, बाकी, remainder. *Eat what you wish and leave the ~.*

restaurant (रेस्त्राँ) noun
जलपान गृह, भोजनालय, place where refreshment may be had. *Taking tea in a ~.*

restrict (रैस्ट्रिक्ट) verb
सीमा बांधना, रोकना, to limit, to confine. *The high rise buildings ~ our vision.*

result (रिज़ल्ट) noun
परिणाम, नतीजा, outcome, effect. *Their negligence ~ed in heavy loss. Undue haste ~s badly.*

resume (रिज़्यूम) verb
फिर से करना, दोबारा शुरू करना, to restart after a pause. *He has ~d his duty after two months.*

retail (रिटेल) noun
खुदरा बिक्री, sale of goods to ultimate consumers. *Most of us buy in ~.*

retain (रिटेन) verb
रोक रखना, याद रखना, keep in check, remember. *I ~ a clear memory of my school days.*

retire (रिटायर) verb
सेवानिवृत्त होना, चले जाना, हट जाना, सोने के लिए जाना, stop working at a certain age, withdraw, go away. *I usually ~ at 9 P.M. Some officers in the army are retiring next month.*

return (रिटर्न) noun
वापसी, to come back. *On your ~.* लाभ, आय-व्यय का विवरण, statement of one's income. *Have you submitted your ~s of income this year?* पुनरावृत्ति, a recurrence. *Many happy ~s of the day!*

revenge (रिवेन्ज) noun
बदला, प्रतिशोध, प्रतिकार, to take vengeance for, inflict punishment for. *He ~ed his brother's death.*

revenue (रेवेन्यू) noun
राज्य की वार्षिक आय, total annual income of the state. *Source of ~. Public ~. A ~ officer.*

reverse (रिवर्स) adjective
उल्टी, opposite in position, विपरीत, *Going in ~ direction. Counting in the ~ direction.*

review (रिव्यू) verb
पुनर्विचार, निरीक्षण करना, समीक्षा करना, consider or examine again. *~ last month's work.* समालोचना *His new drama has been adversely ~ed.*

revise (रिवाइज़) verb
दोहराना, फिर पढ़ना, to amend. *He is revising his notes for the test.*

revive (रिवाइव) verb
फिर से जीवन में लाना, होश में लाना, bring back to life. *~ the person, who has fainted.*

revolt (रिवोल्ट) verb
विद्रोह या क्रान्ति करना, rebel. *The Romans ~ed against Caesar.*

reward (रिवार्ड) noun
प्रतिफल, पुरस्कार, prize. *The ~ of virtue. A ~ of Rs.500 for information about lost child.*

rhyme (राइम) noun
तुक, तुकान्त कविता, similarity of sound of the last words of the line of a verse, e.g., feet, beat, meat, heat; dream, beem, seem, team.

rib (रिब) noun
पसली, a curved bone

extending from the backbone round the chest. *There are 24 ~s in our body.* पत्ती की नस, vein of leaf. *The ~s of leaf keeps it straight.*

rice (**राइस**) noun
चावल, grain used as staple food.

rich (**रिच**) adjective
धनी, मालदार, wealthy. *The ~ should help the poor.* कीमती, शानदार, costly, splendid (clothes, jewels, etc.) मात्रा में अधिक, abundant. *Our country is ~ in iron and coal. A ~ diet, A ~ harvest,* शानदार, sumptuous, भव्य. *To wear ~ dress on one's wedding day.*

rid (**रिड**) verb
मुक्त करना, हटाना, साफ़ करना, निकालना, cleaning away anything undesirable, relief from something. *How I wish I could get ~ of the unwelcome visitor. We were glad to get ~ of bad company.*

ride (**राइड**) verb
सवारी करना, सफ़र, to take a journey on a bicycle, horseback or in a public vehicle. *Go for a ~.*

ridicule (**रिडिक्यूल**) noun
उपहास, हँसी ठट्ठा करना, mockery, making fun of. *You needn't ~ my proposal in public.*

right (**राईट**) adverb
ठीक, सीधी, straight, direct. *Put it ~ in the middle of the field.*

right (**राइट**) noun
ठीक बात, अधिकार, what is just, good. *He has no ~ in that property.*

right (**राइट**) adjective
सीधे हाथ की ओर, opposite of left. *Towards the side of the ~ hand. Taj Mahal stands on the ~ side of Yamuna.*

rigid (**रिजिड**) adjective
सख्त, कठोर, दृढ़, stiff, unbending. *A ~ person he is.*

rim (**रिम**) noun
पहिए का किनारा, ring of the wheel. चश्मा, शीशा आदि का चौखटा, रिम लगाना, किनारा बनाना *The mirror has been ~med.*

ring (**रिंग**) noun
अँगूठी, मुँदरी, circular band worn round a finger. *A wedding ~.* कान की बाली, *Ear ~.* गोला, वृत्त, circle. *The boys stood in a ~.* सर्कस का घेरा जिसके अन्दर खेलों का प्रदर्शन होता है, छुपे तौर पर काम करने का समूह. *A ~ of dope smugglers.*

rinse (**रिन्स**) verb
साफ़ पानी से धोना, wash with clean water to remove soap, dirt, etc. *~ the soap out of the cloth.*

riot (**रॉयट**) noun
बलवा, हंगामा, outburst of lawlessness. *A communal ~.*

ripe (**राइप**) adjective
पका हुआ, पूर्ण विकसित, fully developed, ripe mangoes.

The time is ~ for a new foreign policy.

rise (राइज़) verb
क्षितिज से ऊपर आना, appear from the horizon (sun, moon, stars, etc.) उठ जाना, get up. *He ~s at 5. P.M..* उन्नति करना, पुनः जीवित होना, *Christ rose again from the dead.*

risk (रिस्क) noun
संकट, danger. *There is no ~ in going there by train.*

rite (राइट) noun
धार्मिक रीति रिवाज, संस्कार, आचार, रस्म, way of performing religious service. *Matrimonial ~s.*

road (रोड) noun
सड़क, a way or course.

roam (रोम) verb
आवारा घूमना, walk aimlessly. *How long have you been ~ing here?*

rock (रौक) noun
पत्थर, पाषाण, शिला, चट्टान, hard stone of earth crust, तालबद्ध संगीत, a kind of music.

rod (रॉड) noun
डंडा, छड़, straight piece of wood or metal. *A fishing ~. The ~ of policemen.*

rogue (रोग) noun
बदमाश, आवारा, धूर्त, scoundrel, a knavish person.

role (रोल) noun
नाटक के पात्र का अभिनय, actor's part in a play. *The ~ of Rama in the T.V. serial Ramayana.*

roll (रौल) noun
लपेट कर बनाया हुआ घेर, something rolled up into the shape of a cylinder. *A ~ of cloth. A ~ of bread.*

romance (रोमान्स) noun
प्रेम कहानी, love story, प्रणय, a love affair, वीर गाथा, heroic tale.

roof (रूफ़) noun
छप्पर, छत, top covering. *Put this box on the ~ of the bus.*

root (रूट) noun
जड़, part of plant that keeps it firm in the soil and absorbs water, minerals, etc. from the soil.

rope (रोप) noun
रस्सी, रस्सा, cord, string. *A piece of ~.*

rose (रोज़) verb
उठा, निकला, past tense of rise. *The sun ~ at 6.25 A.M. today.*

rose (रोज़) noun
गुलाब, a kind of sweetsmelling red flower.

rosy (रोज़ी) noun
गुलाबी, pink or pinkish red. *~ cheeks of the baby.*

rot (रौट) verb
सड़ना, खराब होना, decay. *Stale food soon ~s.*

rough (रफ़) adjective
खुरदरा, असमतल, having rugged

surface, मैला-कुचैला, shaggy, *A dog with a ~ coat,* ऊबड़-खाबड़, uneven, गुन्डा, लफंगा, a rowdy, ruffian, खराब, स्वादरहित, tasteless, insipid.

round (राउन्ड) noun
गोल, circular, *A ~ field,* फेरा, चक्कर, दौरा, *The doctor's ~ in the hospital.* चारों ओर, *The earth moves ~ the sun.*

rub (रब) verb
रगड़ने की क्रिया, the process of rubbing. *Give the floor a good ~.*

rubber (रबर) noun
रबड़, hard elastic matter for making tubes, bladder, etc. निरोध, a condom.

rubber (रबर) noun
ताश के खेल में दो बाज़ी जीतना *We have won the ~ by winning two games out of three.*

rubbish (रबिश) noun
कूड़ा-कचरा, refuse, waste, *A heap of ~.* बकवास, nonsense. *That novel is all ~.*

rude (रूड) adjective
असभ्य, गँवार, अभद्र, uncultured, crude, impolite. *It is ~ to keep sitting when your teacher enters the class.*

ruin (रुइन) noun
विनाश, पतन, downfall. *Gambling was the main cause of his ~.*

rule (रूल) noun
पैमाना, फुटा, a straight edged scale, *A foot ~.* नियमावली, conduct, *The ~s of cricket, football, carrom, chess.*

rumour (रूमर) noun
गप्प, अफ़वाह, gossip, hearsay. *There is a ~ of midterm elections.*

run (रन) verb
दौड़ना, going on foot at speed. *A five minute ~ before breakfast. Make ~s in cricket.* क्रिकेट के रन.

rupee (रूपी) noun
रुपया, monetary unit of India, Sri Lanka, Pakistan, Nepal. *The Indian ~ is worth 100 paise.*

rural (रूरल) noun
ग्रामीण, देहाती, of the village. *~ uplift.*

rush (रश) noun
भीड़ crowd. *~ in the market on a festival day,* तेज बहाव, rapid flow, *Swept away by the ~ of the current.* तेजी से झपटना. *~ in front.*

□□□□

S

s मुद्रण में प्रयुक्त लघु अक्षर

मूल उच्चारण **एस**

s लिखने में प्रयुक्त लघु अक्षर

स प्रयोग में उच्चारण – 'श' के लिए h लगाते हैं, ा. बिलकुल नहीं है।

अंग्रेजी वर्णमाला का उन्नीसवाँ अक्षर

sac (सैक) noun
थैली, पुट, कोश, baglike structure of an animal or plant. *A bee brings back nectar in its honey ~.*

sack (सैक) noun
थैला, बोरा, large bag. हटाना, निकालना, dismiss. *Two ~s of potatoes.*

sacred (सैक्रेड) adjective
पवित्र, धार्मिक, holy, religious. *Temples, mosques and churches are ~ places.*

sacrifice (सैक्रिफाइस) noun
बलि, बलिदान, त्याग, the slaughter of an animal for offering to a deity. *The ~ of a goat to Kali.* अर्पण करना, *Laxman ~d his pleasure for Rama's welfare.*

sad (सैड) adjective
दुःखद, खेदजनक, unhappy, sorrowful, mournful. *He is ~ because he has lost his purse.*

safe (सेफ़) adjective
सुरक्षित, निरापद, free from danger, secure. *I am quite ~ here.*

safe (सेफ़) noun
तिजोरी, लोहे की मज़बूत अलमारी, strong chest. *~ fixed in a wall.*

said (सैड) verb
कहा, past tense of say, adjective of say. *On the ~ day the market was closed.*

sail (सेल) verb
नाव या जहाज का चलना, पतवार piece of cloth to manage the boat movement. *The ship will ~ tomorrow.*

sake (सेक) noun
कारण, हित, cause, interest. *For the ~ of my family.*

salad (सैलड) noun
हरी कच्ची, साग सब्जियाँ (टमाटर, मूली, गाजर, ककड़ी, चुकन्दर, नींबू आदि), green vegetables uncooked. *Cold meat and ~.*

salary (सेलेरी) noun
वेतन, तनख्वाह, pay. *A ~ of Rs. 750 per month.*

sale (सेल) noun
बिक्री, विक्रय, offered to be sold. *Is the car for ~?.*

salt (साल्ट) noun
नमक, लवण, sodium chloride (Nacl). *Don't forget to ~ the soup.*

salute (सैल्यूट) noun
सैनिक सलामी, the raising of the hand to the forehead. *The scouts gave a ~ to the chief guest.*

same (सेम) adjective
उसी, वैसा ही, वही, उसी की तरह, unchanged, exactly alike. *We are studying in the ~ school. Put the box in the ~ room where you found it.*

sample (सैम्पल) noun
नमूना, बानगी, specimen, pattern. *~ of a new soap. ~ of tobacco.*

sanatorium (सेनेटोरियम) noun
क्षय रोगियों का आरोग्य धाम, place of treatment of consumptives in hilly areas where the climate is good.

sanction (सैंक्शन) noun
इजाजत, अनुमति approval of an action. *The measures adopted have the ~ of tradition.*

sand (सैंड) noun
बालू, रेत, fine debris of rocks. *Mix ~ with cement for plastering the wall.*

sandwich (सैंडविच) noun
दो ब्रेड के टुकड़े जिनके बीच में मक्खन, टमाटर आदि भरे हों, two or more slices of bread with butter, tomato, or meat in between.

sari (सारी) noun
साड़ी, cotton or silk cloth worn by Hindu women.

sat (सेट) verb
past tense of sit बैठा, *She ~ cross-legged on a wooden plank.*

satisfy (सैटिसफ़ाई) verb
संतुष्ट करना, give somebody what he wants. *Nothing satisfies him, he is very greedy.*

Saturn (सैटर्न) noun
शनि ग्रह, a planet of the sun.

sauce (सॉस) noun
चटनी, a semi liquid preparation used as seasoning of food. *Tomato ~.*

saucer (सौसर) noun
तश्तरी, रकाबी, round shallow dish. *Where is my cup and ~?.*

savage (सैवेज) adjective
क्रूर, भयानक, असभ्य, barbarous, uncivilized. *~ manners.*

save (सेव) verb
बचाना, सुरक्षित रखना, keep safe. *The boatman ~d the child from drowning.*

say (से) verb
कहना, utter, speak. *Have you*

anything to ~?.

scale (**स्केल**) noun
छिल्का, शल्क, horny thin plates covering the body of certain animals, fishes, crocodiles etc., परत, तह, पपड़ी, chalky material deposited on hard water, inside boilers, kettles, water pipes, etc, दाँत की मैल, the tartar on teeth.

scale (**स्केल**) noun
पैमाना, तराजू, a graduated measure, used for weighing. *This ruler has one ~ in inches and other in centimeters. A ~ has two pans, one for weights and the other for goods.*

scalp (**स्कैल्प**) noun
खोपड़ी, सिर के बाल और त्वचा, the skull.

scam (**स्कैम**) **noun**
घपला, गोलमाल, a fraudulent scheme esp., for making quick profit.

scan (**स्कैन**) verb
सावधानी से जाँच करना, to examine carefully.

scandal (**स्कैन्डल**) noun
लज्जाजनक, घृणित कार्य, act that causes public outrage or indignation. *By nature we enjoy a ~ about somebody.*

scar (**स्कार**) noun
घाव या चोट का निशान, mark left by healed wound, sore or burn, *A long ~ on his left arm.*

scarce (**स्केयर्स**) adjective
आवश्यकता से कम, insufficient to fulfil the demand. *Apples are ~ in the summer.*

scarf (**स्कार्फ़**) noun
दुपट्टा, गुलूबंद, a long, broad strip of cloth worn about the neck and shoulders. *The ~ of a scout.*

scatter (**स्कैटर**) verb
तितर-बितर करना या हो जाना, to separate and go off in different directions. *The crowd ~ ed after the speech ended.*

scene (**सीन**) noun
दृश्य, घटनास्थल, place of occurrence, view. *The boats in the river make a beautiful ~.*

scent (**सैंट**) noun
सुगंध, इत्र, an agreeable odour. *The handkerchief ~ed with lavender. The cat ~ed a mouse.*

schedule (**शैड्यूल**) noun
निर्धारित कार्यक्रम, programme of work to be done or of planned events. *Heavy fog disrupted the airline ~.*

scheme (**स्कीम**) noun
रूपरेखा, मानचित्र, representation of something. योजना-बद्ध कार्यक्रम, plan for doing something.

scholar (स्कॉलर) noun
छात्र या छात्रा, boy or girl at school, वह छात्र जिसे छात्रवृत्ति मिलती हो, a student whose merit entitles him to money. *A lady ~.* विद्वान, पंडित, *Be more ~ly in your approach to the problem.*

school (स्कूल) noun
विद्यालय, पाठशाला, a place where formal education is imparted to the children. *The ~ time is 10 to 4 P.M.*

science (साइन्स) noun
क्रमबद्ध ज्ञान, systematic knowledge. विज्ञान

scissors (सिज़र्स) noun
कैंची, cutting instruments with two blades.

scold (स्कोल्ड) verb
डाँटना, फटकारना, झिड़की देना, rebuff, rebuke. *He ~ed his servant for breaking the new plates.*

scooter (स्कूटर) noun
स्कूटर गाड़ी, light motorcycle with small wheels and low seat. *To travel on a ~.*

scope (स्कोप) noun
विस्तार, आशय, गंतव्य, extent, range of outlook. *An investigation of wide ~.*

score (स्कोर) noun
हिसाब, count. खेलों में रनों, गोलों, अंकों आदि का योग. *Are you going to ~ in the match?*

scorpion (स्कॉर्पियन) noun
बिच्छू. an arachnid with poisonous sting in the tail.

scoundrel (स्काउन्ड्रल) noun
बदमाश, दुष्ट, villain, rascal. *He is a first class ~.*

scout (स्काउट) noun
बालचर, *Boy ~, Girl ~.*

scrap (स्क्रैप) noun
बेकार के टुकड़े, small pieces of raw material, discarded matter. *Give these ~s to the dog.*

scratch (स्क्रैच) adjective
खरोंच, मामूली चोट, a slight injury, mark.

screen (स्क्रीन) noun
सिनेमा के चित्र दिखाने वाला पर्दा, black surface on T.V. or computer, चलचित्र। *Write songs for the ~.* यवनिका.

screw (स्क्रू) noun
पेंच, a cylinder grooved spirally, driven into wood or metal.

script (स्क्रिप्ट) noun
लिपि, टंकण के सदृश हस्तलिपि, system of writing. *Written in Devnagri ~. The examiner had to mark 250 ~s.*

scrutiny (स्क्रूटिनी) noun
अनुरीक्षण, जाँच पड़ताल, thorough & detailed enquiry. *A close ~ of election results.*

sea (सी) noun
सागर, समुद्र, the great part of salty water covering the greater part of earth's surface. *Ship rolls on the ~s.*

seal (सील) noun
समुद्र में रहने वाली मछली, a kind of fish eating sea animals.

seal (सील) noun
मुहर, (लाख, चपड़ा, मोम आदि की) जो दरवाजे, बॉक्स, पैकेट, पत्र पर सुरक्षा की दृष्टि से लगाई जाती है, piece of wax, lead, etc., to stamp with a design, a letter, box or door to guard against its being opened by a wrong person.

search (सर्च) verb
खोज, तलाश, तलाशी लेना, examine thoroughly. *~ one's pockets. A ~ for missing purse. ~ out the lost child.*

season (सीजन) noun
ऋतु, मौसम any division of the year according to the weather, spring, summer, autumn, winter, किसी वस्तु का उपलब्ध होना. *The mango ~. The football ~. The nestling ~.*

seat (सीट) noun
बैठने का स्थान, place to sit. *Please take your ~.*

seclude (सिक्लूड) verb
समाज से दूर रखना, keep away from society. *He leads a ~d life.*

second (सैकन्ड) adjective
द्वितीय, दूसरा, next after the first. *Monday is the ~ day of the week. Travelling in a ~ class compartment. A ~ floor apartment, ~ gear in a car.* मिनट का 60वाँ भाग, sixtieth part of a minute.

seconds (सैकन्डस) noun
घटिया किस्म का माल, goods of inferior quality. *Some of the articles you see are ~s.*

secret (सीक्रेट) adjective
रहस्य, गुप्त, mystery. something not known to many. *A ~ door. His arrest is a ~ . What is the ~ of his success?*

secretary (सैक्रेटरी) noun
सचिव, officer appointed to look after certain department. *~ to the Prime Minister. ~ of the Treasury.*

section (सैक्शन) noun
किसी वस्तु का एक अंश, टुकड़ा, खंड, part. *The ~s of a building.*

secure (सिक्यूर) verb
सुरक्षित करना, to make safe. *~ all the doors and windows before leaving the house.*

seduce (सिड्यूस) verb
पथभ्रष्ट करना, कुमार्ग, पाप में लगाना, *~ a man to betray his country.* किसी को बहला फुसला कर शारीरिक संबंध स्थापित करना. *Men are ~d by beauty and wit.*

see (सी) verb
देखना, अवलोकन करना, to perceive

with the eye. *I ~ things differently now.*

seed (सीड) noun
बीज, that which is sown, किसी भावना का प्रारंभ. *Sow the ~s of value in children.*

seek (सीक) verb
किसी चीज़ की तलाश में जाना, to go in search of. *To ~ the truth. To ~ a place of rest. To ~ a person.*

seem (सीम) verb
दिखाई देना, appear. *He ~s to be wise.*

seep (सीप) verb
किसी द्रव का रिसना, चूना, to pass, to flow, or ooze gradually. *Water ~ing through cracks in the wall.*

seize (सीज़) verb
कब्जे में करना, grasp, take hold of forcibly. *~ a weapon. ~ the chance to make some money.*

seldom (सैल्डम) adverb
कभी-कभी, not often. *She ~ leaves her house.*

select (सैलेक्ट) verb
चुनना, छाँटना, to choose, pick out. *~ somebody as the team leader.*

selfish (सैल्फ़िश) noun
स्वार्थी, a man of personal interest. *He is very ~.*

self (सैल्फ) noun
स्व, स्वयं का, अपना, used as suffix in certain pronouns, e.g., myself, yourself, herself, himself, itself, उपसर्ग

sell (सैल) verb
बेचना, बिक्री करना, obtain a price in exchange for. *~ oranges for four rupees a dozen. I ~ insurance.*

semen (सीमन) noun
वीर्य, sperm bearing fluid of male animal.

semi (सेमी) preposition
'आधा' अर्थ देने वाला उपसर्ग, having the sense of half. *~ circle, ~ annual, ~ weekly.*

seminar (सेमीनार) noun
विचार गोष्ठी, a group of students undertaking an advanced course of study.

send (सैन्ड) verb
भेजना, to permit to go. *I sent my son to college. ~ a messenger.*

senior (सीनियर) adjective
अधिक आयु वाला, older in years. *My brother is five years ~ to me.* पद में ऊँचा, of higher rank. *He is a ~ student in the college.*

senior citizen (सीनियर सिटीजन) noun
अवकाशप्राप्त नागरिक (65 वर्ष से ऊपर का), an elderly person.

sense (सैन्स) noun
तर्कशक्ति तथा विचार, faculties of reason and judgement. *~ of*

understanding. To have no ~ of responsibility.

sensual (सैन्सुअल) adjective
शरीरिक आनन्द से संबंधित, related to sexual pleasure, कामी, दुराचारी, *A life devoted to ~ pleasures.*

sentence (सेन्टेन्स) noun
वाक्य, a group of words conveying a complete sense, निर्णय, दण्ड। *The culprit has been ~d to pay a fine of Rs. 10,000.*

sentiment (सैन्टीमैन्ट) noun
मनोभाव, भावना, mental feeling, emotions. *There is a general ~ in the country in favour of cut in defence expenditure.*

sentry (सैन्ट्री) noun
सन्तरी, चौकीदार, watchman.

separate (सैपरेट) verb
अलग अलग करना, to isolate. *France is ~ed from England by the channel.*

septic (सैप्टिक) adjective
सड़न पैदा करने वाला, involving infection, usually a pus-forming microbe. *The wound has become ~.*

septum (सैप्टम) noun
नासिकाओं के बीच का पर्दे जैसा पर्दा a dividing wall.

sequence (सीक्वैन्स) noun
अनुगम, परम्परा, following one thing after another, succession. *A list of books in alphabetical ~. The ~ of events.*

serene (सीरीन) adjective
शान्त, अचंचल, calm, peaceful. *A ~ landscape. A ~ look. A ~ smile.*

sergeant (सार्जन्ट) noun
सार्जन्ट, a non-commissioned army officer of a rank above that of a corporal.

serial (सीरियल) adjective
क्रमानुसार, सिलसिलेवार, in series, in a row. *The ~ numbers of the book. The ~ of Ramayana on T.V.*

series (सीरीज) noun
श्रंखला, परिपाटी, a sequence, *A T.V. ~. A new ~ of readers for students of English.*

serious (सीरियस) adjective
गंभीर, grave, weighty, sincere, *Looking ~. A ~ illness. A worker. I take the threat very ~ly.*

serpent (सर्पेन्ट) noun
सर्प, साँप, snake, शैतान, चालाक, द्वेषपूर्ण व्यक्ति, wily, treacherous, or malicious person. *Beware of ~s.*

servant (सर्वेन्ट) noun
घरेलू अथवा सरकारी कार्य के लिए रखा गया नौकर, person employed for domestic or public work. *Engage a ~. Policeman is a public ~. Science is a good ~ but a bad master.*

serve (सर्व) verb
सेवा करना, नौकरी करना, to work for somebody. *He ~s us as a*

watchman. To ~ a cause.

service **(सर्विस)** noun
सेवा, सहायता, help, aid. *To do someone a ~. The manufacturer guarantees ~.*

session **(सैशन)** noun
सत्र, अधिवेशन, a portion of the year in which instructions are organized at a college. *I was in class VIII during the ~ 1981-82. The winter ~ of the parliament.*

set **(सैट)** verb
क्षितिज के नीचे चले जाना, go below horizon. *The sun ~s in the west.* सही क्रम में रखना, किसी काम को करना, प्रदर्शन हेतु रखना।

set **(सैट)** noun
एक सी वस्तुओं का समूह. *A dinner ~.* एक से व्यक्तियों का समूह. *A literary ~,* एक पूरा यंत्र. *A T.V. ~.*

settle **(सैटल)** verb
स्थायी रूप से बस जाना, establish permanently. *Many Indians have ~ d in the States.* समझौता करना. *The law suit was ~d amicably.*

several **(सैवरल)** adjective
अनेक, कई, कुछ, various, some but not many. *I have read this story ~ times.* अलग अलग, separately. *The partners in this firm are jointly and ~ly responsible to its creditors.*

severe **(सीवियर)** adjective
सख्त, कठोर, असहनीय, strict, grave, difficult to bear. *~ punishment. ~ headache. ~ly dealt with.*

sew **(स्यू)** verb
सिलाई करना, stitch together. *~ a shirt.* वार्ता आदि में सफलता प्राप्त करना. *They ~ed up the deal.*

sewer **(स्यूअर)** noun
मल, गंदे पानी की नाली, public drain to carry off waste matter or filth. sewage.

sex **(सैक्स)** noun
लिंग भेद, नर या नारी, character of either being male or female. कामुकता से आलिंगन करना. *They were really ~ing it up last night.* संभोग करना, to engage in sexual intercourse.

shade **(शेड)** noun
छाया, शरण, shadow, shelter. *Standing in the ~ of a tree.*

shadow **(शैडो)** noun
परछाई, shade cast by an object. *The child is afraid of its own ~.* सदा साथ रहने वाला *The dog was his ~.* निगरानी करना *He felt he was being ~ed.* खिन्नता पैदा करना. *The incident ~ed their meeting.*

shaft **(शैफ़्ट)** noun
बरछे या तीर आदि का डंडा, a pole of various weapons, व्यंग्य बाण, sarcasm. *~s of sarcasm.*

shake **(शेक)** verb
हिलाना, झकझोरना, move from side to side, up and down, घबराहट पैदा करना, disturb profoundly. *They were badly ~n by the*

news of death. We shook the mangoes from the tree, प्रकम्पन, shaken. *A ~ of the head.*

shall (शैल) verb
सहायक क्रिया, (गा, गी, गे). *I ~ reach Lucknow in the evening by this bus.*

shallow (शैलो) adjective
छिछला, of no great depth, *A ~ pond,* तुच्छ, ओछा, *A ~ argument, A ~ writer, A ~ brained fellow.*

shame (शेम) noun
लज्जा, शर्म, humiliation. *I was overcome with ~.* disgrace. *You have put your family to great ~ by your wicked deeds.* अपयश, dishonour. *Put someone to ~. What a ~ to cheat a blind man!.*

shampoo (शैम्पू) noun
बाल साफ़ करने का मिश्रण, a preparation for washing hair. *A new perfumed ~.*

shank (शैंक) noun
पिंडली, leg between the knee and ankle. *Long thin ~s of a lady.*

shape (शेप) noun
स्थिति, अवस्था, condition. *To assume a ~.*

shape (शेप) verb
आकृति प्रदान करना. *The statue is perfect in ~.*

share (शेयर) noun
भाग, खंड, a portion of something. *They had a ~ in the property. I purchased 10 ordinary. ~s of Modi Mills Ltd.* कई भागों में विभक्त करना, divide into many parts. *~ the sweets between them.*

sharp (शार्प) adjective
तेज धार वाला, तीखा, fine edge, *A ~ blade.*

she (शी) pronoun
मादा, नारी, वह स्त्री, female person or animal.

shelter (शैल्टर) noun
आश्रयस्थल, something serving as protection from heat, cold, etc., शरण, पनाह, refuge. *A tin shade is a good ~ against rain and dew.*

shine (शाइन) verb
चमकना, प्रकाश देना, to give light. *The sun is shining.*

ship (शिप) noun
जलयान, पोत, भाववाचक संज्ञा बनाने का प्रत्यय, *friend~, workman ~.*

shirt (शर्ट) noun
कमीज़, man's garment for upper part of the body.

shit (शिट) noun
बेकार वस्तु, मल, बकवास, worthless person or thing.

shock (शॉक)
आघात, धक्का, a violent emotion. *The ~ of a heavy loss.* बिजली से धक्का लगना, effect caused by electric current through the body.

shoe (शू) noun
जूता, boot, घोड़े की नाल, metal plate nailed to the hoof of the horse.

shoot (शूट) verb
गोली मारना, ऊँचा उठाना, move, go, rise suddenly. *Prices are ~ing up suddenly.*

shop (शॉप) noun
दुकान, a place where goods are sold. *A grain ~.*

short (शौर्ट) adjective
छोटा, लघु, opposite of long अल्पकालिक, brief in duration. *He lived here for a ~ time.*

shot (शॉट) verb
चलाई हुई गोली, the act of shooting.

should (शुड) verb
shall का भूतकाल, past tense of shall. *I ~ be pleased.* परामर्श या सुझाव देने में प्रयोग, used to denote advise or suggestion. *We ~ obey our parents.*

shoulder (शोल्डर) noun
कन्धा, स्कन्ध, part of body by which the arm is connected.

shout (शाउट) noun
चिल्लाना, पुकार, loud cry, a call. *~s of joy.*

show (शो) verb
दिखाना, an appearance. *Voting by ~ of hands,* प्रदर्शनी, an exhibition. *A flower ~.*

shut (शट) verb
बन्द कर देना, to close. *~ the door and windows.*

shy (शाई) adjective
शर्मीला, लज्जाशील, bashful, संकोची, डरपोक, timid. *The child feels ~ among strangers.*

sick (सिक) adjective
बीमार, अस्वस्थ, ill, unwell. *He caught cold and fell ~.*

side (साइड) noun
भुजा, bounding surface. *A triangle has three ~s.* तरफ, पहलू, दृष्टिकोण, an aspect or phase. *Consider all ~ s of a problem.*

siege (सीज) noun
चारों ओर से घेरा डालना, besiege. *~ of Leningrad.*

sight (साइट) noun
देखने की शक्ति, power of seeing दृश्य, a view. *His eye~ is weak.*

sign (साइन) noun
चिह्न, निशान, symbol used to represent something. *Dark clouds are a ~ of rain.*

sign (साइन) verb
हस्ताक्षर करना, put one's name on a letter, document. *Please ~ a cheque.*

signal (सिग्नल) noun
चिह्न, sign, सूचक, indicator. *Traffic ~s. A siren is a ~ of an air raid during wartime.*

silence (साइलेन्स) noun
शान्ति, खामोशी, condition of

being quiet. *The ~ of night.*

silk (सिल्क) noun
रेशम, a fine fibre obtained from the cocoon of silkworms. रेशमी वस्त्र Famous Chinese ~.

silver (सिल्वर) noun
चाँदी, रजत, shining white precious metal. *A chain of ~.*

similar (सिमिलर) adjective
मिलता जुलता, एक समान, having resemblance. *Silver is ~ in colour to steel.*

simple (सिम्पल) adjective
साधारण, सामान्य ढंग से, easy to understand. *A ~ child. A ~ way of life.*

sin (सिन) noun
पाप, दुष्कर्म, अनैतिक कार्य, transgression of divine law. *The ~ of Adam.*

since (सिन्स) adverb
तब से, उस समय से, between some time in the past and present time. *He has not been coming to school ~ Monday.*

sincere (सिन्सियर) adjective
सच्चा, ईमानदार, free from deceit, hypocrisy or falseness. *Are you ~ in your efforts?*

sing (सिंग) verb
गाना, कूजना, to produce melodious sounds. *The crickets are ~ing in the bushes.*

single (सिंगिल) adjective
अकेला, केवल एक, one only, one in number, unique. *A ~ example.*

singular (सिंगूलर) noun
अपनी किस्म का एक ही, unusual or strange, outstanding, एकवचन. *A woman of ~ courage.*

sink (सिंक) verb
डूबना, निमग्न होना, sunken, go down. *The sun ~s in the west.* fixed basin गंदे पानी को ले जाने वाला गड्ढा, *A kitchen ~. A bath room ~.*

sir (सर) noun
आदरसूचक शब्द, श्रीमान, used as a polite way of addressing a man. *May I go out, ~? My dear ~.*

Sir (सर) noun
सर का ब्रिटिश खिताब, title used before the first name of a knight. *~ Edward, ~ John Jackson.*

sister (सिस्टर) noun
बहन, भगिनी, a female sibling, प्रधान परिचारिका, a nurse in charge of hospital ward.

sit (सिट) verb
बैठना, rest with body supported by the buttocks either on a seat or on the ground. *Don't ~ there, the place is dirty.*

situation (सिचुएशन) noun
स्थिति, the state of affairs. *The ~ of the house allowed for a beautiful view. The present*

international ~ is alarming.

six (सिक्स) adjective
छः, half a dozen.

size (साइज़) noun
आकार, माप, the spatial dimension. *They are of the same ~.*

sketch (स्कैच) noun
ख़ाका, रेखाकृति, drawing. *A ~ map of India.*

skin (स्किन) noun
खाल, त्वचा, outer covering of an animal body, *Black ~.*

skirt (स्कर्ट) noun
लहँगा, घुटने तक का यूरोपिअन वस्त्र, one piece garment from the waist to the ankle.

sky (स्काई) noun
आसमान, गगन, the blue canopy over our head. *A starry ~.*

slap (स्लैप) verb
थप्पड़ मारना, तमाचा लगाना, strike with the open hand. *To ~ somebody on the face.*

sleep (स्लीप) noun
नींद, निद्रा, slumber, condition of rest at night.

sleeve (स्लीव) noun
आस्तीन, part of garment that covers the arm. *Roll up the ~s of your shirt.*

slip (स्लिप) noun
फिसलना, slide. *One ~ and you could fall off the cliff.* संतुलन खोना, गिर जाना, lose one's balance and fall. *He ~ped on the muddy road and broke his leg.*

slow (स्लो) adjective
सुस्त, not quick. *A ~ worker.* मन्द, धीमा, dull. *A ~ student. My watch is 5 minutes ~.*

small (स्मौल) adjective
छोटा, not large, *A ~ dinner party.* दीन, साधारण, humble. *In ~ circumstances.*

smart (स्मार्ट) adjective
फुर्तीला, bright, clean. *Looking ~ in a new suit.* फैशन वाला, fashionable. चतुर, होशियार, clever, skillful.

smell (स्मैल) noun
बू, सूंघना, सूंघने की शक्ति, sense of smell. *Dogs can find things by ~.*

smile (स्माइल) noun
मुस्कराहट, मुस्कराना, pleased expression. *There was a ~ on his face.*

smoke (स्मोक) noun
धुंआ, sooty vapour and gases. *~ coming out of factory chimneys.*

smooth (स्मूथ) adjective
चिकना, समतल, not rough to the touch. *A ~ piece of wood.*

snake (स्नेक) noun
साँप, सर्प, a reptile, दगाबाज, a treacherous person.

snow (स्नो) noun
तुषार, पाला, बर्फ, soft white flakes of frozen water falling

from the sky. *A heavy fall of ~.*

so (सो) adverb
इस प्रकार से, in such a manner. *As you treat me, ~ I shall treat you.* तदनुसार, to that extent, उसी रीति से, लगभग उतना ही, approximately, इस कारण, therefore. *It was Sunday, ~ the bank was closed.*

social (सोशल) noun
सामाजिक, living in groups. *Man is a ~ animal.*

sock (सॉक) noun
मोजा, जुराब, a short stocking covering ankle and lower part of the leg. *A pair of ~s.*

soft (सॉफ़्ट) adjective
मुलायम, चिकना, smooth to the touch. *Butter is ~. A ~ pillow.*

soil (सौइल) noun
जमीन, मिट्टी, the upper portion of earth's surface. *Erosion of ~.*

solar (सोलर) adjective
सूर्य संबंधी, of the sun.

sold (सोल्ड) verb
past tense of sell. बेचा, बेच दिया गया. *He ~ his pen for 5 rupees.*

soldier (सोल्जर) noun
सैनिक, सिपाही, person engaged in military service.

solid (सॉलिड) adjective
ठोस, not hollow. *A ~ wall. ~ masses of clouds.*

solution (सोल्यूशन) noun
घोल, विलयन. *The ~ of sugar in tea/milk/water.* किसी समस्या का समाधान, हल, solve a problem.

some (सम) adjective
कुछ, थोड़ा, तनिक, ज़रा, an unspecified amount. *There's ~ ice in the fridge.*

son (सन) noun
पुत्र, बेटा, male child. *Come in, my ~, and take your seat.*

song (सौंग) noun
गीत, गाना, a musical piece adapted for singing. *She sang a good ~.*

soon (सून) adverb
जल्दी, अल्प समय में, in a short time. I shall be back ~.

soot (सूट) noun
कालिख, कलौंच, *Black ~.*

sorrow (सौरो) noun
रंज, अफ़सोस, दुःख, grief, sadness, regret. *His ~ is great.*

sorry (सौरी) adjective
खिन्न, उदास, feeling regret. *I am ~ at your loss,* क्षमा या खेद की भावना प्रकट करने हेतु, to express apology or regret. *I am ~, I can't lend you my book.*

soul (सोल) noun
आत्मा, रूह, spiritual part of a person. *His whole ~ revolted against it.*

sound (साउन्ड) noun
ध्वनि, आवाज. *What is this ~ about?*

soup (सूप) noun
रसा, शोरबा, liquid food, broth, *Tomato ~.*

sour (सोर) adjective
खट्टा, bitter or sharp in taste. *The grapes are ~.*

source (सोर्स) noun
उद्‌गमस्थल, origin. *Where does the Ganga has its ~? What is the ~ of your income?*

south (साउथ) noun
दक्षिण दिशा, direction opposite to north. *Sri Lanka lies to the ~ of India.*

sow (सो) verb
बीज बोना, to scatter seeds over land for growth. *~ the field with wheat.*

space (स्पेस) noun
अन्तरिक्ष, शून्य आकाश, the unlimited, 3-dimensional expanse in which all material objects are located and all events occur. *The universe exists in ~.*

spare (स्पेयर) adjective
जिसकी फ़िलहाल ज़रूरत न हो, kept in reserve. कम, अल्प, अपर्याप्त, छोड़ना, क्षमा करना. *He doesn't ~ himself .*

speak (स्पीक) verb
बोलना, to utter words, बातचीत करना, to converse. *To ~ with somebody.*

special (स्पैशल) adjective
खास, विशेष, particular, peculiar. *What are your ~ hobbies?*

specific (स्पैसिफ़िक) adjective
निश्चित, ठीक ठीक, explicate, precise. *Tell me your ~ requirements.*

specs (स्पैक्स) noun
चश्मा, ऐनक, eyeglass, spectacles. *She wears ~.*

speech (स्पीच) noun
आवाज, वाणी, भाषण, the faculty of speaking. *He is very polite in ~.*

speed (स्पीड) noun
गति, फुर्ती, swiftness. *To move with great ~.*

spell (स्पैल) verb
शब्दों के अक्षरों को बताना, give the letters of words. *How would you ~ knowledge?*

spend (स्पैन्ड) verb
व्यय करना, उपयोग करना, गुजारना, दे डालना, त्याग करना, to pay out, wear out, waste. *He ~s too much money on books.*

sperm (स्पर्म) noun
शुक्राणु, male reproductive cell.

spice (स्पाइस) noun
मसाला, aromatic vegetable substance for flavoring food, उमंग, उत्साह, an interesting element, zest. *A ~ of humour in his solemnity.*

spider (स्पाइडर) noun
मकड़ी, eight-legged insect which spins webs.

spinach (स्पिनेक) noun
पालक, a green vegetable cultivated for its succulent leaves.

spirit (स्पिरिट) noun
आत्मा, the principle of conscious life. स्प्रिट, एल्कोहल *Use of ~ in burning lamps.*

spoon (स्पून) noun
चम्मच, a piece of cutlery.

sport (स्पोर्ट) noun
खेल-कूद, athletics. हँसी मजाक, playful trifling, jesting or mirth.

spot (स्पोट) noun
धब्बा, निशान, stain. *~s on the face.*

spot (स्पॉट) adjective
तुरन्त, तत्कालीन, at once. *~ payment.*

spray (स्प्रे) noun
फुहार, बौछार, a jet of fine particles of liquid discharged from an atomizer for direct application to a surface.

spread (स्प्रैड) verb
फैलाना, खोलना, ढकना, to unroll, to unfold. *The bird ~s its wings.*

spring (स्प्रिंग) noun
स्रोत, सोता, an issue of water from the earth, as a stream, pool or lake, लचीलापन, elasticity or resilience. *This board has ~ in it.* कमानी, an elastic contrivance. *The ~ of a clock.* उगना, जन्म लेना, come from. *New leaves ~ up in rains.*

spy (स्पाई) noun
गुप्तचर, जासूस, to observe secretively with hostile intent.

square (स्क्वेयर) adjective
वर्गाकार, a figure having four equal sides, each angle being right angle.

squirrel (स्क्विरल) noun
गिलहरी, small bushy tailed animal with red or grey fur.

stab (स्टैब) verb
चाकू घुसेड़ना, to penetrate sharpely or painfully.

stable (स्टेबल) adjective
दृढ़, स्थिर, firm. *A ~ government.*

staff (स्टाफ) noun
कार्यालय में काम करने वाले कर्मचारी, group of persons as employees. *College ~. ~ car.*

stage (स्टेज) noun
रंगमंच, platform. स्तर, period. *First ~ of cancer.*

stair (स्टेयर) noun
सीढ़ी, सोपान, ज़ीना, series of steps for going from one level to another.

stamp (स्टाम्प) noun
ठप्पा, मुहर, impression.

stand (स्टैन्ड) verb
खड़े होना, a cessation of motion, स्टॉल, माल बेचने का स्थान, a stall. *Don't ~ in the sun.*

star (स्टार) noun
तारा, any of the heavenly bodies, मुद्रण में सितारे का चिह्न, asterisk.

start (स्टार्ट) verb
किसी कार्य का प्रारंभ करना, beginning of any work. *We ~ed at four.*

state (स्टेट) noun
स्थिति, दशा, हालत, अवस्था, the condition of a person or thing. *A solid ~. He dresses in a manner befitting his ~.* राज्य, a sovereign govt.. *The ~ of Haryana.*

station (स्टेशन) noun
रेलगाड़ी रुकने का स्थान, a regular stopping place, लोक सेवाओं का मुख्यालय, *Police ~. Fire ~.*

stationer (स्टेशनर) noun
लेखन-सामग्री विक्रेता, seller of writing materials.

stay (स्टे) verb
ठहरना, remain in a place. *~ where you are.*

steal (स्टील) verb
चुराना, to thieve. *He stole out of the house at midnight.*

steam (स्टीम) noun
वाष्प, भाप, vapour of boiling water. *~ engine.*

steel (स्टील) noun
फ़ौलाद, इस्पात, modified form of iron. *Made of ~.*

stem (स्टैम) noun
पेड़, पौधे का तना, trunk, stalk.

step (स्टैप) verb
पैर रखना, कदम रखना, to move to go. *To ~ forward.*

stick (स्टिक) noun
टहनी, बेंत, छड़ी, *A walking ~.* चिपके रहना, to cling fast to.

still (स्टिल) adjective
गतिरहित, मौन, चुपचाप, motionless, calm, quiet. *He lay ~ on the carpet.* अब भी, even now. *He is ~ unwell.*

stipend (स्टाइपैन्ड) noun
वेतन, छात्रवृत्ति, वजीफा, भत्ता, pay, scholarship, fellowship, allowance.

stich (स्टिच) noun
सिवन, सिलाई, knitting. *Put a few ~ es in the garment.*

stone (स्टोन) noun
पत्थर, शिला, पाषाण, *A pile of ~s.*

stop (स्टॉप) noun
रोकना, अटकाव, विराम. *To come to a ~.*

store (स्टोर) noun
संचय, संग्रह, गोदाम, a hoard. *There is a lot of wheat in the ~.*

storey (स्टोरी) noun
मंजिल, तल्ला, floor in a building. *A house of three ~s.*

storm (स्टॉर्म) noun
प्रचन्ड वायु, झंझावात, तूफान, a violent commotion in the air. *A ~ is blowing.*

story (स्टोरी) noun
कहानी, कल्पित कथा, बीती हुई घटनाओं

का किस्सा, a small tale, fiction. *An interesting ~.*

straight **(स्ट्रेट)** adjective
सीधा, सीध में, having no bend. *Hang the picture ~.*

strange **(स्ट्रेन्ज)** adjective
अजीब, अनोखा, विचित्र, odd, queer, unusual. *That was a ~ remark to make.*

street **(स्ट्रीट)** noun
सड़क, road. *His house is on that ~.*

strength **(स्ट्रैन्थ)** noun
शक्ति, ताकत, दृढ़ता. *~ of character, mind and will.*

strict **(स्ट्रिक्ट)** adjective
सख्त, कठोर, stern, severe. *~ measures were adopted to suppress terrorism.*

strike **(स्ट्राइक)** noun
हड़ताल, a concerted stopping of work. *A ~ by factory workers.* मारना, hit. *He struck me on my nose.*

strong **(स्ट्रान्ग)** adjective
हृष्ट–पुष्ट, हट्टा–कट्टा, having great bodily power. *A ~ boy.* दृढ़, अटल, firm, unfaltering. *He has ~ views about non- alignment.* मजबूत, financially sound. *Japan has a ~ economy.*

struggle **(स्ट्रगल)** noun
संघर्ष, झगड़ा, लड़ाई, scuffle, fight, conflict.

student **(स्टूडैन्ट)** noun
विद्यार्थी, छात्र, शिक्षार्थी, pupil at a school or college.

study **(स्टडी)** noun
अध्ययन, चिन्तन, acquisition of knowledge.

stupid **(स्टुपिड)** adjective
सुस्त, मूर्ख, mentally dull, foolish. *I found him ~ when I went to meet him.*

style **(स्टाइल)** noun
फ़ैशन, आकार, किस्म, a mode of fashion. *A very short hair ~.*

subject **(सब्जैक्ट)** noun
विषय, basic matter of thought. *A ~ for discussion.* नागरिक, citizen. *A British ~.* परतंत्र, dependent. *We are ~ to the law of the land.*

submit **(सबमिट)** verb
प्रस्तुत करना, स्वीकृति के लिए पेश करना, झुक जाना, मान लेना. to yield in obedience. *To ~ an application. ~ to superior judgement.*

subordinate **(सबआर्डिनेट)** noun
कनिष्ठ पदाधिकारी, junior in rank. *I will get it done by my ~.*

subtract **(सबट्रेक्ट)** verb
घटाना, कम करना, to take away something. *~ 14 from 25.*

success **(सक्सैस)** noun
सफलता, the prosperous termination of attempts.

such (सच) adjective
इसी प्रकार का, ऐसा. *The food, ~ as it was, was plentiful.*

suck (सक) adjective
चूसना, बच्चे द्वारा स्तन पान करना, draw into mouth. *A child ~s the mother's breast.*

sudden (सडेन) adjective
यकायक, आकस्मिक, अचानक, happening unexpectedly. *A ~ change in the weather.*

suffer (सफर) verb
तकलीफ पाना, हानि सहना, to undergo pain or distress. *The patient is still ~ing.*

sufficient (सफ़ीशेन्ट) adjective
पर्याप्त, काफी, enough to meet the requirement. *~ proof of honesty.*

sugar (शुगर) noun
गन्ने, चुकन्दर की चीनी, sweet substance obtained from sugarcane.

sum (सम) noun
योग, कुल, जोड़, total, whole. *The ~ of 6 and 8 is 14.*

summary (समरी) adjective
सारांश, संक्षेप, सार, brief, concise. *To treat someone with ~ dispatch.*

summer (समर) noun
ग्रीष्म, season between spring and autumn.

sun (सन) noun
सूर्य, सूरज, the central star that controls the body of solar system. *The ~ rises in the east.*

sunday (सनडे) noun
इतवार, रविवार, सप्ताह का प्रथम दिवस, the first day of the week.

super (सुपर) noun
ऊपर, श्रेष्ठ, उससे भी आगे, best, above, beyond. *A ~ fast train.*

supreme (सुप्रीम) adjective
सर्वोच्च, highest in rank. *The ~ court.*

sure (श्योर) adjective
निश्चित, certain. *I am not ~ of his return.*

surface (सरफेस) noun
सतह, outer face of any object. *A cube has six ~s.*

surprise (सरप्राइज़) noun
आश्चर्य, wonder, astonishment. *He looked at me in ~.*

surround (सराउण्ड) verb
चारों तरफ से घेरना, encircle. *To be ~ed by admirers.*

suspect (सस्पैक्ट) verb
शक करना, doubt. *I ~ed his statement.*

suspend (सस्पैंड) verb
ऊपर से लटकाना, to hang, कुछ समय के लिए अधिकार से वंचित कर देना, to debar for a limited period. *He was ~ed on a charge of bribery.*

swan (स्वान) noun
हंस, राजंहस, a large, beautiful water bird.

sweat **(स्वैट)** noun
पसीना, secreted from the sweat glands. *Wipe the ~ off your face.*

sweep **(स्वीप)** verb
झाड़ू लगाना, सफ़ाई करना, to clean by broom, etc. *To ~ away the dust.*

sweet **(स्वीट)** adjective
मीठा, tasting like sugar आकर्षक, ललित, सुन्दर, charming, beautiful, शुद्ध एवं स्वच्छ, fresh and pure.

swim **(स्विम)** verb
तैरना, move the body through water.

switch **(स्विच)** noun
बिजली का बटन, a device for turning on or off an electric current.

sword **(सोर्ड)** noun
तलवार, शमशीर, कृपाण, a weapon.

symbol **(सिम्बल)** noun
चिह्न, निशान, sign, mark. *Swastika was the official ~ of Nazi party.*

syrup **(सिरप)** noun
चाशनी, मीठे स्वाद की द्रव के रूप में दवा, a medicine in a sweet tasting liquid. *A cough ~.*

system **(सिस्टम)** noun
समान क्रिया करने वाले अंग, *The digestive ~.* व्यवस्था, संगठन, any assemblage or set of correlated members. *A ~ of shorthand characters.*

□□□□

T

t
मुद्रण में प्रयुक्त लघु अक्षर

t
लिखने में प्रयुक्त लघु अक्षर

मूल उच्चारण **टी**

ट द थ प्रयोग में उच्चारण — h के साथ द और थ, चाहें तो ठ भी - इनके लिए अलग अक्षर नहीं हैं।

अंग्रेजी वर्णमाला का बीसवाँ अक्षर

table (टेबल) noun
मेज, an article of furniture with four legs and a flat top. *A dressing ~.*

tact (टैक्ट) noun
व्यवहार-कुशलता, सूझबूझ, चतुरता, acting wisely.

tail (टेल) noun
पूँछ, दुम, flexible appendage to the trunk. *The dog's ~.*

tailor (टेलर) noun
दर्जी, a person whose occupation is the making and mending of garments. *An expert ~.*

take (टेक) verb
लेना, हाथ से पकड़ना, grasp, receive with hands. *Who has ~n my watch?*

tale (टेल) noun
कहानी, story, अफवाह, rumour. *Fairy ~s.*

talent (टेलेण्ट) noun
निपुणता, योग्यता, skill, ability. *He is a man of ~.*

talk (टौक) noun
वार्तालाप, बातचीत, conversation. *They had a friendly ~.*

tall (टौल) noun
ऊँचा, high. *He is ~er than his sister.*

tame (टेम) adjective
पालतू, domesticated, दब्बू, docile. *A ~ dog.*

tank (टैंक) noun
ताल, झील, जलाशय, कुंड, pool, pond, lake, तोप से सुसज्जित इस्पाती गाड़ी, *A ~ commander.*

tap (टैप) noun
टोंटी, stopper, चुपके से किसी का फ़ोन सुन लेना, act of tapping a telephone, खटखटाना, blow, knock.

tape (टेप) noun
फ़ीता, strip.

tare (टेअर) noun
बारदाने का भार, weight of the container. *Gross weight minus ~ is equal to the net weight.*

task (टास्क) noun
सौंपा गया काम, work assigned.

taste (टेस्ट) noun
स्वाद, the sense given by tongue. *It's bitter to ~.*

tax (टैक्स) noun
कर, राजस्व, money levied on goods, income tax, *Sales ~.*

tea (टी) noun
चाय, an aromatic beverage. *~ time in the afternoon.*

teach (टीच) verb
शिक्षा प्रदान करना, give lessons to somebody. *I ~ him English.*

team (टीम) noun
किसी काम, खेल अथवा व्यापार में लगे व्यक्तियों का दल, a group of persons. *A ~ of football players.*

tear (टियर) noun
आँसू, saline watery fluid secreted from eyes. *His eyes filled with ~s at his failure.*
फाड़ना, टुकड़े-टुकड़े कर देना, wrench away. *~ a sheet of paper in two.*

teeth (टीथ) noun
दाँत, plural of tooth

telephone (टेलीफ़ोन) noun
दूरभाष, phone. *Send messages by ~.*

tell (टैल) verb
कहना, बताना, to express in words. *~ me your name.*

tender (टैन्डर) noun, verb
मुलायम, नाजुक, soft, delicate, ॠण चुकता करने हेतु धन, an offer as of money, निविदा, प्रस्तुत करना, offer. *He ~ed his services on the occasion.*

tension (टेन्शन) noun
बैचेनी, क्षोभ, तनाव, खिंचाव, emotional stress, nervous strain. *Working under ~ is a major cause of heart disease.*

term (टर्म) noun
एक निश्चित समय, fixed period of time. *Elected for a ~ of six years.*

terminate (टर्मीनेट) verb
समाप्त करना, come to an end. *The meeting ~d in disorder.*

terrible (टैरिबिल) adjective
भयानक, डरावना, खौफ़नाक, awful, dreadful, fearful.

test (टैस्ट) noun, verb
परीक्षा, जाँच करना, परीक्षण करना, विश्लेषण करना, examination, analysis. *Blood ~. Stool ~.*

text (टैक्स्ट) noun
मूल पाठ, main part or matter of any script, कोई विषय, subject. *Read the ~ carefully before answering the question.*

than (दैन) conjunction
से, अपेक्षा, तुलना में, in comparison with. *He is wiser ~ his brother.*

thank (थैंक) verb
धन्यवाद देना, आभार प्रदर्शन करना, कृतज्ञता, expression of gratitude. *He returned the books with ~s.*

that (दैट) adjective
वह, कौन, इतने पर भी, used in various special constructions.

the (दी) definite article
अनेक वाक्यों और शब्दों के पूर्व उपयोग होता है *~ boy.*

their (देयर) adjective
उनका, possessive case of they. *They have lost ~ cow.*

them (दैम) pronoun
उनको, उन्हें, objective case of they. *We met ~ yesterday.*

then (दैन) adverb
तब, उस समय, at that time. *I was siting idle ~.*

there (देयर) adverb
उस स्थान पर, वहाँ, in that place. *He went ~ in the evening.* किसी वाक्य को प्रारंभ करने के लिए। *~ is somebody at the gate.*

therefore (देयरफोर) adverb
अतः, इस कारण से, thus, hence. *~ it must be wrong.*

these (दीज़) adjective
ये, यह का बहुवचन, pl. of this. *~ books are mine.*

they (दे) pronoun
वे pl. of he, she, it. *~ are going home.*

thick (थिक) adjective
मोटा, घना, गाढ़ा, dense, a thick paper. *~ milk,* घनिष्ठ, intimate. *Joseph is very ~ with Portia now.*

thief (थीफ़) noun
चोर, तस्कर, one who steals, one guilty of theft or larceny.

thigh (थाई) noun
जंघा, उरु, flesh portion of the upper part of the leg above the knee.

thin (थिन) adjective
पतला, दुबला, not flat or plump. *A ~ girl.*

thing (थिंग) noun
वस्तु, any material object. *What ~s do you like to eat?*

think (थिंक) verb
सोचना, ध्यान देना, विचार करना, to intend. *~ twice before saying anything.*

third (थर्ड) adjective
तृतीय, तीसरा, next after the second. *March is the ~ month of the year.*

thirst (थर्स्ट) noun
प्यास, तृष्णा, strong desire for water or anything.

this (दिस) adjective
यह *Look at ~ picture.*

thorn (थौर्न) noun
काँटा, sharp stem.

thorough (थौरो) adjective
पूरा, पूर्ण, complete, perfect. *A ~ gentleman.*

though (दो) conjunction
यद्यपि, not withstanding that. *~ they are poor, they are not dishonest.*

thought (थौट) noun
विचार, चिन्तन, reasoning. *All his ~ went into his work.*

thread (थ्रेड) noun
धागा, सूत, डोरा, रेशा, thin and twisted string. *A reel of silk ~.*

threat (थ्रैट) noun
धमकी, घुड़की, *Under a ~ of suspension.*

throat (थ्रोट) noun
गला, कण्ठ, passage from mouth to the stomach.

through (थ्रू) adjective
एक सिरे से दूसरे सिरे तक, from end to end, सारे समय, *Pass ~ the gate.*

thumb (थम्ब) noun
अँगूठा, shortest and thickest finger, किसी के दबाव में. *She has got her husband under her ~.*

thus (दस) adverb
इस प्रकार, in this way, इसलिए *So ~ he ruined his future.*

ticket (टिकट) noun
अधिकार पत्र. *Cinema ~. Railway ~.*

tide (टाइड) noun
ज्वारभाटा, the ebb and flow of the sea.

tidy (टाइडी) adjective
सुव्यवस्थित, arranged neatly. *A ~ room.*

tie (टाई) noun
गले में बांधने वाली टाई, necktie, बंधन, a bondage.

tiffin (टिफिन) noun
तीसरे पहर का भोजन, lunch.

tight (टाइट) adjective
तंग, कसा हुआ, closely fit. *A ~ collar.*

till (टिल) conjunction
उस समय तक, up to the time when. *He won't go ~ it is five.*

time (टाइम) noun
समय, काल, बेला, *In the present ~.*

tip (टिप) noun
सिरा, the end. बख्शीश *~ the porter a rupee.*

tire (टायर) noun
ring of rubber placed over rim. टायर

tire (टायर) verb
थकाना, to exhaust. *Hard work ~d him.*

title (टाइटिल) noun
मुखपृष्ठ, नाम, लेखपत्र, distinguishing name of something.

to (टू) preposition
ओर, तरफ़ को, the direction of. *He is coming ~ me.*

to be (टू-बी) adjective
भावी, भविष्य में बनने वाली, soon to be the thing specified. *Bride ~.*

today **(टुडे)** adverb
आज this day. ~ *is a holiday.*

together **(टुगैदर)** adverb
एक साथ, किसी के साथ में, in company.

toilet **(टॉइलेट)** noun
श्रंगार, श्रंगारसामग्री, articles used in dressing. *She is busy at her ~.*

tomato **(टोमेटो)** noun
टमाटर, red pulpy fruit.

tongue **(टंग)** noun
जीभ, जिह्वा, a muscular organ inside the mouth.

too **(टू)** adverb
भी, और भी, बहुत अधिक, in excess, over much. ~ *hot to drink.*

top **(टॉप)** noun
चोटी, the highest point. *At the ~ of his fame.*

torture **(टॉर्चर)** noun
कड़ी यातना, वेदना, severe pain. *She died under ~.*

toss **(टॉस)** verb
हवा में ऊपर फेंकना, to throw up in the air. *She ~ed the beggar a rupee coin.*

total **(टोटल)** adjective
सम्पूर्ण, समग्र, complete, whole. *He is a ~ flop.*

touch **(टच)** noun
स्पर्श, छूने की किया *Act of ~ing.*

tough **(टफ़)** adjective
सख्त, कड़ा, strong and durable. ~ *rubber is needed for tyres.*

tour **(टूर)** noun
भ्रमण, यात्रा, देशाटन, journey from one place to another. *Our class is going to Varansi on a ~.*

towel **(टॉवेल)** noun
तौलिया, an absorbent cloth used after bath.

tower **(टॉवर)** noun
मीनार, लाट, बुर्ज. *The ~ of a church.*

town **(टाउन)** noun
नगर, कस्बा, an area of habitation.

toy **(टॉय)** noun
खिलौना, a plaything.

track **(ट्रैक)** noun
लीक, पगडंडी, line of marks left by a moving thing. *The ~s of a tiger. Tyre ~s.*

trade **(ट्रेड)** noun
व्यवसाय, व्यापार, process of buying. *Domestic ~. Foreign ~.*

tradition **(ट्रेडीशन)** noun
परम्परा, beliefs, customs, *Family ~s.*

tragedy **(ट्रैजिडी)** noun
दु:खान्त, with a sad ending. *Julius Caesar of Shakespeare is a ~.*

train **(ट्रेन)** noun, verb
रेलगाडी, a self propelled conne-

cted group of rolling stock, शिक्षा देना, प्रशिक्षण देना, educate, instruct. ~ *up students for a march past.*

transact (ट्रान्सैक्ट) verb
कार्य सम्पन्न करना, निपटाना, act of transacting, लेन-देन. *The banks ~s in the share market.*

transfer (ट्रान्सफ़र) noun
तबादला, स्थान-परिवर्तन, act of transferring. *He is under orders of ~.*

transit (ट्रान्ज़िट) noun
गमनागमन, the fact of passing through.

translate (ट्रान्सलेट) verb
परिणत करना, अनुवाद करना, to turn from one language to another.

transparent (ट्रान्सपेरेन्ट) adjective
पारदर्शी, स्पष्ट, pervious to light. *Glass is ~ to light.*

transport (ट्रैन्सपोर्ट) noun
परिवहन, being conveyed. The ~ of goods by air.

travel (ट्रैवल) verb
यात्रा करना, सफ़र करना, to go from one place to another. ~ *round the world.*

treasure (ट्रेज़र) noun
खजाना, संचित धन, wealth, riches stored.

treat (ट्रीट) verb
किसी विषय पर कुछ कहना, लिखना, to deal with a subject, व्यवहार, बर्ताव करना, the act of behaving, मनोरंजन, आनन्द, भोज, a special delight.

tree (ट्री) noun
वृक्ष, पेड़, large perennial plant.

tribe (ट्राइब) noun
जाति, वर्ग. *The Red Indian ~s of America.*

tribute (ट्रिब्यूट) noun
श्रद्धांजलि, आभार प्रकट करना, statement symbolizing one's regard.

trim (ट्रिम) adjective
साफ़ सुथरा, सुव्यवस्थित, in good order, neat and tidy.

trip (ट्रिप) noun
लघु यात्रा, excursion, short journey. *Our class is going on a pleasure ~.*

trophy (ट्रॉफ़ी) noun
विजय स्मारक, evidence of victory.

trouble (ट्रबल) verb
तकलीफ़ देना, उठाना, कष्ट सहना, to cause worry, give or take discomfort. *My arthritis ~s me greatly.*

trouser (ट्राउज़र) noun
पायजामा, पतलून, pentaloon. *A pair of grey ~s.*

true (ट्रू) adjective
सत्य, यथार्थ, opposite of false. *Is the news of his death ~?*

trunk (ट्रंक) noun
वृक्ष का तना, main stem of a tree, धड़ torso, संदूक, a large

box, हाथी की सूँड़, nose of an elephant, दूरभाष द्वारा बातचीत, telephone call to a distant place.

trust (ट्रस्ट) noun
भरोसा, विश्वास, reliance on the integrity.

try (ट्राइ) verb
कोशिश करना, make an attempt. *I can't promise to have a ~ on something.*

tube (ट्यूब) noun
नली, नलिका. *~ of a bicycle.*

tumor (ट्यूमर) noun
गिल्टी, गाँठ, abnormal growth in some part of the body. फोड़ा, रसौली.

tune (ट्यून) noun
सुर, धुन, राग, melody, गीत, आलाप, musical note.

turn (टर्न) noun
घुमाव, चक्कर, an act of turning. *He took a ~ and went to the left.*

turtle (टर्टिल) noun
समुद्री कछुआ, a reptile of the order chelonia.

tutor (ट्यूटर) noun
निजी शिक्षक, private teacher.

twice (ट्वाइस) adverb
दो बार, two times.

type (टाइप) verb
टंकण करना, use of a typewriter. *I can ~ at a speed of 60 words a minute.* चिह्न, नमूना, symbol, specimen. *Her face is of the Japanese ~.*

□□□□

U

u

मुद्रण में प्रयुक्त लघु अक्षर

U u

लिखने में प्रयुक्त दीर्घ और लघु अक्षर

मूल उच्चारण **यू**

अ यू

प्रयोग में उच्चारण ज्यादातर अ, एकाध यू मूल उच्चारण — कैसी उपेक्षा है!

अंग्रेजी वर्णमाला का इक्कीसवाँ अक्षर और पाँचवाँ तथा अंतिम स्वर – बिलकुल आख़िर में याद आई!

ugly (अग्ली) adjective
भद्दा, बदसूरत, unpleasant to look at. *An ~ fellow.*

ulcer (अल्सर) noun
व्रण, फोड़ा, an open sore discharging pus.

ultimate (अल्टिमेट) adjective
अन्तिम, सबसे अधिक दूर, furthest, farthest. *The ~ style in shirts.*

ultimatum (अल्टिमेटम) noun
अन्तिम माँग, अन्तिम प्रस्ताव, आखिरी चेतावनी, a final warning. *Deliver an ~.*

umbrella (अमब्रैला) noun
छाता, छतरी, that protects from rain, किसी तरह की रक्षा का साधन, any kind of general protecting force. *American nuclear ~.*

umpire (अम्पायर) noun
मध्यस्थ, निर्णायक, पंच, one who acts as judge. *~ of tennis match.*

unable (अनेबल) adjective
असमर्थ, not able. *He is ~ to see because of old age.*

uncertain (अनसर्टेन) adjective
अनिश्चित, not definitely ascertainable. *~ weather.*

uncle (अंकल) noun
चाचा, मामा, brother of one's father or mother.

unconscious (अनकौन्शस)
अचेत, बेहोश, without awareness. *Lying ~.*

under (अण्डर) adverb
नीचे, below, beneath. *The boat went ~.*

undergo (अण्डरगो) verb
सहन करना, अनुभव करना, to experience. *To ~ surgery.*

underground (अंडरग्राउन्ड) adjective
ज़मीन के नीचे, below the ground, गुप्त क्रियाओं में लिप्त, involved

in illegal activities. *He went ~ to avoid arrest.*

understand (अन्डरस्टैन्ड) verb
अर्थ समझना, follow the sense. *Do you ~ what I mean?*

underworld (अन्डरवर्ल्ड) noun
पाताल, यमलोक, रसातल, antipodes, पतित वर्ग, चोर, डाकू, criminal elements of society.

uniform (यूनिफौर्म) adjective
एक सी, अपरिवर्तित, not changing. *Maintain ~ temperature.* एक सी पोषाक, परिधान, वर्दी. *Children wearing ~s.*

union (यूनियन) noun
मिलाप, संघ, गठबन्धन, *~ is strength.*

unit (यूनिट) noun
इकाई, मापतौल का मानक. *The family is considered to be a ~ of society. The kilo is a ~ of weight.*

unite (यूनाइट) verb
मिलाना, जोड़ना, एक करना, make one. *~ one state to another.*

unique (यूनीक) adjective
अनोखा, अद्वितीय, matchless. *A building.*

universal (यूनिवर्सल) adjective
विश्वसंबंधी, व्यापक, the whole. *~ brotherhood.*

universe (यूनिवर्स) noun
अखिल विश्व. *The ~ is the creation of Almighty God.*

university (यूनिवर्सिटी) noun
विश्वविद्यालय, institution for higher education and research.

unless (अनलैस) conjunction
यदि, नहीं, जब तक कि, if not. *You will get late ~ you run fast.*

unseen (अनसीन) adjective
अदृश्य, not seen. अपठित गद्यांश या पद्यांश,

until (अनटिल) conjunction
जब तक, up to the time when. *Wait ~ the rain stops.*

unto (अनटू) preposition
को, to. *Hard work brought him ~ success.*

up (अप) adverb
ऊपर, ऊँचा, to a higher place. *Prices of articles are still going ~.* समाप्त, over, expired. *Stop writing, the time is ~.*

update (अपडेट) verb
आज तक के तथ्यों का समावेश करना, to bring up to date. *An ~d dictionary.*

upon (अपौन) preposition
ऊपर, on, floating. *~ water. Heavy food ~ his stomach.*

upset (अपसैट) verb
अस्तव्यस्त करना, गड़बड़ा देना, to disturb. *Heavy food ~ his stomach.*

urge (अर्ज) verb
आग्रह करना, to insist on. *To ~ a plan of action.*

urgent (अर्जेन्ट) adjective
अति आवश्यक, immediate necessity. *An ~ matter.*

us (अस) pronoun
हमें, हमको, objective form of we. *Let ~ go.*

use (यूज़) verb
काम में लेना, to employ for some purpose. *You can ~ my book for some days.*

usual (यूजुअल) adjective
प्राय:, अधिकतर, often. *Coca Cola is the ~ drink in summers.*

utensil (यूटैंसिल) noun
बर्तन, उपकरण, vessel. *Baking ~s.*

uterus (यूटेरस) noun
गर्भाशय. *Of the ~.*

utility (यूटिलिटी) noun
उपयोगिता, useful. *Pen has no ~ for an illiterate person.*

utter (अटर) verb
कहना, मुँह से बोलना, speak. *The last words he ~ed were inaudible.*

□□□□

V

v मुद्रण में प्रयुक्त लघु अक्षर

मूल उच्चारण **वी**

v लिखने में प्रयुक्त लघु अक्षर

व प्रयोग में उच्चारण

अंग्रेजी वर्णमाला का बाईसवाँ अक्षर

vacancy (वेकेन्सी) noun
रिक्त स्थान, being vacant. *Vacancies for typist in an office.*

vacate (वैकेट) verb
खाली करना, कब्जा छोड़ना, quit, leave the possession of. *To ~ the house.*

vacation (वैकेशन) noun
खाली करने की क्रिया, act of vacating, लम्बी अवधि का अवकाश, long leave. *Summer/winter ~ in a college.*

vacuum (वैक्युअम) noun
शून्य, खाली स्थान, निर्वात, space empty of air, *Create a ~.*

vagina (वजाइना) noun
योनि, स्त्रियों का प्रसव मार्ग, a passage from uterus to vulva.

vague (वेग) adjective
अस्पष्ट, indistinct. *I have simply a ~ idea of the incident.*

vain (वेन) adjective
व्यर्थ, बेकार, meaningless. *A ~ attempt.*

valentine (वैलंटाइन) noun
प्रेम पत्र, sentimental greeting card sent on St. Valentine's day (14th Feb.) to a sweet-heart, प्रेमिका, प्रेमी, *Will you be my ~?*

valid (वैलिड) adjective
वैध, न्यायसंगत स्थिति, effective. *A ~ procedure.*

value (वैल्यु) noun
मान, मूल्य, worth of something. *This tea is good ~ at five rupees a packet.* जीवन मूल्य, esteem.

valve (वाल्व) noun
एक ओर खुलने वाला कपाट, device to control the flow in one direction. *~ of a cycle tube.* हृदय में रक्तवाहक कपाट, heart valve.

van (वैन) noun
ढँकी हुई गाड़ी, a large covered wagon.

vanish (वैनिश) verb
लुप्त होना, विलीन हो जाना, गायब हो जाना, to disappear.

vanity (वैनिटी) noun
घमंड, खोखलापन, conceit, worthlessness.

vapour (वेपर) noun
भाप, धुआँ, कोहरा, smoke, mist. गैसीय अवस्था.

variable (वैरीएबल) adjective
परिवर्तनशील, अस्थिर, fluctuating. *Changing ~ prices.*

variety (वैराइटी) noun
प्रकार, किस्म, भेद, different form of something. *A large ~ of patterns to choose from.*

various (वेरिअस) adjective
विविध, अनेक, भिन्नभिन्न, different kinds. *They are reading in ~ classes.*

varnish (वार्निश) noun
पेन्ट, *A coat of ~ on the doors.*

vast (वास्ट) adjective
विशाल, बहुत बड़ा, बृहद, huge. *~ empire.*

veg (वैज) noun
तरकारी, सब्जियां, *vegetables.*

vehicle (वाइकल) noun
सवारी, यान, वाहन, conveyance.

veil (वेल) noun
घूँघट, पर्दा, बुर्का, to cover with, to conceal.

vein (वेन) noun
शिरा जो हृदय तक रक्त पहुँचाती है, a vessel that conveys blood to the heart.

velocity (वैलोसिटी) noun
वेग, rapidity of motion.

vengeance (वैन्जिएन्स) noun
बदला, to avenge.

ventilate (वेंटिलेट) verb
हवा आने जाने के लिए खोलना, expose to free passage of air.

venture (वेंचर) noun
साहसिक कार्य, an adventurous job.

venue (वैन्यू) noun
किसी घटना का स्थान, स्थल, the locale of any event. *A last minute change of ~.*

verdict (वर्डिक्ट) noun
पंचायत, न्यायालय का फ़ैसला, judgement. *The jury's ~ was that he was guilty.*

verge (वर्ज) noun
किनारा, सीमा, edge, rim or margin. *On the ~ of nervous breakdown.*

verify (वैरीफाई) verb
प्रमाणित करना, to prove the truth of. *~ the contents of the letter.*

verse (वर्स) noun
कविता, पद, poem. *Blank ~.*

version (वर्ज़न) noun
भाषान्तर, अनुवाद *An English ~ of Ramayana.*

versus (वर्सस)
विपरीत, विरुद्ध, against. *India ~ Pakistan.*

very (वैरी) adverb
बहुत, अत्यंत, in a high degree. *It is ~ gracious of you to do this.* बिल्कुल वही, precise, particular. *He is the ~ boy who has broken my pen.*

via (वाया) preposition
रास्ते से होकर, by way of, माध्यम से. *This train goes to Mumbai ~ Nagpur.*

vice (वाइस) preposition
स्थान पर, उप, in place of. दुर्गुण, दुष्टता, भृष्टता, opposite of virtue. *Greed is a terrible ~.*

victim (विक्टिम) noun
शिकार, किसी के द्वारा सताया या मारा गया, one who sustains injury.

victory (विक्टरी) noun
विजय, जीत, फ़तह, success. *The ~ of Trafalgar.*

videlicet (विडैलिसिट) adverb
(abbr. viz.) अर्थात्, namely.

view (व्यू) noun
दृष्टि, sight. *The chief guest stood in full ~ of the students.*

village (विलेज) noun
गाँव, ग्राम, rural area. *He lives in a ~.*

villain (विलेन) noun
खलनायक, devoted to crime. खलनायिका.

violence (वाइलन्स) noun
हिंसा, uncontrolled rough force.

virgin (वर्जिन) noun
कुमारी, कुमार, जिसने कभी सम्भोग न किया हो a girl/boy who has never had sexual intercourse. chaste.

virtue (वरचू) noun
सद्गुण, noble quality. *Lead a life of ~.*

virus (वाइरस) noun
विषाणु, ultramicroscopic infectious agent.

visible (विज़िबल) adjective
दृष्टिगोचर, that can be seen. *The lunar eclipse will not be ~ in India.*

visit (विज़िट) verb
मिलने के लिए जाना, भ्रमण करना, go to see somebody or place, निरीक्षण करने जाना, go for official inspection.

visual (विजुअल) adjective
दृष्टि संबंधी, concerned with seeing. *~ images.*

vital (वाइटल) adjective
परम आवश्यक, सजीव, जानदार, essential, प्राण डालने वाली, imparting life.

vivid (विविड) adjective
सजीव, जीवन्त, lively. *A ~ painting.*

vocal (वोकल) adjective
वाणी से संबंधित, मुख से उच्चारित, uttered with the voice, *A ~ sound.*

vocation (वोकेशन) noun
व्यवसाय, पेशा, profession. *A*

nurse by ~.

voice (**वॉयस**) noun
वाणी, आवाज, बोली, sound uttered through the mouth of living creatures. *Her ~ trembled with emotion.*

volume (**वॉल्यूम**) noun
पुस्तक, पुस्तक का खंड, book, one part of a big book. *A book in three ~s.* आयतन, घनफल, विस्तार, space occupied by a substance, आवाज़ की प्रबलता, degree of sound intensity.

vomit (**वौमिट**) verb
वमन, उल्टी करना, regurgitate, throw up. *She began to ~ blood soon after she slipped on the ground.*

vote (**वोट**) noun
मत, मतदान, formal expression of choice.

voucher (**वाउचर**) noun
व्यय का लिखित प्रमाण पत्र, receipt of an expenditure. *Collect gift ~s for free gifts.*

vowel (**वावेल**) noun
स्वर की ध्वनि, letter symbolizing such a sound. *a,e,i,o,u are ~s.*

vulture (**वलचर**) noun
गिद्ध, large bird which feeds on carrion.

vulva (**वल्वा**) noun
भग, external female genitalia.

❑❑❑❑

W

W
मुद्रण में प्रयुक्त लघु अक्षर

w
लिखने में प्रयुक्त लघु अक्षर

मूल उच्चारण **डब्लू**

व / हव / ह / र

प्रयोग में उच्चारण – h के साथ हव और ह और r के साथ र। व के लिए क्या v काफी नहीं था और दो v जोड़कर बनाया यह अक्षर क्या तमाशा नहीं लगता?

अंग्रेजी वर्णमाला का तेइसवाँ अक्षर

wafer (वेफर) noun
पपड़ीदार बिस्कुट, thin flat biscuit.

wage (वेज) noun
पारिश्रमिक, money that is paid or received for work. *Employed on daily ~s.*

wagon (वैगन) noun
ठेला गाड़ी, रेलगाड़ी का डिब्बा (माल ढोने का), a railway freight car.

waist (वेस्ट) noun
कमर, the part of body between the ribs and hips. *Wear a belt round the ~.*

wait (वेट) verb
प्रतीक्षा करना, to stay in expectation. *I have been ~ing here for an hour.*

walk (वाक) verb
पैदल चलना, टहलना, the act of going on foot. *~ across the street.*

wall (वौल) noun
दीवार, structure of brick serving as fence. *The eastern ~ of the house.*

wander (वान्डर) verb
बिना किसी उद्देश्य के घूमना, roam aimlessly.

want (वान्ट) verb
चाहना, इच्छा करना, to require, to need. *I ~ a good dictionary.* अभाव, कमी, lack. *The house is collapsing for ~ of repairs.*

war (वार) noun
युद्ध, armed conflict between nations. *The second world ~ ended in 1945.*

ward (वार्ड) noun
जेल का एक भाग, separate division of jail. अभिभावक की देखरेख में अवयस्क बालक. *This child is my ~.*

warm (वार्म) adjective
गरम, between hot & cool. *Woollen clothes keep us ~.*

warn (वार्न) verb
सचेत करना, to advise caution. *He ~ed me of the impending danger.*

warrant (वारंट) noun
न्यायालय का गिरफ़्तारी आदेश, court order of arrest. *A ~ to arrest a vagabond.*

was (वाज़) verb
था, singular of the verb 'be'.

wash (वाश) verb
धोना, साफ़ करना, to clean. *Give the car a ~ing.*

waste (वेस्ट) adjective
रद्दी, बेकार, निरर्थक, वीरान, desolate, useless, हानि, क्षय, to ravage. *What a ~ of time!*

watch (वाच) noun
रक्षा, चौकसी. *The act of ~ing.* हाथघड़ी, wrist watch.

water (वाटर) noun
जल, पानी, liquid as in rivers, canals, seas, oceans, etc. *Fish live in ~.*

watt (वाट) noun
विद्युत शक्ति की इकाई, unit of electric power. *A 40 ~ bulb.*

wave (वेव) noun
तंरग, लहर, तंरग-आयाम, a strong emotional movement. *A ~ of anger.* रेडियो टेलीग्राफ़ी में लहरों के शिखर पर का अंतर.

wax (वैक्स) noun
मोम, a plastic substance secreted by bees or by product of petroleum. *A candle of ~.*

way (वे) noun
मार्ग, path, पथ, road, दूरी, distance. *They have come a long ~.*

we (वी) pronoun
हम, plural of I. *~ want to go now.*

weak (वीक) adjective
दुर्बल, कमजोर, feeble, frail. *It is a ~ team.*

wealth (वैल्थ) noun
धन, दौलत, सम्पत्ति, riches, money and property. *Personal ~.*

weapon (वैपन) noun
हथियार, अस्त्र-शस्त्र, an instrument of defence or offence. *A bull uses its horns as its ~s.*

wear (विअर) noun
पहनना, act of wearing. *A shirt for winter ~.*

weather (वैदर) noun
मौसम, state of atmosphere with respect of wind, temperature, cloudiness, moisture, etc.

wed (वैड) verb
शादी करना, marry. *They will be ~ded shortly.*

week (वीक) noun
सप्ताह, a period of seven days. *Last ~ I was on medical leave.*

weep (वीप) verb
रोना, आँसू बहाना, to shed tears. *The baby came to ~ as it was hungry.*

weight (वेट) noun
भार, वजन, heaviness as found in a balance. *My ~ is 72 kilos.*

welcome (वैलकम) noun
सत्कार, स्वागत, अभिनन्दन, a kindly reception. *The chief guest was given a warm ~.*

well (वैल) noun
कुआँ, a hole drilled into the earth to obtain water, petroleum, brine, etc.

well (वैल) adjective
स्वस्थ, अच्छा, in good health, उचित, ठीक, proper, gratifying, संतोषजनक, satisfying. *He is ~ now.*

went (वैन्ट) verb
past tense of 'go'. गया।

wept (वैप्ट) past tense
of 'weep'. रोया

were (वर) past tense
of 'be'. थे

wet (वैट) adjective
गीला, भीगा, soaked in water. ~ cloth.

what (व्हाट) adjective
कौन सी, which. क्या, कैसा. *~ a lovely child!*

wheat (व्हीट) noun
गेहूँ, गन्दुम, an edible seed of a plant which is ground into flour.

wheel (व्हील) noun
चक्र, पहिया, a circular frame revolving on an axis.

when (व्हैन) adverb
कब, at what time. *~ did you come?*

where (व्हेअर) adverb
जहाँ, जिस जगह पर, at which place, कहाँ, at what place. *This is the place ~ we met.*

whether (व्हैदर) conjunction
यदि, if, दोनों में से एक, one of the two. *I don't worry ~ he wins or loses.*

which (विच) adjective
कौन सी, what किस प्रकार का, of what sort. *~ book do you like most?*

while (व्हाइल) conjunction
समय, अवधि, a space of time. *I will be back in a short ~.*

whisper (व्हिस्पर) verb
बहुत धीमी आवाज में बोलना, कानाफूसी करना, *What are you ~ing about?*

whistle (व्हिसल) noun, verb
सीटी, सीटी बजाना, *To blow a ~.*

white (व्हाइट) adjective
सफ़ेद, श्वेत, the colour of milk. *Snow is ~.*

who (हू) pronoun
कौन, what person. *~ is knocking at the door?*

whole (होल) adjective
पूर्ण, सम्पूर्ण, complete, entire. *That's the ~ story of his misfortune.*

whom (हूम) pronoun
किसे, किसको, जिसको, objective

form of who. ~ *do you want to meet?*

whose (हूज़) pronoun
किसका, जिसका, of which. *The boy ~ father loved me is my friend.*

why (व्हाई) adverb
किसलिए, किस कारण से, क्यों, for what reason. ~ *are you late today?*

wide (वाइड) adjective
चौड़ा, broad, बृहद, extensive. *A man of ~ experience.* बल्लेबाज की पहुँच के परे, beyond the reach. ~ *ball.*

widow (विडो) noun
विधवा, a woman whose husband is dead, esp. one who has not remarried.

widower (विडोअर) noun
विधुर, a man whose wife is dead and who has not married again.

wife (वाईफ़) noun
पत्नी, भार्या, a married woman in relation to her husband.

wild (वाइल्ड) adjective
जंगली, not domesticated. *The wolf is a ~ animal.*

will (विल) noun
इच्छा शक्ति, mental power, वसीयत, legal document, इच्छा करना, चाहना, to desire. 'गा' (भविष्य काल प्रकट करने को) *Tomorrow ~ be Sunday.*

win (विन) verb
जीतना, विजय प्राप्त करना, to gain victory.

wind (विन्ड) noun
पवन, वायु, air in natural motion. *The ~ blew my cap off.*

window (विन्डो) noun
खिड़की, वातायन, an opening in the wall for air and light.

winter (विन्टर) noun
शीतकाल, season between autumn and spring. ~ *vacation.*

wipe (वाइप) verb
पोंछना, रगड़ कर साफ करना, rub in order to clean. ~ *the plates.*

wire (वायर) noun
तार, तार समाचार, telegram. *Send them a ~ to come soon.*

wise (वाइज़) adjective
शिक्षित, विद्वान, ज्ञानी, learned. *They are ~ enough.*

wish (विश) verb
चाहना, इच्छा करना, to desire. *I ~ to be a doctor.* शुभकामना करना. *I ~ you success.*

with (विद) preposition
साथ, अधिकार में, in possession of. *My books are ~ him.*

withdraw (विदड्रौ) verb
निकाल लेना, वापस लेना. *Take away ~ money from the bank.*

witness (विटनैस) noun
साक्षी, गवाह, one who sees some thing. *You are a ~ to the accident.*

woman (वुमन) noun
स्त्री, नारी, औरत, adult female of human being.

womb (वूम्ब) noun
गर्भाशय, uterus.

wonder (वन्डर) noun
अद्भुत, चमत्कार, strange thing, अचरज, surprise.

wood (वुड) noun
लकड़ी, timber. *Doors are generally made of ~.*

wool (वूल) noun
ऊन, soft hair of sheep, goat or other animal.

word (वर्ड) noun
शब्द, combination of letters which have some meaning.

work (वर्क) noun, verb
कार्य, परिश्रम, labour, exertion, रोजगार, धंधा, employment, काम करना, to labour. *Always ~ hard to succeed.*

world (वर्ल्ड) noun
विश्व, संसार, जगत, universe. *The whole ~.*

worry (वरी) verb
परेशान होना, चिन्ता करना, to cause anxiety. *I am worried by my wife's illness.*

worship (वर्शिप) noun
पूजा, पूजन, उपासना, a religious service.

worst (वर्स्ट) adjective
superlative of bad, ill, or, evil सबसे बुरा, दुष्टतम, bad to greatest extent.

worth (वर्थ) adjective
की कीमत, के योग्य, of value equal to. *The old cycle is not ~ more than Rs 250.*

worthy (वर्दी) adjective
योग्य, लायक, deserving. *~ of respect.*

would (वुड)
past tense of will, वर्तमान तथा भूत काल में घटनाओं को प्रकट करने के लिए. *~ you please bring a chair for me?*

wound (वुन्ड) noun
घाव, चोट, injury. *A deep ~ in his right arm.*

wrap (रैप) verb
लपेटना, ढँकना, cover or roll up.

wrestle (रैसल) verb
कुश्ती लड़ना, to fight with.

wrist (रिस्ट) noun
कलाई, पोंचा, carpus. *He seized me by the ~.*

write (राइट) verb
लिखना, to trace or form letters on the surface of paper.

wrong (रौन्ग) adjective
गलत, not correct. *Your answer is ~.* त्रुटिपूर्ण. *He did no ~ in my opinion.*

□□□□

X

x
मुद्रण में प्रयुक्त लघु अक्षर

X x
लिखने में प्रयुक्त दीर्घ और लघु अक्षर

मूल उच्चारण **एक्स**

एक्स ज़
प्रयोग में उच्चारण—बहुत थोड़े शब्द हैं इसमें, बेचारा!

अंग्रेजी वर्णमाला का चौबीसवाँ अक्षर

xerox (ज़ीरोक्स) noun
छपे हुए चित्रों अथवा कागजों की नकल उतारने की मशीन, to reproduce by xerography.

Xmas (एक्समस)
Christmas, ईसाइयों का पर्व क्रिस्मस

x-ray (एक्सरे) noun
एक प्रकार की रश्मि जिससे शरीर के भीतर की तस्वीर उतारी जाती है, form of short wave ray that penetrates solids and makes it possible to see into or through them.

□□□□

Y

y
मुद्रण में प्रयुक्त लघु अक्षर

y
लिखने में प्रयुक्त लघु अक्षर

मूल उच्चारण **वाई**

य प्रयोग में उच्चारण

अंग्रेजी वर्णमाला का पच्चीसवाँ अक्षर

yahoo (याहू) noun
असभ्य जंगली आदमी, rough uncouth person.

yard (यार्ड) noun
आँगन, प्रांगण, enclosed space around a building, वह स्थान जहाँ गाड़ी तैयार की जाती है तथा इस्तेमाल न होने के समय खड़ी रहती है, area where trains are made up, where wagons and coaches are kept when not in use.

yard (यार्ड) noun
गज़, लम्बाई की इकाई, unit of length. 3 ft or 36 inches as exactly 0.9144 metre.

yawn (यौन) verb
जंभाई, उबासी लेना, drowsiness.

year (इयर) noun
वर्ष, period from 1st Jan. to 31st Dec. 365 ¼ days.

yellow (यैलो) noun
पीला, the colour of lemon or gold. *The yolk of hen's egg is ~.*

yes (यस) adverb
हाँ, स्वीकृति, consent. *Are you ready? ~.*

yesterday (यैस्टरडे) adjective
बीता हुआ कल, previous day. *~ was Monday.*

yet (येट) adverb
अब तक, तब तक, by this or that time. *They have not gone ~.*

yield (ईल्ड) verb
उत्पन्न करना, प्रदान करना, देना, to provide, to give forth. *Mango trees ~ mangoes.* सम्मान या हार के कारण समर्पण करना, to surrender.

yoga (योग) noun
इन्द्रियों की गहन साधना. Hindu system of meditation and self control

you (यू) pronoun
तुम, तुम सब, . आप. *Are ~ going home?*

young (यंग) adjective
तरुण, युवा, being in the early stage of life. *A ~ woman.*

your (योर) adjective
तुम्हारा, आपका, belonging to you. *This is ~ book.*

youth (यूथ) noun
युवक, युवतियाँ, state of being young, यौवन. *A ~ful appearance.*

❑❑❑❑

Z

z
मुद्रण में प्रयुक्त
लघु अक्षर

लिखने में प्रयुक्त
दीर्घ और लघु
अक्षर

मूल
उच्चारण
ज़ेड

ज़
प्रयोग में उच्चारण

अंग्रेजी वर्णमाला का अंतिम अक्षर

zeal (ज़ील) noun
उत्साह, जोश, enthusiasm, ardour. *Show ~ on the occasion of the festival.*

zebra (ज़ैब्रा) noun
अफ्रीका का धारीदार घोड़ा, an striped horse of Africa.

zebra-crossing (ज़ैब्रा-क्रॉसिंग) noun
सड़क का वह भाग जिस पर चौड़ी सफ़ेद धारियाँ पड़ी होती हैं जहाँ पर वाहन रुक कर पैदल चलनेवालों को सड़क पार करने की सुविधा देते हैं. part of a road, marked with white stripes, where vehicles must stop if pedestrians wish to cross.

zenith (ज़ैनिथ) noun
उच्चतम स्थान, highest point. *His fame was at its ~ during the Presidentship.*

zero (ज़ीरो) noun
शून्य, सिफ़र, a cypher, nothing, the number 0. *His progress is ~.* किसी कार्य को शुरू करने का समय, critical time at the commencement of an action, point between plus (+) and minus (-) on a scale. *The thermometer fell to ~ last night.*

zigzag (ज़िगज़ैग) noun
टेढ़ा-मेढ़ा रास्ता, मोड़, a line, course, characterized by sharp turns. *An expert driver is needed to drive a car over ~ hill roads.*

zip (ज़िप) noun
जंजीर, chain, एकाएक कपड़ा फटने की आवाज़, sound made by the sudden tearing of cloth.

zone (ज़ोन) noun
क्षेत्र, मण्ड़ल, घेरा, कटिबन्ध, area.

zoo (ज़ू) noun
चिड़ियाघर, प्राणी संग्रहालय, place where animals are kept, bred and exhibited. *They went to see the ~.*

zoom (ज़ूम) verb
तेजी से सनसन की आवाज करते हुए उड़ना या चलना, move quickly with a loud humming, तेजी से वृद्धि होना, rise sharply. *Inflation causes prices to ~.* कैमरे के विशेष प्रकार के लैन्स, camera lens that can be adjusted to make the object being photographed appear gradually bigger or smaller so that is seems to be getting steadily closer or more distant.

□□□□

भारतीय भाषाओं के अंग्रेजी में लिये जा रहे कुछ शब्द

अंग्रेजी उदार भाषा है और अन्य भाषाओं के प्रचलित शब्दों को अपने भीतर समाने में संकोच नहीं करती। नए कोशों में ऐसे ढाई हजार शब्द शामिल कर लिये गये हैं। इनमें से कुछ, लगभग 150 शब्द, यहाँ नमूने के रूप में दिये जा रहे हैं। समय के साथ इनका प्रयोग दुनिया के अन्य देशों में भी होने लगेगा – कुछ का तो होने भी लगा है।

aarti (आरती)
पूजन के उपरान्त थाल, दीप सजाकर ईश्वर की आरती करना

abhinaya (अभिनय)
नृत्य, मंच अथवा सिनेमा में किसी पात्र की हूबहू नकल करना

achar (अचार)
खाद्य जिसे तेल और मसालों से सुरक्षित रखा जाता है – आम, नींबू का अचार

acharya (आचार्य)
ब्राह्मण धार्मिक गुरु

achkan (अचकन)
शेरवानी, पुरुष वस्त्र

adalat (अदालत)
न्यायालय

adharma (अधर्म)
अनैतिक व्यवहार जो कर्तव्य या रिवाज़ों के विपरीत हो

adivasi (आदिवासी)
मानवों का समूह जो वनों में कई पीढ़ियों से रहता आ रहा हो

admi (आदमी)
मनुष्य

agarbatti (अगरबत्ती)
(also धूप) ऊदबत्ती

Agni (अग्नि)
हिन्दुओं के अग्निदेव

akali (अकाली)
सिखों के राजनीतिक दल का सदस्य

artha (अर्थ)
धन

asura (असुर)
दुष्ट आत्मा, राक्षस

atman (आत्मा)
जीवन का मूल तत्व, soul,

azan (अज़ान)
मस्जिद की प्रार्थना में जाने के लिए पुकार

babu (बाबू)
कार्यालय में काम करने वाले व्यक्ति

badam (बादाम)
सूखा मेवा, almond nut

baiji (बाईजी)
वेश्या, जो नृत्य, संगीत में चतुर हो

bai (बाई)
स्त्री (पश्चिम भारत में स्त्री के लिए नम्र संबोधन), घरों में काम करने वाली स्त्री

bakwas (बकवास)
मूर्खतापूर्ण बात करना

bandar (बन्दर)
monkey

bania (बनिया)
व्यापारी, trader

begum (बेगम)
मुस्लिम रानी

Bhagwan (भगवान)
God, ईश्वर

bindi (बिंदी)
टीका, स्त्री के मस्तक पर लगाने वाला सज्जात्मक टीका

Brahma (ब्रह्मा)
देवता जिन्होंने दुनिया बनाई

bulbul (बुलबुल)
छोटी सुन्दर चिड़िया जो बहुत प्रिय गाती है

burra (बड़ा)
burra din. (Christmas)

bursati (बरसाती)
बरसात में पहनने का बड़ा कपड़ा

butter oil (बटर ऑइल)
घी

cat (कैट)
फ़ैशनेबिल, catwalk.

chaat (चाट)

chai (चाय) चा,

chappal (चप्पल)

chaprasi (चपरासी)

chhokra (छोकरा)
a young boy

chhokri (छोकरी)
a young girl

chini (चीनी)
sugar

chivda (चिबड़ा)

chor (चोर)
thief

chullah (चुल्हा)
a stove that uses coal to burn

dada (दादा)
बड़ा चचेरा भाई

dahi (दही)
curd or yoghurt

dargah (दरगाह)
also durgah

dehati (देहाती)
ग्रामवासी

devta (देवता)
god, deo, dewa

desi (देसी)
स्थानीय, local

dhokla (ढोकला)
एक गुजराती व्यंजन

dhol (ढोल)
ड्रम, drum

diya (दिया)
मिट्टी का दीपक

dosa (डोसा)
चावल के आटे से बना दक्षिण भारतीय व्यंजन

dupatta (दुपट्टा)
स्त्रियों द्वारा गले और गर्दन पर पहना जाने वाला परिधान

darwaza (दरवाज़ा)

darwan (दरबान)
द्वारपाल

eedgah (ईदगाह)
Idgah.

esraj (इसराज)
एक वाद्ययंत्र

ekdam (एकदम)
तुरन्त

Eid (ईद)
मुस्लिम त्यौहार

faltu (फ़ालतू)
व्यर्थ

fatwa (फतवा)
इस्लाम धर्म में आदेश जारी करना

fatiha (फ़ातिहा)
fateha, इस्लाम में किसी व्यक्ति के मरने पर प्रार्थना करना

feringhee, firangi (फिरंगी)
सफ़ेद चमड़ी वाला आदमी, अमेरिकन, एंग्लो-इंडियन

foujdar (फ़ौजदार)

funda (फन्डा)
ज्ञान, knowledge

gajra (गजरा)
स्त्रियों द्वारा बालों में पहना जाने वाला फूलों का गजरा

Ganapati (गणपति)
also Ganesa, Ganesh. हिंदू देवता

ganja (गाँजा)

ganna (गन्ना)

garba (गरबा)
गुजराती नृत्य

garibi (गरीबी)
poverty

ghat
नदी किनारे का घाट

gherao (घिराओ)
घेरना

gobar (गोबर)
dung

golgappa (गोलगप्पा)
पानीपूड़ी

gond (गोंड)
मध्य भारत की एक जाति,

hafta (हफ़्ता)
हर हफ़्ते पैसे वसूलना

haldi (हल्दी)
turmeric

hamal (हमाल)
कुली

haramzada (हरामज़ादा)
हरामी

havala (हवाला)
विदेशी धन को अनुचित ढंग से रुपए में बदलना

henna (हिना)
मेंहदी, mehendi

hijra (हिजड़ा)
eunuch.

Hindustan (हिन्दुस्तान)
India

hungama (हंगामा)
शोरगुल

iftar (इफ़्तार)
दिन भर के रोज़े के बाद शाम का खाना (इस्लाम)

imambara (इमामबाड़ा)
मोहर्रम के दिन मुस्लिम जहाँ अपने ताज़िए लाते हैं

inquilab (इंकिलाब)
क्रांति

izzat (इज्ज़त)
honour

Jagannath (जगन्नाथ)
विष्णु देव का मानव रूप

jai (जय)
victory

jaiphal (जायफल)
nutmeg

jaldi (जल्दी)
quickly

jalebi (जलेबी)
एक मिष्ठान्न

jamun (जामुन)
jamul

janata (जनता)
people

jawan (जवान)
a solidier in Indian Army.

jehad (जेहाद)
धर्मयुद्ध

jharu (झाड़ू)
broom

jheel (झील)
lake

jhelo (झेलो)
tolerate

Jnana, Jnana Yoga (ज्ञान योग)
spiritual practice

kafir (काफ़िर)
caffir, ऐसा व्यक्ति जो इस्लाम में विश्वास नहीं करता

kahar (कहार)
हिन्दू परिवार में झाड़ूपौंछा कार्य करने वाला

kaju (काजू)
cashew nut

keema (कीमा)
finely chopped meat

laddu (लड्डू)
a ballshaped sweet

ladli (लाड़ली)
much loved girl

lafanga (लफंगा)
a rogue, आवारा

linga (लिंग)
a black stone sacred as Shiva, शिव

malai (मलाई)
cream

mandir (मंदिर)
temple

maska (मस्का)
मक्खन, butter

maulvi (मौलवी)
मुल्ला, a muslim teacher

naka (नाका)
स्थान जहाँ कर वसूला जाता है

namaj (नमाज)
also namaz

namak (नमक)
salt

nirodh (निरोध)
a condom

nulla (नाला)
नल्ला, a stream

odhani (ओढनी)
दुपट्टा

om (ओम)
ॐ a sacred sound

pagri (पगड़ी)
pugri, सिर पर बाँधने की पगड़ी, मकान किराए पर लेने के लिए एजेन्ट को पैसा देकर बात पक्की करना

pakora (पकौड़ा)
also pakoda

pan (पान)
betel leaf

pani (पानी)
water

puri (पुरी)
पूड़ी

qabristan (कब्रिस्तान)
a muslim graveyard.

koi hai
कोई है

qurbani (कुरबानी)
त्योहारों पर धार्मिक रूप से जानवरों का काटा जाना

saag (साग)

sabzi (सब्जी)
(also sabji, subji, subzi), सब्जी

sadhvi (साध्वी)
a virtuous woman

sadhu (साधु)
a holy man, a virtuous man

safai (सफ़ाइ)
act of cleaning

Sankhya (सांख्य)
हिन्दू दर्शन पर आधारित द्वैत सिद्वान्त. पदार्थ और आत्मा, matter and soul

satya (सत्य)
truth

sufi (सूफ़ी)
मुस्लिम रहस्यवादी

taka (टका)
बांग्लादेश की पैसे (धन) की इकाई

talak (तलाक)
also talaq कानूनी रूप से शादी तोड़ना

tawaif (तवायफ़)
a prostitute

tava (तवा)
griddle

ulema (उलेमा)
मुस्लिम व्यक्ति जो कानून का ज्ञाता हो

upnishad (उपनिषद्)
दर्शन ग्रंथ

urs (उर्स)
मुस्लिम संत की पुण्यतिथि पर मनाया जाने वाला समारोह

vaid (वैद्य)
आयुर्वेद का डॉक्टर

vilayat (विलायत)
England

vir (वीर)
brave

vada (बड़ा)
पिसी हुई दाल का गोल-गोल तेल में सेंककर बनाया गया

yajna (यज्ञ)
ritual sacrifice

yama (यम)
Hindu god of death

yar (यार)
दोस्त

yoga (योग)
Hindu system of ascetic practice

yoni (योनि)
मादा जनन अंग, जन्मांतरों तक विभिन्न प्राणियों के रूप में जन्म

zafran (ज़ाफ़रान)
also kesar, saffron

zarda (ज़र्दा)
सुगंधित तम्बाकू

zeera (जीरा)
also jeera

zila (जिला)
district

zenana (ज़नाना)
स्त्री

zulm (जुल्म)
अत्याचार

□□□□

Other Books on

LOTUS ILLUSTRATED DICTIONARIES

Healing Power of Gems

Published by
Lotus Press Publishers & Distributors